Music Films

Music Films

Documentaries, Concert Films and Other Cinematic Representations of Popular Music

Neil Fox

THE BRITISH FILM INSTITUTE
Bloomsbury Publishing Plc
50 Bedford Square, London, WC1B 3DP, UK
1385 Broadway, New York, NY 10018, USA
29 Earlsfort Terrace, Dublin 2, Ireland

BLOOMSBURY is a trademark of Bloomsbury Publishing Plc

First published in Great Britain 2024 by Bloomsbury
on behalf of the
British Film Institute
21 Stephen Street, London W1T 1LN
www.bfi.org.uk

The BFI is the lead organisation for film in the UK and the distributor of Lottery funds for film. Our mission is to ensure that film is central to our cultural life, in particular by supporting and nurturing the next generation of filmmakers and audiences. We serve a public role which covers the cultural, creative and economic aspects of film in the UK.

Copyright © Neil Fox, 2024

Neil Fox has asserted his right under the Copyright, Designs and Patents Act, 1988, to be identified as author of this work.

For legal purposes the Acknowledgements on p. ix constitute an extension of this copyright page.

Cover design by Louise Dugdale
Cover image: A Hard Day's Night, The Beatles, 1964.
Courtesy Everett Collection / Mary Evans.

All rights reserved. No part of this publication may be reproduced or transmitted in any form or by any means, electronic or mechanical, including photocopying, recording, or any information storage or retrieval system, without prior permission in writing from the publishers.

Bloomsbury Publishing Plc does not have any control over, or responsibility for, any third-party websites referred to or in this book. All internet addresses given in this book were correct at the time of going to press. The author and publisher regret any inconvenience caused if addresses have changed or sites have ceased to exist, but can accept no responsibility for any such changes.

A catalogue record for this book is available from the British Library.

A catalog record for this book is available from the Library of Congress.

ISBN: HB: 978-1-8390-2344-6
PB: 978-1-8390-2343-9
ePDF: 978-1-8390-2346-0
eBook: 978-1-8390-2345-3

Typeset by RefineCatch Limited, Bungay, Suffolk
Printed and bound in India

To find out more about our authors and books visit www.bloomsbury.com and sign up for our newsletters.

For Beth

Contents

List of Illustrations	viii
Acknowledgments	ix
Foreword by Gruff Rhys	xi
Introduction	1

Part One   Form and Feel

1	'What Should I Say?' – Milestones and Innovations	33
2	'We'll try for a groove' – Music Making and the Careers of Musicians	89

Part Two   Politics and Place

3	'Secret Black Technologies' – Black Music	115
4	'Wherever we are, we are' – Place	143
5	'I just have to deal with it' – Women	163

Part Three   Performativity and Performance

6	'Fuck continuity' – Truth and Myth	187
7	'Walk on stage and fucking 'ave it' – Concert and Tour Films	213

Endnotes – Omissions, Alternative Histories and Further Watching	241
References	245
Filmography	251
Index	259

Illustrations

0.1	Bunch of Kunst (dir, Franz, 2017)	25
1.1	Finisterre (dir. Evans and Kelly, 2003)	74
1.2	Delia Derbyshire: The Myths and Legendary Tapes (dir. Catz, 2020)	85
2.1	Elephant Days (dir. Caddick and Cronin, 2015)	97
3.1	Milford Graves Full Mantis (dir. Meginsky, 2018)	120
3.2	Lee Morgan performing with Art Blakey and the Jazz Messengers, Amsterdam, 1960; featured in I Called Him Morgan (dir. Collin, 2016)	122
3.3	Syl Johnson: Anyway the Wind Blows (dir. Hatch-Miller, 2015)	125
3.4	Devil's Pie: D'Angelo (dir. Bijlsma, 2019)	128
3.5	Inna De Yard (dir. Webber, 2019)	132
4.1	Sound It Out (dir. Finlay, 2011)	150
5.1	Poly Styrene: I Am A Cliché (dir. Sng and Bell, 2021)	176
5.2	The Ballad of Shirley Collins (dir. Curry and Plester, 2017)	183
6.1	Orion: The Man Who Would Be King (dir. Finlay, 2015)	195
6.2	King Rocker (dir. Cumming, 2020)	203
7.1	Be Pure. Be Vigilant. Behave (dir. Evans, 2019)	214

Acknowledgments

The guiding principle for writing this book was Norman Mailer's writing advice to Andrew O'Hagan to 'enter your times, write your heart out, and never settle for having the correct opinion' (2020). There is something meaningful, cinematically, in music films as a broad, longstanding genre and this is my attempt to wrestle with that. It is one set of ideas, and one that would not be possible without the input and support of so many people. Cue the following list of gratitude. I don't care if it reads like Father Ted's 'Golden Cleric' speech. I may never be here again. So, thank you to my dear friends, collaborators and colleagues Justin, Dario, Kingsley and Laura. To my family, Mum, Dad, Jordi (& his gang). To the editors and conference organisers who have helped improve and supported my writing and ideas in this area; MarBelle, Ben Hopkins, Mat Colegate, Laura Mayne, Bobby Barry, Ella Kemp, Neil Mitchell, Gabriel Solomons, Tom Puhr, Georgina Guthrie, Kieron Moore, Ben Halligan, Robert Edgar, Kirsty Fairclough-Isaacs, Nicola Spelman and Mark Duffett. To the critics, academics, programmers and filmmakers, some of whom I am honoured to call friends, who have shared their contacts and ideas and their voices, ears and work with me; Tom Shone, Jeanie Finlay, Ryan Gilbey, Mark Jenkin, Stewart Lee, Michael Cumming, Ashley Clark (so many recommendations and introductions to films came via him), Alex Barrett, Racquel Gates, Carl Hunter, Rob and Puloma, Carine Bijlsma, Colm and Vanessa at Doc N Roll Fest, Karen Shook, Christopher Morris, Gruffydd Davies, Dylan Goch, Luc Roeg, Jenna and James at Fire Records, Johnny Fewings, Kieran Evans, Nicky Wire, Tony Palmer, Kasper Collin, Jake Meginsky, Christine Franz (& Oliver), Tim & Rob, Felicity Gee, Pamela Hutchinson, James Bell, Niall McCann, Joanna Wright, Ian Mantgani, Mary Davies, Annabel Grundy, Jason Wood, Sam Davies, Paul Sng, Toby Amies, Peter Webber, Don Letts, Lily Keber, Julien & Amanda Temple, Caroline Catz, Liv Proctor and Posy Dixon. To Elizabeth Aubrey and Gregoire at Society Magazine for talking to me about this subject for their own work, which coincided with key moments in the writing of this book. To friends who offered encouragement throughout; Chuck Baker, James Dean, Craig, Adam Lannon, James Maitre, Raf, Adam Gunton, and particularly to Craig Green who tracked down a copy of the Tom Waits concert film *Big Time* (1988) on VHS as well as a VHS player, and David Litchfield for saying just the right thing at just the right time. To Ashley at MoMA and the staff at Falmouth University library and the BFI library and archive. To Camilla Erskine, Veidehi Hans and Anna Coatman at Bloomsbury for their support over the entirety of the process. To Paula Devine for thoughtful copy editing. To Gruff Rhys for a beautiful foreword. Finally, to my children Tessa and Miles for reminding me it doesn't matter what anyone says about this book because being with you is what counts, and to my wife Beth. She has read thousands of acknowledgements at the start of books and given her reading experience I worry that what I write here will be cliché, derivative, trite. I worry about that here more than in the rest of the book, weirdly. From before and throughout the process of writing this book, she has consistently encouraged me to write my way, to write from the heart, and to believe in myself. She has been kind and critical, challenging me and cajoling me with love and respect as she does in our daily life. I am so grateful to and for her. Beyond words. In so many ways this book would not have been possible without her. Trite as that may read it is the absolute truth. I love you Beth.

Foreword

Zoom

I met Dr Neil Fox in a very cinematic way, a three-way Zoom call during the pandemic.

He was interviewing people for a book on Music Films, and as a touring musician in the 21st century I had naturally left some documentary residue, a small trail of filmic artefacts in my wake. Most notably a couple of movies that document what I call 'investigative concert tours' [*Separado!* (2010) and *American Interior* (2014)], shot by my director friend Dylan Goch (who came to cinema from his background of mixing live VHS tape projections at raves in West Yorkshire) and who was also on the call.

Blue

That an academic was interested in our creations felt encouraging and out of the blue as financing them had been problematic. My somewhat ambitious and perhaps misguided aim to be documented as *Musician by Night, Private Investigator by Day* didn't always cut it in the regular film world. A TV executive commented 'sorry we don't fund vanity projects' whilst even a friendly critic fairly commented 'this film has no relation to theatre, it's just like a long music video'.

Funk

How do you make sense of a form that isn't like it's close relative *the film*, a descendant of a marriage between theatre, technology, and landscape painting? A bastard child of music (the most *outlaw* of all mediums) and cinema itself that's been allowed to spiral away in its own funk, largely unattended by critical eyes into an overcrowded kaleidoscope of the crude and righteous? Or as Neil explains it, through an anti-late capitalist post-modern lens, 'a real mess'?

Boogie

But what a mess! Entire circuits of Music Film festivals have emerged worldwide, in an attempt to contain some of these marvels. In the book Neil details the emergence of 'Direct Cinema' in the 1960s as 16mm cameras revolutionised the portability of film making. The digital age has similarly facilitated an era of ultra-direct cinema for musicians and directors to capture an array of hagiography, portraiture, fantasia, and realism for audiences to attempt to process. The key to its cinematic success in my opinion is subversion. Music works best as a subversive medium so why shouldn't any attempt to document it be any different? Start low then aim lower. Dig for fire!

Trash

At this critical juncture, before the Tik ToK age of infinite celluloid, Neil's book dances and digs deep into crevices of trash beyond the tired usual 'best of' lists and finds gems and unacknowledged voices to sit side by side with some universally loved films. And forms it into a considered and comprehensive overview of Music Film.

Feel

Musicians often lead messy lives, and the road gives great mileage to the Music Film genre with its infinite backdrops. But musicians, unlike the actors of regular films or the politicians and orators of documentaries, are often self-conscious, verbally inarticulate or prefer just to let the music talk. The vocabulary of musicians alludes to this. The Music Film then is the cinema of *feel* more than of performance. It's an attribute that is hard to pinpoint but it's clear when it doesn't work. And at last, someone with heart and taste and a critical eye has attempted to corral and make comprehensive sense of this encyclopaedic mess. And that mess is this book.

Gruff Rhys
December 2022

Introduction

'[I] really don't understand any of it'[1] – Introducing Music Films

Music films are an important yet derided and overlooked part of the cultural historical narrative of both music and film. Whilst 'Music Film' is not a stable term, and never has been, in this book I want to grapple with it and try and find some real meaning in it. Mark Fisher's assertion that at 'the end of history, the impasses of politics are perfectly reflected by the impasses in popular music' (2018: 382) resonates with a sometimes-justified critique of music films as passive artefacts that do not engage with tensions in art, culture, history, or society in any meaningful way. Yet as this book will show, when understood as cinematic objects created in the context of many competing forces, trying to do multiple things at once and always with an only partial ability to reflect reality, they can reveal much about music, film, and filmmaking. Ultimately this book argues that music films are messy objects, characterized by their tensions and inconsistencies, but full of potential meanings and varying levels of insight into their subjects.

I want to wrestle with music films in a manner that moves them away from being understood merely as marketing documents, egotistical self-portraits, fan-service or social commentaries into something that incorporates all those elements and more in a messy, slippery object doing multiple things at once. At their best, music films are objects fully engaged with these different elements, which can compete with and contradict each other. I see them as sites of both 'critique and complicity', a phrase borrowed from Linda Hutcheon's work on

---

[1] Singer Lee Brilleaux's mum talking about the music of Dr Feelgood in *Oil City Confidential* (2009).

postmodernism (2000). This idea gives validation to a genre that has long been widely disregarded in terms of formal and contextual complexity, dismissed as 'just' a music film.

That 'just' has allowed some filmmakers to distance their own apparently unique take on the genre from all the other trite, sycophantic, and formally stolid examples that are beneath them as artists. That qualifier, 'just', was part of the music film's earliest days when DA Pennebaker said of *Dont Look Back* (1967) that he didn't want it to be 'just' a music documentary (even though the genre was barely a few years old with hardly any examples to refer to). This 'just' has put the music film in a box, and they are often trapped in that box – perceived as largely unworthy of in-depth critique as valid cinematic objects barring a few examples that supposedly transcend the genre. This book tries to (re)open that box and allow the music film to be regarded in all its messy glory as a form that is always a combination of 'complicitous critique' (2000: 2) in Hutcheon's useful words.

This book asserts that within a large body of work such as that collected under the banner music film, there are significant works that push against the accusations levelled against the form in the collective, namely that they are, particularly since the turn of the twenty-first century, objects of nostalgia aimed squarely at building myth and filling coffers. Those critical of the form are not completely wrong in expounding such views. Their accusations have validity and accuracy. However, as with so much, it is not that simple, and music films have never really had their moment of critical championing as a cinematic genre.

Music film has always been an unstable and contested genre, a sub-genre, a bastardized variant. Innumerable lists of the 'best music documentaries' and 'best concert films' spring up with regularity across the critical spectrum in film magazines like *Sight and Sound* and music magazines like *Rolling Stone*, but rarely are the films given serious consideration as cinematic objects. Th films are largely seen through the lens of music, analysed for what information and knowledge about music artists they can provide. This is a significant part of what they do, but deeper questions of how they provide that information and what approaches are used to access insight and emotional charge, have long been neglected.

The explosion in music film since 2000 has been met in the 2010s with an increasing scholarly focus on the genre. This book extends vital work done to validate and legitimize the music film by a variety of writers using a variety of approaches. As the title suggests, Thomas F Cohen's Playing to the Camera: Musicians and Musical Performance in Documentary Cinema (2012) looks at several films, including some covered in this book such as *Jazz on a Summer's Day* (1959) and *Ornette: Made in America* (1985), through the lens of performers and performance. The edited collection *The Music Documentary: Acid Rock to Electropop* (2013) tackles a variety of genres and periods in discrete chapters that do sterling work in broadening the scope of texts worthy of analysis. Keith Beattie's BFI Film Classics monograph *Dont Look Back* (2016) is, at the time of writing, the only critical monograph dedicated to a single music film title. Benjamin J Harbert's *American Music Documentary: Five Case Studies of Ciné-Ethnomusicology* (2018) applies his own methodology, the ciné-ethnomusicology of the title, to better understanding a variety of texts including, again, some covered in this book, such as *Depeche Mode: 101* (1989) and *Instrument* (1999), a film about Fugazi. These books exclusively cover documentary and non-fiction cinema. All are drawn on throughout this book, explicitly and in implicit dialogue.

Other key writing on popular music and cinema positions non-fiction works, including concert films, in a broader lineage of cinema that, in addition to documentary, incorporates narrative-fiction film and those in the liminal space between, such as Richard Lester's *A Hard Day's Night* (1964). These works include David E James's *Rock 'N' Film: Cinema's Dance with Popular Music* (2016), which features a good overview of country music on film, a music genre lamentably neglected in this book, and John Scanlan's *Rock 'N' Roll Plays Itself* (2022), which features a discussion of films released close to the writing of this book, which is encouraging to see. Also, the edited collections *Celluloid Jukebox* (1995) and *The Arena Concert: Music, Media and Mass Entertainment* (2015),[2] Dave Saunders' vital analysis of the important 1960s period of Direct Cinema, *Direct Cinema: Observational Documentary and the Politics of the Sixties* (2007), John Mundy's *Popular Music on Screen: From Hollywood Musical to Music Video* (1999) and Garry Mulholland's *Popcorn: Fifty Years of Rock 'n' Roll Movies* (2011). From a purely jazz perspective there is Scott Yanow's *Jazz on Film: The*

---

[2] I have a piece in this collection, on the Beastie Boys film *Awesome: I Fuckin' Shot That!* (2006)

Complete Story of the Musicians & Music Onscreen (2004). Some films turn up in books focusing on specific periods, such as the inclusion of *A Hard Day's Night* in Peter Cowie's *Revolution! The Explosion of World Cinema in the 60s* (2004). As you can imagine, the Beatles are well served by books about their cinematic output, most recently, at the time of writing, by Stephen Glynn's excellent *The Beatles and Film: From Youth Culture to Counterculture* (2020). For the most part – particularly in Cohen, Harbert and James's work – the books looking at music films have a much narrower approach in terms of texts, ensuring greater detail on single titles. It is necessary and exceptional work, but not the approach of this book, which seeks to be broader in terms of quantity, cinematic and musical style, and also to try and create a field survey that ends as close to the manuscript submission as possible.

These works, and numerous articles and book sections drawn upon elsewhere, have done great critical work in taking the music film seriously, opening it up to a variety of theoretical and analytical viewpoints. There has been no attempt to create a unified way of accessing music films critically, where they are seen as films that share a set of conventions and complex relationships, or that asks questions of the music film that have been asked about its parent/sibling/guardian, the documentary. Also, as alluded to above, the deep focus in several of the texts mentioned sees the films included taking the music film up to the 1990s and in a few cases just beyond. This book posits 2000's *The Filth and the Fury* directed by Julien Temple as the moment when new possibilities and directions entered the music film. It's my belief that the first 20 years of this century have resulted in some of the most dynamic, innovative, powerful and moving works in music film. Hutcheon writes that 'knowing the past becomes a question of representing, that is, of constructing and interpreting, not of objective recording' (2000: 70). Longstanding critical analysis of documentary texts as sites of contested reality and perspective have not been extended in the main to the music film, yet many of them are works that question their ability to record, represent and reproduce 'reality', often within their very form.

This book brings together a series of films from across 70 plus years of cinema and builds dramatically on an emerging conversation that asks for them to be taken seriously and considered a valid genre of cinema beyond documentary representation of musical artists. A genre that contains within it a constant, universal tension between the commercial and the artistic. The music film is a site of complicity and critique. In the examples that are cited in this book as doing important work cinematically, the level of complicity and the level of critique is always on a spectrum. One significant reason for this is the unique formulation in music films of answers to Roland Barthes' (1977) conundrum 'Who is the author?' Music films are sites of tension between several parties, often with competing ideas and ideals about the film being made. There are record labels, management companies or concert promoters – the capitalist arm of the enterprise – wanting a product that leads to economic increases via record sales, concert tickets, merchandise etc. On the other side is the filmmaker, not wanting to make 'just' a music documentary (because music is assumed to be such a frivolous subject).

In the middle, between label and filmmaker, is the artist, often wanting to present as authentic but also to further enhance their persona to retain or restore their career, to remain relevant but also to show a 'real' side to themselves, to make a 'real' connection, often shifting over the course of the film and sometimes over the course of scenes or sequences. This messy combination of voices, often reduced to a belief that all are complicit, and no critique is occurring, has led to music films being dismissed, generically, as tools of capitalism. It is this mess that makes them interesting. Often different ambitions and tensions are present in the work, which admittedly makes them disjointed at times, but also makes them critical artefacts when considering the complex machinery of the neoliberal moment. In an interview for *Filmmaker* magazine about the latter's Radiohead tour film *Meeting People Is Easy* (1998), filmmaker Jem Cohen remarks to Grant Gee that 'you made a pretty unhappy documentary there Grant. When did you know that you were going to do that?' To which Gee replies 'from the start really' (1999). *Meeting People Is Easy* follows Radiohead on tour for their 1997 album *O.K. Computer* and finds them exhausted, bored, annoyed, distant and at odds with the job of being a famous, adored rock band. It was funded by their record label Parlophone, who, despite it not being a flattering portrait of their leading lights at the time, released the film anyway. It's gripping, but can hardly be called promotional, even though it weirdly did do that work as well.

In addition to shared and competing authorship there is the added tension that there is often an existing audience for the films coming to the cinematic object because of music fandom or appreciation. The idea that the text itself is a further site of complicity and critique beyond the conscious impact of the record industry, artist and filmmaker, needs to be taken seriously. One of the most common criticisms of music films can be reduced to dissatisfaction amongst fans whose subjective desires for information or focus has not been met. This is combined critically with an assumption that a music film is, and should be, an exhaustive or definitive biography, as if such a thing were possible or desirable. One of the critiques of music films that recurs in this book is such an approach from filmmakers, resulting in what critic Guy Lodge calls 'facts and footage' (2020) movies, or what musician Robert Lloyd calls 'Wikipedia films' (2020). This boils down to a belief that fans wish to have their experience of an artist represented and a belief, subconscious possibly, that a music film lives and dies by what it shows, rather than how it shows it. There is a similar general criticism levelled at music books, and this book is clear-eyed in that it is not exhaustive, definitive, or even correct in its assessments. It presents a way of seeing music films, one that will hopefully lead to more ways of seeing down the line that contradict or support this one.

'I'm sure it will be on the DVD'[3] – What is a music film?

I use the term 'music film' to incorporate films defined as music documentaries and concert films, as well as those that fall between the cracks of both of those terms. This includes the odd narrative film where artists play versions of themselves doing heightened versions of things that their 'real' counterparts would do, such as *A Hard Day's Night*, or narrative fiction films that utilize documentary and concert film aesthetics to critique or satirize popular music films, such as in Rob Reiner's *This Is Spinal Tap* (1984). A music documentary is different to a concert film is different to a tour film, though often conventions and aspects of all three are present in the others. Most concert films feature some level of backstage or behind-the-scenes footage, and most music documentaries feature their subjects in some form of performance. However, just calling them 'music documentaries' also isn't appropriate. Patricia Aufderheide writes that

---

[3] *24 Hour Party People* (2002).

'documentaries are about real life, they are not real life. They are not even windows on real life' (2007: 02). Or as Wim Wenders wrote, 'if you go to the cinema to see a film that claims to document something you're likely to be disappointed' (1991: 62). This quote pinpoints something fundamental to the music film, given how the participants are performers for whom performativity is a crucial component of their on-stage and promotional life.

There is no doubt that the films discussed in the book fulfil many of Bill Nichols' modes of documentary,[4] often utilizing several modes within the same text. It is not just films such as *The Rutles: All You Need Is Cash* (1978) that appropriate the formal properties of documentary to tell a fictional tale. It could be argued that music films have at their core a tension between the real, the authentic and the performative and constructed. Hutcheon attests that 'parody can be used to point to art as art, but also to art as inescapably bound to its aesthetic and even social past' (2000: 97) and, at their peak, this is what music films do. The hesitation to call the films discussed in the book documentaries, even though that is itself a contested and slippery term, is because the subject at the heart of them is performance, a person or people whose job, vocation, calling, is to craft narrative or inhabit a persona. Even when that persona is closely connected to their so-called 'real' self, there is still a distance to travel between person and performer.

As with complicity and critique this is a sliding scale. For example, in *Madonna: Truth or Dare* (1991), Madonna is presenting a version of herself to the world very deliberately, using the clever blend of shock and awe and personality subterfuge she has always been so brilliant at. There is very little belief we are seeing a 'real' Madonna even if the candid environment of her dressing room, the hand-held camera, and the grainy black-and-white film stock prompts us to feel otherwise. Conversely, there is little doubt that blues singer Leo 'Bud' Welch in Mississippi, all 80 plus years of him when the film *Late Blossom Blues* (2017) was made, is being himself. The film follows Welch as a friend of his seeks recognition for the bluesman following a call put out by the record label Fat Possum to capture blues musicians before they die. By the time the music industry and the film catch up with Welch, his decades of quiet

---

[4] Nichols' six modes of documentary are poetic, expository, observational, participatory, reflexive and performative (2001: 138). While often contested they do provide a good starting point for conceptualizing what music films are doing.

existence playing weekly in church as choir accompaniment have taken root and, charming as he is for the camera, he is who he is. Even so, the book assigns the term 'music film' to all the titles herein, and one of the thrills of *Late Blossom Blues* is watching Welch perform in front of an audience, fully engaged with the power of his music and abilities. Music films incorporate stories from both ends of the music career spectrum and every point in between. They utilize documentary conventions such as archive material, interviews and voiceovers to provide information, yes, but they also act as access points for audiences.

The examples of films about Madonna at one end and Leo Welch at the other end of a spectrum highlight tensions in both film and music about authenticity and truth and what audiences can and should expect in terms of those ideas from artists, across different genres. Expectations that they be 'real' or 'authentic', have long been prevalent for artists in genres such as punk and Hip Hop and there is a common (again perceived) notion that documentary or non-fiction is a space where authenticity and truth are absolute. However, the reality is different in both forms. As Nichols (2011) writes of documentary film:

> The apparent authenticity or indexicality of the image, the location shooting [...] do not clinch the case for a single argument or conclusion any more than the forensic evidence put before a jury automatically clinches the case for guilt or innocence.
>
> 2011: 176

Context, and interventions from the filmmaker and the artist(s) always impact the footage and its presentation and knowing an artist through their existing visual media representations is often a good indicator of the level of authenticity that may be present in a music film. It may be naïve to think a music film will provide access to the 'real', which has previously been concealed in other attempts and artefacts. Documentary and other cinematic conventions allow filmmakers to craft portraits of artists and provide space for the artists to present their story and themselves to audiences. Performance is part of the story, pretty much always, even if it is the performativity of fandom in one of the many films focusing on that side of the story, or in the stories of studios, record labels and record shops for whom some concession to 'selling' is vital to maintain and sustain. Often in these stories there is a crafted identity that draws people to the studios, labels, and stores in the first place. For this reason, the term music film – as well as being easier than constantly writing music documentaries and concert films or such like – is apposite. They are about music, or music is the foremost lens and entry point through which they are experienced. But they are also films, made by filmmakers seeking to represent something truthful about their subject while accepting the limitations of that. Filmmakers are also frequently interested in putting the performer or their work in a wider social or cultural context because they fear, without it, pop music as a subject could only ever be classed as frivolous.[5] The book's definition of popular music is like everything herein, slippery and contradictory at points. It takes in jazz and some experimental outposts but stops short of classical music.

The term music film is also apposite when considering another of Hutcheon's ideas, that of the paratext. This is the idea that some texts self-consciously use form to 'represent historical events within narrative design', something that is 'highly artificial and un-organic' (2000: 80), which feels very close to what the music film is doing. Ultimately, because of the configuration of authors and the funding, idea or basis for music films often stemming from artists or their backers (managers, labels etc.) the notion that they are para to the text of the artist, or the music is one that must be considered. This should not be taken as a negative, a way of ghettoizing or stigmatizing, but of freeing the genre. If this complicity is taken as read, that a music film is only ever going to be a paratext to music, a vehicle for artist promotion, what can be done in terms of critique? How can a film or filmmaker formally or otherwise complicate that narrative and mess with the capitalist system? Over the course of many music films, artists themselves do this work, sometimes wittingly and sometimes not. Hutcheon notions that perhaps the paratext 'is deliberately awkward, as a means of directing our attention to the very processes by which we understand and interpret the past through its textual representations'. Music films are textual representations, often of textual representations. These films are always going to be seen via the lens of the artist or the music; that is why they are

---

[5] I don't agree with this idea, but I like how that tension that filmmakers can feel plays out in music films.

being made in the first place, either because they are funding the film or because their story has been deemed worth telling cinematically. So, they are paratexts, but that doesn't mean they are passive. On the contrary, paratexts can be vital ways of adding and examining critical tensions in terms of an artist, genre, or event. They remind us of the curation, point of view and contextual elements that can, but don't always, go into telling an historical narrative – even as they are occurring, such as in *Gimme Shelter* (1970), a film discussed throughout the book.

A music film is one – creative and commercial agenda-driven – representation of limitless possibilities. Even as a paratext to music, the film serves a vital critical role and its formal properties constantly remind the audience of that critique, if the audience is paying attention. In this context, this book is also a paratext. In addition to being 'deliberately awkward' Hutcheon also claims that paratexts are 'central to historiographic practice, to the writing of the doubled narrative of the past in the present' (2000: 80). In that vein, footnotes,[6] as opposed to endnotes,[7] are deployed regularly in the book and vary in their form from personal asides to recommendations for further information, or watching, or to additional context that might be useful but would detrimentally interrupt the flow of the idea being laid out.

'You want the waiters to move around a bit?'[8]
The Roots of the Music Film

There's no question when looking at what are considered the canonical titles in both magazine 'best of' lists and critical texts that the 1960s are when the genre explodes in a major way, with a series of feature films that set the conventions of the music film and showcased its potential for capturing significant cultural moments. Fisher writes how, in the period following the Second World War, music 'became the centre of the culture because it was consistently capable of

---

[6] Hutcheon claims that 'publishers hate footnotes (they are expensive and they disrupt the reader's attention)' (2000: 80). Are you disrupted?
[7] Though, (annoyingly? Ironically?) I do have a final, short section called 'Endnotes'.
[8] A club manager draws attention to the filmmaking form in *Lonely Boy* (1962), a short film about Paul Anka considered by many to be the first music documentary.

giving the new a palpable form; it was a kind of lab that focused and intensified the convulsions that culture was undergoing' (2018: 368). Cinema was not far behind and, not long after the pop explosion, it was being deployed to capture the fallout. From the Maysles Brothers' *What's Happening: the Beatles in the USA* (later retitled *The Beatles First US Visit*) and Lester's *A Hard Day's Night,* both 1964, via Pennebaker's *Dont Look Back* (1967) and *Monterey Pop* (1968) to the Maysles [again] and Charlotte Zwerin's *Gimme Shelter* and Michael Wadleigh's *Woodstock,* both 1970. This period remains regarded as the formative years of the music film, as I am seeking to define it here, and when its generally regarded high points occurred. This book challenges the latter notion, that the genre was all but done by the late 1980s, in a chapter looking at the music film's milestones and innovations but also in its overwhelming focus, quantity wise, on films from outside this canonical period. It is a vital period, and the films are worthy of the critical focus they have received. However, they weren't the first music films, even if they benefitted from a cultural zeitgeist where the subjects at the heart of the films were prominent in the wider cultural consciousness – Beatles, Dylan, Stones, Hendrix, Woodstock – in ways that subjects in later films could only dream of being, due to the changing role, shape and position of pop music in society and culture.

Before this mid 1960s explosion came several films that set the formal and thematic parameters of the genre in interesting ways. Consensus suggests that *Lonely Boy* (1962), a short film featuring Paul Anka as he traverses being a young star, is the first music documentary. Certainly, it contains the conventions that have come to define the music film. There is live footage performance, the star is seen backstage and offstage, and the press, the fans and the star himself are interviewed. There is privileged access to information about the star that feels exciting. Indeed, there is a candidness to some of the information relayed, particularly Paul's views on sex and his manager's open discussion of the singer's plastic surgery on his nose, that is markedly absent from films that follow in *Lonely Boy's* wake, almost as if it showed artists from the start what they didn't want to reveal about themselves. Even though it's only twenty-seven minutes long, it has the shape and contents of a music film as would become recognizable, with a freshness because of the lack of other examples, that still feels raw and unusual sixty years on, at the time of writing this book. Even so, it didn't arrive fully formed with no precedents. There are other examples of films that formulated the ideas, conventions and approaches of the music film before *Lonely Boy*, and several key examples revolve around jazz.

This is unsurprising given that in Hollywood cinema jazz musicians had been playing versions of themselves throughout the decades, bringing a verisimilitude to films about jazz due to the music itself being a key art-form of the first half of the twentieth century. As an art-form jazz was both popular and innovative (not that those two things are mutually exclusive). However, the majority of those films including *The King of Jazz* (1930) and William Dieterle's *Syncopation* (1942), while formally innovative and progressive in terms of the class struggle of jazz artists nevertheless suggest a narrative regarding the evolutions of the music that are White-centric, and the latter particularly is exclusive and limiting regarding the Black[9] artists that developed jazz in ways that don't sit well as time has passed. And, while they bring a level of authenticity to proceedings or get to grips with the 'real' life of jazz musicians they are still fictional narrative features. And unlike films that would emerge following the 1960s and 1970s such as *The Rutles: All You Need is Cash* or *This Is Spinal Tap* they do not draw on documentary aesthetics as a storytelling device. Aside from these examples, and short performance films known as 'jazz soundies' that were made for video jukeboxes in the 1930s and 1940s, the first examples of [short] documentaries that foreground popular music, introduce staged documentary elements and seek to balance live performance with fan behaviours and wider social and cultural contexts can be found in the decade from the mid-1940s to the mid-1950s.

Gjon Mili's ten-minute short *Jammin' the Blues* (1944) starts with cigarette smoke rising up the screen as the credits do the same. A voiceover announces, 'this is a jam session' and what follows is a staged version of just that, with Lester Young leading a group of tightly grouped jazz musicians through a couple of numbers as two energetic dancers emerge and recreate that element of a 'real' late-night session. This is a performance film, shorn of narrative, capturing musicians at work. There's a cool craft to it, as, following the credits, a hat lifts and reveals Lester Young whose saxophone rises to his lips and joins

---

[9] The reason I have chosen to capitalize Black when referring to Black artists and music originating from Black culture, alongside the more common capitalization of White, is rooted in the arguments put forward by Kwame Anthony Appiah see www.theatlantic.com/ideas/archive/2020/06/time-to-capitalize-blackand-white/613159/

the piano, bass and drums we've heard so far. Against a black box studio, there are close-ups of fingers, mouths and burning cigarettes as the musicianship and atmosphere is communicated to the audience. When Marie Bryant arrives to sing 'On the Sunny Side of the Street', the camera reveals an adjacent white box studio space, opening the visuals out to embrace the lightness of the song. It's an exhilarating piece of performance capture, with the editing and closeness of the lens making it feel swinging, intimate and tactile. There is even room for moments of playful flourish when the foregrounding of Young, with Bryant on a chair in the distance, conjures the image of her as if tiny and sitting on the end of his saxophone.

A decade later Roger Tilton's *Jazz Dance* (1954) would seek to capture the feeling of the general public dancing to jazz in an American club rather than in the staged setting of *Jammin' the Blues*. An inter-racial band play for the dancing delight of a mostly White crowd and the film captures the whole spectrum of physical activity on display, from cool leaning against walls to uninhibited joyous floor-filling. Similar to *Jammin'*, the camera captures details such as the scuffed, tapping shoes of the pianist, but also includes the details of the attending public. One woman, automatically and without thought tugs nervously at the thread of her checked blouse. Late in the film a conga line breaks out, making the band smile as they soundtrack its winding promenade around the venue. The main focal point of the film, however, is the dancing of two Black men. Featured prominently, their exuberance thrills and inspires their fellow attendees and the camera revels in their energy. Writing about this time of the century and Black dancing, Hanif Abdurraqib explains how Black dancers 'were about celebrating their ability to move like no one else around them could move, for whatever time they could. Pushing themselves to the brink of a short, blissful exhaustion, as opposed to a slow, plodding, death-defying one' (2021: 09). *Jazz Dance* captures that. The Black men's dancing veers between solo, almost dance-off-esque, routines and time dancing together, hand-in-hand, in footage that still feels sadly revolutionary today but that must have been incendiary upon the film's release.

Karel Reisz and Tony Richardson's *Momma Don't Allow* (1955) extends the work of *Jazz Dance* and introduces a British enquiry by following three young people – a butcher's assistant, a cleaner and a dental nurse – as they finish work and head to Wood Green Jazz Club for a night out watching and dancing to the

Chris Barber Jazz Band, featuring Lonnie Donegan. The film opens with the band arriving and setting up for the gig – a far cry from the sequence in something like Jonathan Demme's *Justin Timberlake + the Tennessee Kids* (2016) with its gargantuan set build – and as they tune their instruments and warm up, staff put out the accoutrements of the night around them. While the cinema audience hears the tuning and gentle warm-up sounds, they see the three young people finishing work and getting ready to go out. Once they arrive at the venue it's a whirl of dancing, unwinding, drinking and courting. The camerawork and editing captures a freedom from the outside world, a freedom enabled by the music's liberating invitation to dance, that results in the space becoming hermetically sealed from the 'real' world outside. The music is great and, as the film ends, the applause for the performance permeates beyond the last image as the screen goes black, a convention numerous music films employ to this day to convey the uncontainable power of the music and the idea that it continues, somewhere, in some form, long after the film is over.

As much as music and music performance plays a key role in *Jazz Dance* and *Momma Don't Allow,* it is fair to say that it is limited to music's role in the evening's proceedings. *Momma Don't Allow* is not a portrait of the band and it is not a Chris Barber Band concert film. The films are portraits of [mostly] White, working-class youth in the mid-1950s and the role that music and dancing plays in their lives. Nestling between this film and *Lonely Boy* in the early examples of the music film and one that heralds the genre's true arrival is the feature-length concert film *Jazz on a Summer's Day* (1959). This book positions this as truly the first music film because it not only contains live performances from a concert or festival, in this case the Newport Jazz Festival, but because it also includes contextual footage which raises questions of the viewer rather than, as has been suggested, merely providing a visual backdrop for the music. As such, I contend that these choices can be read as a critical commentaries or interventions by the filmmakers. The non-musical footage that accompanies the musical performances has and can be read as window dressing – nice images that accompany the nice sounds – but that is to ignore the potential charge they carry in providing critique and a layer of insight on the part of the filmmakers and their subject. This film raises questions about the role of similar footage in other music films, often written off as simple, aesthetically pleasing, accompaniment to sounds or narrative information. Also, it is a feature film conceived for the cinema screen. It is not a TV film, a TV series,[10] or a short film. In his book *Direct Cinema,* Dave Saunders expertly analyses how the combination of 16mm cameras and synch sound – and the ability to capture image and audio at the same time and while being mobile, discreet and flexible – coupled with the youth culture explosion – saw a greater awareness of and interest in popular music forms and performances, in the late 1950s and 1960s. This awareness was positive on the part of youth cultures and sceptical, if not downright hostile, on the part of older audiences and music lovers. This hostility between the old and the new is something that plays out repeatedly, with every wave of new musical form and genre.

Jazz on a Summer's Day is a feature-length documentary that precedes the 'Direct Cinema' wave that Saunders writes about, but contains within it tensions and reflections that would come to be part of emerging cultural and cinematic conversations around popular music and cinema. It is also, importantly, a film that presents a mode of how to feature, edit, incorporate and contextualize popular music performance in an extended, aesthetically pleasing form. In footage of his performance Thelonious Monk sits in his own musical world, oblivious to the surroundings and who is watching. On arrival on stage the announcer proclaims him a musician 'unconcerned with any opposition to his music' and his posture and performance backs this up, making criticisms of the film regarding how it cuts away from his performance (discussed shortly) seem redundant. Monk is beautifully unfazed by it all.[11] Elsewhere, the film seeks to include the traditional – Mahalia Jackson's performance is fantastic – and the new. *Jazz on a Summer's Day*'s feature film length allows it to do certain things that make it important as a standalone work portraying music and musicians and put in motion conventions and editorial decisions that have ramifications in nearly all the music films that have followed in its wake.

---

[10] More on this later in the introduction.
[11] For what we see of him. Criticisms that say how frustratingly little of Monk performing is shown feel appropriate as he is given very short shrift visually.

'Nerds like me want every film to be *Get Back*'[12] – Who are music films for?

Another key legacy of *Jazz on a Summer's Day* is how it sparked critical conversations around what a music film should do and should contain that remain in force more than 60 plus years and counting. Jazz fans and critics criticized the film on release for the way it interrupts performances, cutting them short or cutting away to show images of fans, or boats. The idea of a music film for many fans and critics was and remains to present performance footage, if possible in its entirety, and as un-authored as possible. Even a film as successful and popular as *Summer of Soul* (dir. Questlove, 2021) suffered this critique. Typically, this has to do with the access to performance material that has not been previously seen. Either because it was filmed for a film, released at a time when viewing live performance footage was harder than it has become, or because the material has been archived, ignored, or thought to have been lost. In *Jazz on a Summer's Day*, it is the former reason. Jazz fans and critics wanted to see the performances untrammelled because recorded performances of the musicians were so rare. It was also criticized for prioritising footage of Louis Armstrong of the Big Band tradition over performances of artists emerging in the later modes, such as Thelonious Monk.

What such critiques do not address is the question of authorial choice and the role of the filmmaker. It is as if the only purpose of a music film is to serve footage of an artist or event and that the filmmaker should get out of the way. This book takes the view that music films are authored by filmmakers seeking to be creative and imaginative while working within constraints. They negotiate the demands of record labels or management companies (who are often funding the project), as well as artists who are often presenting a version of themselves rather than their real self (one that is not a stable or coherent object in the first place), and they do so from a position of fan as well as filmmaker. There is also the artistically unpleasant consideration of the general cinema audience and return of investment, something that criticisms of why there is more Louis Armstrong than Thelonoious Monk in a 1959 film released in

---

[12] Critic and fan, Geeta Dyal, on the Film Comment podcast, January 2022. Available at: www.filmcomment.com/blog/the-film-comment-podcast-music-documentaries/

cinemas fail to take into account. The reason that music fans and music critics don't always like music films is that they don't like the choices filmmakers make, while film critics often don't grapple with those choices and how they may have come to pass. Geeta Dyal ponders this when she says 'nerds like me want every film to be *Get Back*', the 2021 Beatles series directed by Peter Jackson from footage stored from the *Let It Be* album and film sessions. At eight hours it delivers an unparalleled deep dive into the Beatles' process. Dyal acknowledges that this is a luxury many artists, or filmmakers seeking to make films about different artists, would not be able to afford, and that many music documentaries don't work for her because she goes in knowing so much about the artists already.

Even at eight hours long and giving the appearance of being unauthored or 'objective', there are, of course, decisions made to present events in a certain combination of shots, or in a certain chronology, that lead to certain readings and exclude others. The keen eyed may be able to ascertain alternative narratives that might have emerged had different parts of the supposed hundred or so hours of footage been utilized instead. This places emphasis back on the filmmaker and returns thought back to who these films are for. Are they for music fans? Are they for general audiences seeking to learn more about an artist or experience an approximation of an event or a scene? Or are they for fans of the filmmakers making the work? As with any cinematic genre the answer is that a diverse array of audiences would be desired and catered for. However, the collision and tension between these three very distinct and overlapping but often individualized types of audience may account for music films receiving less attention than other cinematic genres. Often music films try to cater to all three audiences, plus the demands of the artist and the funder, which makes them messy. When it works, when a general audience plus fans of the band and fans of the filmmaker are pleased, it feels miraculous.

A deeper critical stance engaging with questions of choice and authorship more prominently can advance understandings of the music film beyond dismissals of the 'I wanted more of this aspect' variety. Within these messy texts there are moments of artistic significance that deserve due attention, even if the text as a whole doesn't cohere as expected or desired by fans and/or critics. Of course, this is not to say that criticisms of what a film shows and how it shows it are not valid. It is more that too often the driving force is a subjective desire to see fandom or fan curiosity repaid, which overawes the conversation and reduces a film to success or failure on such terms. Many films are messy in their coherence due to authorial factors and others including rights and footage access, interview access, funding, screening contexts and more. They are complicated works, often with cinematic elements buried within them. Criticism of *Jazz on a Summer's Day* which decries the way the film cuts away from performances to feature boats fails to see what happens when the question is asked 'What can be gleaned from the cutaways to boats?' Certainly, some films don't hold up to analysis of this kind. Cutaways from performance can fail to reveal anything of note that adds to the context and experience, but the investigation should, nonetheless, be undertaken.

In *Jazz on a Summer's Day,* the construction of footage leads to a variety of potential readings.

Thomas F Cohen's take in his book *Playing to the Camera* is that the film's 'numerous cutaways to shots of the boating event imply as much concern for yacht racing' (2012: 24) as for jazz. There is also the reading that the choice to cut away and reveal the nature of the event's surroundings and the concurrent America's Cup sailing race nearby is part of a commentary on the filmmaker's part. A cursory understanding of jazz history as a Black American art-form reveals that Black musicians were side-lined as White musicians took up the form.[13] Additionally, Black artists were forced to take up roles as a specific (acceptable) kind of entertainer, as was the case for Louis Armstrong. This knowledge imbues footage of Black musicians on a stage playing for a wealthy, predominantly White audience with socio-political charge. When Cohen writes that the frequent cutaways, particularly during Monk's performance, amount to the music 'accompanying White people's amusements' (2012: 32) he is correct, but this can be seen as a critique by the filmmaker. As musicians such as Monk play, the new sound of jazz on a rare excursion from cities where earning a living playing such music was incredibly hard and demoralizing – as attested by the writing and interviews in Hal Wilmer's *As Serious As Your Life*

---

[13] The narrative film *Syncopation* (1942) captures the labour struggles and class dynamics of jazz musicians really well, but in its approach to casting and character unfortunately creates a whitewashed narrative of the form's development.

(1977) – the footage of carefree White people watching yachts sail, or simply exist in a privileged, sun-dappled leisure time feels incongruous, possibly deliberately so. The brief for photographer Bert Stern was to create a document of the 1958 Newport Jazz Festival, and he did that. Critic Richard Brody, writing in *The New Yorker*, is conflicted about the film and Stern's choices but does claim, poetically, that the music is 'filmed with a rare artistry, a rare attention to making images of music that are themselves musical' (2016).

Most of the film is performance footage. However, the film has a restlessness in its editing that is suggestive of a desire on the part of Stern to capture something of the otherness of the event, giving the film a restlessness. It may be that this restlessness disrupts and undermines the so-called purity of the performance footage (something Brody writes about in the review cited above), but it also injects something else into the film that enables the footage to be seen in a different way. It is a choice, one that makes an artistic stand and one that, at the dawn of the genre, challenges its audience and invites critique. In one reading it's a missed opportunity to show legendary artists in uninterrupted flow, in another reading it's making a comment about the lives and situations of those artists, drawing attention to them performing in that context. Ultimately though, it is both at the same time. *Jazz on a Summer's Day*, like many music films, is an unstable, messy object, with still-killer if truncated musical performances.

'What's missing is the likes of us'[14] – Filmmaking Choice in Music Films

The majority of music films – and each year brings more into the fold – take the 'facts and footage' approach, serving fans and general enthusiasts and taking an overview approach, trying to include as many key moments of biography and career triumph and challenge as possible. However, the perseverance and dominance of this approach has contributed to the widespread notion that music films are merely visual documents for artists to sell their wares or estates to repackage back catalogues, rather than viewed

---

[14] Critic AO Scott discussing *The Velvet Underground* (2021) participant roster on the New York Times *Popcast* podcast and his 'joy' at the lack of critics . Available at:-www.nytimes.com/2021/11/16/arts/music/popcast-velvet-underground-documentary.html.

through a lens of how audiences are being given access and what the filmmaking is saying about the subject. Too often it feels as though the 'what to show' has not been engaged with deeply enough.

One example of the difficult and constrained choices filmmakers must make is who to include in a music film. It takes more than a plethora of famous or familiar faces to convince of a subject's value, even if that subject is Miles Davis. *Miles Davis: Birth of the Cool* has many, many 'talking head' contributors spreading the gospel; the impact is diluted by the volume. By contrast, Jake Meginsky's film about a different jazz musician, *Milford Graves Full Mantis* (2018) has one contributor, Graves, and is more impactful as a storytelling and cinematic experience. This approach is not always appropriate, but the choice of whom to include as testimonial and whom to leave out says a lot about the filmmaker's approach to a subject and how they want to tell their story. Recent examples, at time of writing, that have stirred up questions based on participant choices include *Joe Strummer: The Future Is Unwritten* (2007), *Cobain: Montage of Heck* (2015) and *The Velvet Underground* (2021), all films whose release caused protracted conversations amongst critics and fans because of who wasn't on screen. These choices and others like them are mostly the desired approach the filmmakers wish to take, but one limitation they can come up against is participants who do not wish to be involved. However, sometimes the choices are down to the involvement of the artists and how they want their life events, personality and work to shape the story.

Sometimes, where the artist is heavily involved in the filmmaking process as a collaborator the 'what to show' can come across as self-indulgent, irrelevant or, in some cases, ill-conceived, working against the narrative they might want to present. At times, the film reveals much about the artist that does not track with the rest of the film's narrative. In other cases, the artist is at the centre of that process, doing something that doesn't show them in the light they may have intended. Two examples are in *Gaga: Five Foot Two* (2017) and *A Dog Called Money* (2019), both analysed later in the book. Some of the ways that music films can miss the mark in terms of representing the subject at the centre of the films can be traced back to the race and gender of the filmmakers, missing out on key aspects of a subject's story because of a lack of subjective experience coupled with a lack of criticality in addressing that subjective dissonance. Sometimes, there are valid criticisms that can be made regarding how films about women or musicians of colour, made by people outside those subjectivities, reinforce the problems, cinematically, that are faced by the subjects in the context of their life and career.¹⁵ It's not always the case though. This book attempts to wrestle, both in its analysis and discussion of films and in its curation of texts, with the problems of representation in music films. Even so, the limitations of time, space and making the whole mean something larger than its component parts that represent a challenge for music filmmakers also represent a challenge when writing about them.

'You got a doc, I got a doc'¹⁶ – The Book's Formal Approach

During an interview for this book Tony Palmer, a seminal music filmmaker responsible for many of the formal conventions that have become commonplace, and whose Leonard Cohen film *Bird on a Wire* (2010) is discussed in the chapter on concert and tour films, described his work as 'propaganda'. He claims he felt it his job to 'have the audience whistling the tunes at the end' of the film (Palmer, 2022). Undoubtedly there is some of that ethos at play in this book, where I hope to introduce readers to new films they may have previously overlooked, or to reconsider previous viewings anew. A more thoughtful term may be that I am engaged in 'advocacy criticism', described by music critic Jon Caramanica (2022) as when a critic uses their platform to draw attention to the overlooked and the under-considered. The book's curation of texts to focus on and explore results in an archive (a subjective one) that creates a music film history, a canon that will hopefully please and reward as well as rile and infuriate fans, critics and scholars. It is exclusive and associative by design and necessity. While in nearly all cases music is the central element of each film, there are examples where something else is central and music is contextual in some form. This varies again. In films such as *Requiem for Detroit?* (2010) or *The Black Power Mixtape 1967–1975* (2011), musicians are used to provide context

---

[15] The critic Simran Hans has written variously about this. Simran's piece on two Whitney Houston films, both discussed later in the book, is insightful in this regard. See https://mubi.com/notebook/posts/my-love-is-not-your-love-two-documentaries-misunderstand-whitney-houston-s-magic.

[16] Pop stars compare their documentary films crews in the wonderfully meta mockumentary *Popstar: Never Stop Never Stopping* (2016).

for stories centred on social and political histories because of music's often key role in the time and fabric of those histories. Music and Detroit, and music and the fight for Black liberation are tightly connected, frequently symbiotic.

Where possible the book promotes the work of non-White and non-male filmmakers and films about non-White and non-male artists. This is sometimes to the exclusion of expected films, which suggests a bias in terms of taste and value judgements on the part of the author, me. The focus is intended to be on films that say something of the relationship between form and content. There are some very good examples of the genre in a simple sense, films that do a good job of conveying music or performance. For example, Murray Lerner's *Listening to You: The Who at Isle of Wight Festival 1970* (1998) is a very pleasurable concert film, well filmed and edited and leading to an enjoyable time watching a 'classic' band at the height of their powers. It doesn't really add anything to the conversation the book is promoting though, about films where there is a relationship between the formal choices and approaches and what might nebulously be termed the 'spirit' of the music or the artist in the film. Also, it was made for television and, where possible, the book focuses on films made for the cinema, for a theatrical experience. There are notable exceptions – because there have to be. For example, Martin Scorsese's *No Direction Home: Bob Dylan* (2005) was technically conceived and produced for television, but not discussing it, particularly in how it works with archive, would be antithetical.

More information can always be delivered over more time. Content can, theoretically, go deeper when expanded over a series, but as a lover of cinema I wanted to write a book about what can be felt and experienced by compression, exclusion and limitation. What can the necessity of less information reveal through its telling? What can it free up? As a result, there is no discussion of the work of Ken Burns who has many extensive series for television on subjects such as jazz and country music.[17] Personally, this experience of watching is very different to, for example, the bursts of joy that can be felt in a standalone work such as *Dave Chappelle's Block Party* (2005). The formal invention of television documentaries historically is less pronounced, with a more considered

---

[17] Increased length doesn't automatically mean that the material presented is more authentic, more or less authored or the experience more rewarding. Writing about Burns' *Country Music* (2019), Alex Abramovich describes it variously as a 'drag', 'dishonest' and 'insidious'. Available at: www.lrb.co.uk/the-paper/v42/n19/alex-abramovich/even-when-it-s-a-big-fat-lie.

foregrounding of content in television documentaries – though there are exceptions including Scorsese's Dylan film – and there is no question that the rise of streaming services and the glut of films flooding services due to the greater demand from traditional and emerging broadcast outlets in the mid-2010s muddied that water of music films considerably, but that needs a different book to this one. And of course, pretty much all the films discussed here have been screened on television in some country at some point. So, the book mostly focuses on films that played film festivals and/or cinemas at some point in their release life. The focus on theatrical and festival features predominantly is exclusionary of films about artists and by filmmakers most outside the mainstream, but that again is a vital other book/text.

Where possible there is inclusion of 'indie films' and short films that sit outside this screening and release context but, as with any task of cultural criticism that seeks to provide an overview, concessions and compromises must be made. It also became a question of containment for a book that already has a considerable number of films under analysis. Readers may feel that some films included here may be overtly content driven as opposed to formally interesting. Their inclusion will likely be due to them being the most prominent moving image representations of a certain genre or artist, or to make a point about the mainstream and overriding perceptions of the music film. Formal considerations about filmmakers' choices are paramount to the analysis here, along with the relationship between form and content. However, the book is reaching for as wide a portrait of the music film as possible. Even with so many films covered, there are still some omissions that smart.[18] The book was written after/while watching or re-watching every film mentioned, however briefly in the text. I wanted the book to be written from a perspective of familiarity with a text, even if only one or two things were mentioned about the work ultimately. Films including Peter Whitehead's *Tonite Let's All Make Love in London* (1967) are incredibly hard to see if you live in rural Cornwall, England and are working on a book in addition to a full-time job.

Other films are hard to see in a different sense. Films such as *Let It Be* (1969), *Cocksucker Blues* (1972) and *Eat the Document* (1972) have been disavowed or removed from circulation by the artists they feature. All these works are discussed in the book's opening chapter on milestones and innovations because in the

---

[18] More on this in the 'Endnotes' at the close of the book.

digital age they can be found online in various bootleg versions. Not around for long, sometimes the transfers are very poor quality (hard to see, see?) and incomplete, making it difficult to forge a definitive response to them as texts, even subjectively. There is, however, a thrill upon stumbling upon these works, knowing that even within the fuzz and blur there are things to see and experience that the artists don't want you to. There is a frisson of authenticity that more sanctioned and sanitized works cannot offer. Hence their inclusion here. From this idea of what the artists and filmmakers want audiences to see, emerges another side of the music film, that of the place that music has in the story being told.

A different example again of a film that is hard to see would be *Leaving Neverland* (2019), the account of victims of serial sexual abuse by Michael Jackson. Following an initial contextual segment showing Jackson performing, the film becomes a harrowing, detailed and austere account of abuse, manipulation and trauma. It is not a film about music, but it is a film about a musician – the world's most famous one no less – and how they utilized the power afforded them by their musical success to enable years of heinous abuse. These are music films even if they are not films that tell a musical story or capture a musical performance centrally. They also represent the end of a spectrum that includes many music films and ties together so many of the films discussed in this book. This is the relationship between music and wider contexts such as race, sex, gender, class and other social, political and cultural constructions and contexts. Whilst it is inarguable that music's place in culture, like cinema, has shifted dramatically from its position in the 1960s when the music film emerged in earnest, there is no question that music in cinema can be accessed and understood through a variety of contextual lenses, in addition to the music film being a place where the art-form of music can be captured with extraordinary poetic and aesthetic effect.

'Aretha is just a stone singer'[19] – Thoughts on the art of the music film

To close out this introduction I will attempt to capture what is meaningful about music films to me. When asked what makes a good music film, my

---

[19] Aretha Franklin's father talks about her to the assembled crowd in *Amazing Grace* (2019).

Figure 0.1 Bunch of Kunst (dir, Franz, 2017).© Christine Franz.

nebulous response is something akin to 'a film that captures the spirit of the music'. This admittedly vague response is hardly appropriate critique for a book. However, within that vagueness is something specific and something that can be and indeed has been felt repeatedly in engagement with music films for this book and in the years that led up to it. Music films can access something cinematic and something that captures, elevates and contextualizes their subject when there is a matching of cinematic spirit with musical spirit. Ian Penman laments how some biographies simply aren't 'up to the multi-hued complexity of the artist in question' (2019: 22) and the same can be felt in many music films. It is thrilling to feel when watching music films that the filmmaker understands the music, personality, art, or politics of their subject and has found a way to translate that understanding cinematically. Richard Lester's *A Hard Day's Night* is maybe the first great and still leading example of this. There is a sense, because of how the filmmaking invention is capturing the performances and representing the lives of the Beatles, albeit in heightened fashion, that Lester understands the music and the people making it in a way that translates to the screen beautifully. It looks effortless, as though the camera is simply there capturing chaotic artistic life as it happens.

Often, music films are an invitation to live in the mess and the contradiction of popular music and the artists who make it. Sometimes they're an invitation to witness the extraordinary simplicity and intangibility of musical genius. Sometimes they are both. Sometimes there is an invitation to access feeling, as opposed to thought. When invited to compile a list of favourite music films, Les Blank's *A Poem is a Naked Person* (1973), the Aretha Franklin concert film *Amazing Grace* (2019) and Christine Franz's Sleaford Mods portrait *A Bunch of Kunst* (2017) always feature highly. These films exemplify how choice and feeling are integral to a resonant cinematic experience. Somewhat ironically, two of these films were ones that the artists didn't want released for reasons that in both cases never became clear. *A Poem is a Naked Person* is a loose, freewheeling portrait of Leon Russell that follows him on tour, recording and hanging out. Beyond the usual rock'n'roll paraphernalia associated with the period, the early 1970s, such as drugs and 'girls', there is little incriminating for Russell who appears separate and aloof for most of the film. His antics never tip into the debauchery found in *Cocksucker Blues* from the year before, and his pronouncements on life and music never feeling as vacuous as those in *Metallica: Some Kind of Monster* (2004).[20]

A Poem is a Naked Person is a wondrous example of where a filmmaker's feel for the subject is all. The content covers the usual conventions, but it's Les Blank's fascination with and empathy not just for Russell, whose performances he captures beautifully, but the environment that Russell comes from and makes work within that gives the film such textural depth. In Nick Pinkerton's words, Les Blank 'doesn't deny sadness but dwells longer on joy' (2015). Russell was born in Oklahoma and spent most of his life living and recording in the American South. The film follows him performing in New Orleans and recording in Nashville. As a filmmaker, Les Blank had a fascination with the American South and its musical forms, making numerous films including the short portrait *The Blues Accordin' to Lightnin' Hopkins* (1968) in that milieu. His interest in the people in the places Russell is from, and ends up in, as well as the Americana roots-based music Russell played, both on his own records and as an in-demand session musician and songwriter, results in a poetry of curiosity. Russell is captured as a musician who wants to play and make music constantly – his own

---

[20] Apologies to Metallica for using them as the example here. As the first chapter shows, I am a big fan of that film and how it portrays the heavy metal titans.

and other people's[21] – including playing at a band-mate's wedding. Around him Blank tries to capture the beauty of the music visually. At one point a single shot of a sunset with clouds moving slowly across the sky accompanies a heartbreaking Russell version of Hank Williams' 'I'm So Lonesome I Could Cry'. Blank also captures the unique sensibilities of the American South, as in one sequence a random parachuter crashes into a cameraman while Blank is filming a sport parachuting event in Oklahoma. Throughout, the film invites the audience to make connections if there are any or to simply enjoy the sounds and images if not.

Russell was still alive, just, when *A Poem is a Naked Person* was finally released, officially, in 2015. *Amazing Grace*, however, was not released until after Aretha Franklin died, as per her wishes. More accurately she expressed the wish that the film never be released, a fact that complicates the restoration of the film from its original source material in 2019. There is the valid opinion that her wishes be respected and the film never be released, yet this stands in tension with the overwhelming joy of witnessing her performance in the film. Franklin, like Russell, never expressed why she felt the way she did, after a mishandling of the film recording process over the two nights she performed at Los Angeles' New Temple Missionary Baptist Church in 1972, meant the footage was unusable for decades until the technology evolved to restore it. However, it seems unlikely it is because of how Franklin performs in the footage, which is possibly the greatest record of a performer performing ever captured on film.[22] Taking a different approach to the similar (re)discovery of material long since lost that was seen in *Summer of Soul* (2021), *Amazing Grace* has very little contextual information. There's just a title card and the short inclusion of some rehearsal footage edited to seamlessly join the live performance that followed. Otherwise, the film just allows the audience the extended privilege of seeing peak Aretha perform.

Watching the film, her brilliance is undeniable. *Amazing Grace* captures Franklin in command of her instrument, her voice. In close ups, seeing Franklin standing at a small pulpit in a simple church, singing for a couple of

---

[21] There is a fractious sequence involving Russell trying to play on a session for Eric Anderson where Russell snaps 'you don't know me well enough to say that about me' to Anderson.
[22] The audio of the performances became her biggest selling record and the biggest selling gospel record of all time, also called *Amazing Grace*.

hundred people, and yet summoning magical sounds with nary a hand flutter or backward arch is exhilarating. The exhilaration is captured in the film on the faces and in the more expressive movements of both the incredible choir backing her and in the devout audience compelled to stomp, dance and holler at receiving this music. The film is a masterclass in understanding the material you have and getting out of its way as much as *A Poem is a Naked Person* is a masterclass in what to add to conjure feeling and giddy associations. Even the gate-crashing of Mick Jagger and Charlie Watts in the *Amazing Grace* audience for the second night, which makes up the second half of the film, can't detract from the experience. Their appearance summons two questions after watching the film; who gets to watch and who gets to be filmed?

The sight of Jagger and Watts amidst the tiny, predominantly Black congregation speaks volumes about the privilege of stardom and the taking up of space at the expense of others. The same year that *Amazing Grace* was filmed, The Rolling Stones squashed a film of their own, Robert Frank's *Cocksucker Blues,* but by that point they had already been the subject of several key music films and cinematic performances. The Stones would continue to find their way onto cinema screens for decades, yet this remains the only cinematic document of Aretha Franklin.[23] A melancholy aspect of watching *Amazing Grace* is wondering what the terrain of the music film would have looked like in its peak product (volume-wise) years of the 1970s had it been released in 1972.

Christine Franz didn't have to worry about the artist in question blocking the release of her film *A Bunch of Kunst* (2017). The band in question were willing and supportive collaborators throughout the entire process. The film is an observational documentary following the rise of Nottingham electronic-punk duo Sleaford Mods as that rise is occurring. It is a feat of timing, showcasing Franz's instincts, from interviewing the band in her day job as a music journalist early in their career, that the band were of importance. Important enough to be the subject of a film. The result, Franz's first film, is a feat of filmmaking. Embedded with the band as they record, tour and live a simple life in Nottingham, the level of trust shared between artists and

---

[23] Until the release of biopic Respect (2021) starring Jennifer Hudson as Franklin.

filmmaker allows for Jason and Andrew, the Mods, to reveal how funny they are, their politics and motivation, creative process, ambitions and idiosyncrasies. Franz is interested in the band, and their charming and awkward manager Steve, as people as much as subjects and allows so much of the footage to run long, to include space and pause, to listen, that the result is a sense of time being slowed in order to capture the moments, as around the band their stock rises, the shows get bigger and a life-changing record deal looms on the horizon.

Franz's major influence was Shane Meadows' *Le Donk & Scor-zay-zee* (2009) a mockumentary that follows a rapper on the rise and his manager's ambition to get him on a bill with the Arctic Monkeys, viewing that as the breakout moment for his client. What the films share is the excitement and anxiety of working towards recognition and sustainability as well as a love and empathy for the people at the centre. And yet, what is remarkable is how (relatively) objective Franz remains in the filmmaking, most notably the edit. The sense of construction is superb, never feeling sycophantic. It feels intimate, trying to avoid leading the audience to a conclusion, but honouring the oddness that is two middle-aged, or nearing middle-age, men whose music and live show on the surface seems anti-entertainment. The sight of Andrew, bobbing with beer can in hand, at the rear of the stage as Jason sweats and convulses and rants his intricate poetry into the mic and faces of the adoring, socially agitated crowd, is thrilling. In his review of Sleaford Mods' 2021 album *Spare Ribs,* Sasha Frere-Jones writes that 'the aggression and chanted vocals qualify Sleaford Mods as a cousin of hip-hop, though the gestalt is closer to punk'. The accumulation of thoughts and images in Franz's film makes any question of whether Sleaford Mods are punk, indie, electro or Hip Hop moot. Franz thinks they are punk and, by the end, the audience does too. Not just because the film ends with Iggy Pop's validation by way of watching them from side stage at Flow festival in Finland and then reciting some of Williamson's lyrics from the book *Grammar Wanker* (2014) on camera, but because Franz intercuts this moment with the band watching a clip of the footage on a laptop, backstage at the festival. Just the two of them, laughing and disbelieving. No airs, no graces, just the manifestation of Williamson's hope for the film uttered at its outset, that 'they can't take this away from us'. *Bunch of Kunst, Amazing Grace* and *A Poem is a Naked Person* are films that prompt complicated, engaging, contradictory and sensorily challenging questions about music, films and music films. Reading music films as cinematic objects puts them at both a distance from and in tension with their other functions as marketing/brand/fan objects, arguing they are a genre to grapple with critically. Understanding them this way makes them harder to dismiss as 'just' music docs or concert films.

Part One

Form and Feel

1

'What Should I Say?'[1] – Milestones and Innovations

To look at pretty much any list proclaiming the greatest music documentaries of all time is to be left with the impression that, bar a few notable exceptions, the medium stopped evolving in the mid-1980s. So, as with other cinematic genres, the common perception is that its best days are behind it, with all that is exciting, fresh or innovative having already been claimed. 2021 was a year that challenged this myth more than any in recent memory[2] and saw the release of several significant and invigorating films, some discussed here and in later chapters of this book. These releases were high profile, including *Summer of Soul* (2021), *The Velvet Underground* (2021) and *The Sparks Brothers* (2020) as well as at the independent end of the spectrum, including *Poly Styrene: I Am A Cliché* (2020), *King Rocker* (2020), *Sisters With Transistors* (2020), *Delia Derbyshire: The Myths and Legendary Tapes* (2020) and *Keyboard Fantasies* (2019). Yet, whilst a stellar year of invention and quality, these releases did not single-handedly reinvigorate the music film. Music films have continued to evolve since they first emerged in earnest in the 1960s. The first section of this chapter looks at that period and into the 1980s, where so many conventions were established, before looking at how things have grown, changed and improved since those early gold rush years.

1964 – *A Hard Day's Night* and The Beatles

From the increasingly distant hindsight of 2022 it is easy to comprehend that, given the cultural impact of The Beatles, not just in music but in fashion and

---

[1] Lead singer Dave Gahan in *Depeche Mode: 101* (1989)
[2] At time of writing in 2022.

style, celebrity and pretty much everything associated with the 1960s, they would have had such great impact on music films. Even so, it's still remarkable how Richard Lester's *A Hard Day's Night* (1964) put in place so many conventions that are still de rigueur for the genre,[3] how it captured a genuine phenomenon in motion and how it instilled a formal playfulness that, sadly, quickly was superseded by earnestness and has been slow to return. While not strictly the first film about the band – that honour goes to Albert and David Maysles' account of their first trip to America *What's Happening! The Beatles in the U.S.A.* (1964)[4] crafted for American television – *A Hard Day's Night* is still the high watermark in terms of the content that would come to make up so many music films. It also perfects the idea of musicians performing persona variations on their real selves. Cowie claims that 'the appeal of the [film]' lay as much with the engaging personalities of [the band] as with the songs' (2004: 124). While ostensibly a narrative film – with the band playing versions of themselves – the band's surging popularity and difficulty travelling, in addition to being engaged in so much recording and publicity, meant production time and narrative scope were limited. However, Lester, the astute filmmaker he is, used these limitations to his advantage. As a result, the film features the band travelling to gigs and appearances, engaging with the press, rehearsing for a TV appearance, loitering in hotel rooms and backstage areas all the while yearning for the hedonistic freedom of a night out.

While many of those conventions appear in the Maysles film of the same moment, they are different here. Richard Lester was an experienced television director, so he was used to working quickly. This, coupled with his penchant, eye and ear for comedy – the inclusion of Wilfrid Bramble as Paul's mischievous grandfather is a masterstroke in this regard – resulted in *A Hard Day's Night* having a particular, special energy whereby narrative sequences feel as if they are happening naturally and a camera just happens to be present. It crafts what documentaries are always seeking to capture. The film is also an example of what happens when a filmmaker's vision and an artist's willingness to invest in the cinematic meet perfectly. *A Hard Day's Night* is, arguably, the first time this potential is apparent in a music film, and this is one of the reasons the film

[3] Lester refers to the film as a 'fictionalized documentary' in Peter Cowie's *Revolution! The Explosion of World Cinema in the 60s* (2004: 127).
[4] Latterly retitled *The Beatles' First U.S. Visit*.

remains so revered and watchable. This legacy is further helped by Lester's understanding of the different Beatles' personalities and strengths. In the film, each Beatle feels distinct and unique, which sets it apart from the Maysles film, where they are less distinct. In many ways, how people would think of the Beatles and their individual traits, were placed in amber by Lester's film. The band became voices for and symbols of both 1960s cheeky anti-establishment sentiment and also Lester's own. The follow-up film, *Help!* (1965) has more pointed satirical moments inserted by Lester, but here he presents the band as a group of smart, bawdy scamps who are game for a laugh and poke fun at the seriousness of the world in a way that would become virtually non-existent in subsequent music films.

This is in addition to the songs and the performances which are, naturally, spellbinding.[5] By the time of *Help!*, just a year later, the band were savvier about the process of making films and a bit more jaded and tired from performing so much, so their investment in the production and someone else's vision was markedly lower. As a result, what stands out in *Help!*, are the performances of songs such as 'Hide Your Love Away' and the film's title track. There are moments of formal wonder. Lester's decision to put a camera on Paul's bass neck for the performance of 'The Night Before' allows for a unique perspective on the performance of the song and creates a warped intimacy that is riveting. The film shines a spotlight on Ringo in a way that he was still mostly denied on record at this time in the Beatles' discography and as a performer he rewards Lester's faith in him. He's eminently watchable as a dupe caught up in the international espionage plot because of a fondness for costume jewellery. Elsewhere, as the 'plot' of the film descends into a chaotic battle between British and Indian forces, Lester manages to drop in delightful, satirical sight gags including having 'equal to exactly one millionth of all the high explosive exploded in one week of the second world war' emblazoned on a box of dynamite being wielded by the villainous Clang, played by Leo McKern. However, the film comes across as markedly racist in many ways. If the film presented diminishing returns to a certain degree considering the peerless *A Hard Day's Night,* it was certainly a stronger overall entry into the Beatles' cinematic oeuvre than that which followed in the 1960s.

---

[5] Despite being lip-synched.

Ringo is again thrust into the role of protagonist in TV movie *Magical Mystery Tour* (1968) as he takes a jaunt around Britain with his aunt. Directed, ostensibly, by the band, there are influential moments, as in the music video-esque interludes for performances of 'The Fool on the Hill' and 'I Am The Walrus'. Otherwise, it leans heavily on the bawdiness hinted at in *A Hard Day's Night* to resemble *Carry on at Your Convenience* (1971) more than anything else. By the time of the animated *Yellow Submarine* (1968) the band are less involved, providing songs and context for a film that draws from the band's iconography in fascinating ways, and the animation retains a warm, crude tactility. Like other 1960s legends who will be discussed shortly, the band had their moment of disavowing a cinematic work when they disowned Michael Lindsay-Hogg's *Let It Be* (1969). It was seen as a too invasive and raw account of the band's last days making their final album of the same name, though there is a happy ending for Beatles fans regarding this film. In 2021, *The Beatles: Get Back* (2021) was released. This near eight-hour mini-series is an archive work that restores and reframes the original footage to give a more nuanced and balanced account of their final work together. However, *Let It Be* feels unfairly maligned. Lindsay-Hogg's choice to reflect some of the distance and tension, at the expense of the more congenial moments that pop up in *Get Back,* is a choice to try and bring forth some of the atmosphere that led the band to call it a day shortly after the film was made. This bookends the period from *A Hard Day's Night* with a bittersweet coda, but one that reflects the cost of the band's journey.

Get Back is one of several Beatles films that have emerged in the twenty-first century. Some have received official patronage, like Ron Howard's misleadingly titled *Eight Days A Week: The Touring Years* (2016). Others have not, such as the charming and insightful *Good Ol' Freda* (2013) about the band's secretary Freda Kelly. *Eight Days A Week,* despite suggesting a performance focus, is the most formally conventional feature documentary about the band yet released. It does include some excellent interview material with Richard Lester talking about the films he directed, putting them, in particular *A Hard Day's Night*, high on the list of the band's many achievements. It serves as a reminder of how unique that film is. After its production and release the band would steadily lose interest in their films, even if Lennon maintained an interest in acting that saw him turn in a superb performance in Lester's *How I Won the War* (1967). As they lost interest and simultaneously could afford the luxuries of lavish productions and storylines, the cinematic representations of the band and their music never quite scaled the heights of that initial celluloid rush, one that opened with the band running away from screaming fans, the camera struggling to keep up as George trips, Ringo falls over him and they both, with John, crack up, enjoying it all, nary a care in the world, making it all look so effortless even if it was a hard day's night. Even so, within those lesser works there remain fascinating insights, performances and cinematic pleasures. *A Hard Day's Night* justifiably remains a high watermark of pop music cinematic storytelling. For excellent analysis and discussion of the Beatles' 1960s cinema, I highly recommend Stephen Glynn's *The Beatles and Film: From Youth Culture to Counterculture* (2020).

1967 – *Dont Look Back*, Bob Dylan and Martin Scorsese

In many respects, *Bob Dylan: Dont Look Back* (1967) – with its missing apostrophe – is the foremost music film. Often regarded, in lists no less, as the greatest music documentary of all time, it is the only music documentary to date to have a monograph dedicated to it – Keith Beattie's illuminating BFI Film Classic (2016).[6] One of the reasons the film retains its power as a cinematic object is because of how temporally unstable it is and has become since it was made. Shot in 1965 while Bob Dylan was on tour in the UK, the film didn't see release until 1967, meaning that by the time it was released its subject had already moved on creatively and culturally. The sense of dislocation is also due to the film not following the chronology of the tour that Dylan is undertaking. This temporal incongruity is further heightened within the film itself by its subject pushing against what is expected of him at that moment in his career. The Dylan that tours the UK in 1965 is expected to, and obligingly does, play the folk protest songs that made his name and (early) legend status but at this point he has already recorded his first 'electric' record, *Bringing It All Back Home* (1965), and is personally at odds with the Bob Dylan that his fans and the press expect. It is genuinely thrilling to witness an artist wrestling with his own rate of change and the public's unwillingness to let him.

---

[6] In the book, Beattie quotes Pennebaker's assertion that the film is not a documentary (2016: 21).

Like *A Hard Day's Night* and *Gimme Shelter* (1970, discussed shortly), *Dont Look Back* captures one of twentieth-century popular music's most famous and revered artists at a defining moment. Also, like those films, it defines the artist in a way that is under-discussed. Beattie writes that the film has an 'intense focus on the performance of persona' (2016: 67), which feels apt, but this performance is witnessed while watching a performer do their job. *Dont Look Back* and *A Hard Day's Night* with it, contain so many features that become the conventions of the music film, staples for the films made in their wake. *Dont Look Back* is ostensibly the first tour film – a sub-genre of the concert film discussed in the final chapter of the book – and as such it puts in place the expected scenarios that become engrained not long after its release. Dylan is seen entertaining in hotel rooms before and after shows. He spends a lot of time talking to the press,[7] on stage and travelling between them. All the while, in the background stands DA Pennebaker and his tiny crew, capturing it all on nascent film and sync sound equipment that allows them to get into nooks and corners and just watch and listen. Following this film, Dylan would take greater control of, or work at a greater emotional remove from, the films made about him because of the representation that comes across in this film. Even so, much of the mythos of Dylan as a mysterious, biting, provocative, combustible, funny and brilliant artist is here for the world to see; he leans into and exaggerates the Dylan that comes across here, weighed down by the unavoidable rigours of touring.

There are moments that have burned into the cinematic cultural consciousness, not always positive, including his cruelty and dismissal of Donovan and Joan Baez – the latter his tour companion. There are frenzied scenes of fans hurtling down alleyways after him and throwing themselves at him[8] and exchanges, particularly with journalists, that reveal a tension at the heart of Dylan that has remained constant throughout his career. Namely, the idea that he is a protest singer and that his songs should be about direct political change. Towards the end of *Dont Look Back* he gets really annoyed with a(nother) journalist and stands firm that he sees himself as an entertainer, and

---

[7] I wrote about the relationship between the press and Dylan & The Beatles for the 1960s British Cinema Project in 2016. Available at: https://60sbritishcinema.wordpress.com/2016/01/04/would-you-ask-the-beatles-that-how-bob-dylan-and-the-beatles-shaped-perceptions-of-the-music-press/

[8] Literally. At one point, Dylan screams to his driver 'get that girl off our car'.

that his songs are just songs. When he asks the journalist 'Who wants to go and get whipped?' in response to the idea that he is confronting his audience masochistically by veering from an expected path, there is pain in his voice, an exasperation that what he is trying to do is not obvious and needs explaining.[9] Pennebaker follows this exchange with Dylan's final performance in the film, an extended sequence of his set at the Royal Albert Hall. In the final moments, Dylan performs 'Love Minus Zero/No Limit' and he is shot from high above, a single spotlight picking him out on the stage. The camera tracks back revealing him isolated in light before, as applause rings out, the camera swings up to the lights in the rafters. His performance is incredible, the crowd invisible, in rapt silence until the climactic explosion of adulation. Then Dylan is in the car, banging on the window and shouting 'go driver go!' He wants away from the fans and press who don't get it, who can't see what Pennebaker's camera has captured: the stubborn, brilliant performance. He is laughing, though.

By the time *Dont Look Back* was released, Dylan had fully 'gone electric' and undertaken the famous UK tour that saw a fan declare him 'Judas', voicing the feeling that he had deserted his folk roots and his fanbase. Also, by the time of *Dont Look Back*'s release, Dylan had made another film of a UK tour, *that* UK tour, with DA Pennebaker. *Eat the Document* (1972). If the temporal coherence of *Dont Look Back* is slippery, the production details of *Eat the Document* are similarly so. Again shot by Pennebaker, the editing and directing was taken over by Dylan who clearly wanted more control of the narrative. It was eventually released six years after the tour and was soon buried by Dylan. At time of writing the film is incredibly hard to see, existing in a similar mode to Robert Frank's infamous *Cocksucker Blues* film of the Rolling Stones discussed shortly. It is sometimes available to see online, the twenty-first century equivalent of the bootleg tape. The editing is fractured and jittery, moving quickly from moment to moment without any space to settle or be still. In this aspect, whether this is part of the design or the shredded version available to view on YouTube, the genius of *Dont Look Back* emerges further. Pennebaker's editing in that film takes on new power in its ability to stop time amid chaos,

---

[9] Decades later this tension is still part of the music film's documentation process. In *Meeting People Is Easy* (1998) Radiohead's Thom Yorke is similarly vexed about the questions he's asked, positing that music should speak for itself.

to allow Dylan's musicality and focus on writing and crafting songs to come through despite the constant motion of touring.

In *Eat the Document,* the most telling moment that gets at Dylan's restlessness in terms of how to come across is when John Lennon, in the back of a taxi, reminds him (from experience no doubt), that 'it's only a film boy'. The film turns up occasionally at screenings, in music documentary and Bob Dylan retrospectives, but the best place to see its footage of the 'Judas' tour is in Martin Scorsese's *No Direction Home: Bob Dylan* (2005). The first of two epic accounts of musicians directed by Scorsese, the latter being *George Harrison: Living in the Material World* (2011) and discussed shortly. *No Direction Home* is long, clocking in at three- and-a-half hours,[10] yet it is not exhaustive and, as with most music films, better for that. The focus is on the rise and making of Dylan, taking his story from his early days to the moment, not long after the 'Judas' incident, when a motorbike accident stopped him in his tracks, and he took a moment to stop and reflect on who and what he was. In *No Direction Home,* much of the tour footage that makes up *Eat the Document* is restored and presented in a new context, one that. with the benefit of hindsight, remakes the moment of one of, if not the, pivotal creative and formative episodes of Dylan's life.

More than that, it positions one moment, one song as the centre of the Dylan universe, 'Like a Rolling Stone'. As mentioned, *Dont Look Back* is the only music film befitting a dedicated monograph (at time of writing) and that feels apt given how many books have been written about Bob Dylan. One, Greil Marcus's *Like a Rolling Stone: Bob Dylan at the Crossroads* (2006), is dedicated to the song that forms the nucleus of Scorsese's film. Scorsese and Marcus both see Dylan's 1965 six-minute-and-nine-second opus as the ultimate Dylan text and *No Direction Home* (the film's title comes from the song) presents the argument of the song's greatness by presenting footage of its recording and performance in glorious colour and with repetitious reverie. The recording and performance of the song and the album it sits on, and the tours that presented it to the world, are woven around recollections on Dylan and his trajectory from the artist himself and others involved or admiring from afar. Dylan's unease at having to look back and discuss the past is in

---

[10] *No Direction Home* was technically made for television – American broadcaster PBS.

tension with a desire to try and be open and honest and play along with the film's treatise. Even the 'going electric' that is Scorsese's thesis as to the cementing of Dylan as a cultural icon for the ages, is met with well-meaning deflection as Dylan says, 'it didn't really happen in the ways that I read about'. The disconnect between Dylan as he sees himself and how he is 'read' is still a cause for tension forty years on from *Dont Look Back,* but here he is at least less combative about it.

If *No Direction Home* makes the case that mid-60s Dylan is the ultimate – not only the Dylan persona, but maybe also the ultimate cultural figure. It also, through the amount of time spent discussing an artist's early years, suggests that post-accident and retreat from touring there is little of note to focus on cinematically in Dylan's life. Scorsese's potential unease at his own framing finds a rebuttal in 2019's *Rolling Thunder Revue: A Bob Dylan Story by Martin Scorsese.* The film does a similar restoration act to *No Direction Home,* this time taking footage from Dylan's own semi-narrative directorial folly *Renaldo and Clara* (1978), rescuing its incredible performance footage and recontextualizing it without the banal improvizations that make up the rest of that film's near four-hour running time. The repurposing of the performance footage brings it to life, and it stands as one of the best cinematic documents of Dylan as a performer. It smashes the idea that only the 'Judas' Dylan is of note cinematically and, around scintillating live footage, Scorsese weaves a mythical recollection of the tour that birthed said footage. John Scanlan writes how:

> It works as a film of our time, two decades into the twenty-first century – a time when we can be easily overwhelmed by the availability of images of the past through the exponential increase in media content, including a vast proliferation in the screen presence of popular music [...] – because it is an example of how to exist within that culture.
>
> 2022: 260

Scorsese and Dylan know that the 'truth' is less interesting than the 'idea of Dylan', especially when the performances are so powerful. Due to the relaxed approach to recounting fact, Dylan here is much more playful and charmingly mischievous as the film leans into his persona of self-mythologizing perpetual re-maker.

The film follows the conventions of the tour film. It sets the context up front. This is Dylan's return to touring after a long absence on the back of a few shows the year prior with The Band – formerly The Hawks who played on the 'Judas' tour – against the backdrop of America's bicentennial and Dylan's unease at the historiographical narratives[11] emerging to celebrate that event. There is backstage footage to accompany the extended and exceptional footage of Dylan performing with his roadshow comrades. Joan Baez is back and along for the ride. The 'revue' of the film's title is how Dylan imagined the touring show, a revolving and melding slew of performers playing shows in places normally bypassed by 'rock legends'. The band includes Joni Mitchell, Roger McGuinn and Ronnie Hawkins as it roves along. Contemporary production interviews, collected to supposedly put the original footage in context, tell a tale of their own. They don't just fail to recollect accurately what happened but actively create a new mythology. Sharon Stone tells of how she was picked out as a teenager from the crowd before a show, serenaded by Dylan singing 'Just Like a Woman' and ended up on tour with the revue. Not true. Elsewhere, Senator Jack Tanner talks about his experiences of the revue. Not true. Tanner is a character in Robert Altman's miniseries *Tanner '88,* played here as in that film by actor Michael Murphy in a wonderfully meta-cinephillic moment. An additional layer of cinephillic in-joking is found in recalling Murphy's role as John Triplette, fixer for the presidential candidate, in Robert Altman's sublime music film *Nashville* (1975).

Scorsese knows what he is doing, just as across this film and *No Direction Home* his preservationist side comes across in tandem with his directorial.[12] Just as is the case in narrative cinema, it is hard to recount the story, legacy and form of the music film without including an extended discussion of the work of Martin Scorsese. For many his foremost work in this field is 1978's concert film *The Last Waltz*. To call *The Last Waltz* a concert film is (as with so many concert films, to be fair) reductive, as it undermines the way Scorsese crafted a cinematic narrative – largely after the fact – so that the concert footage is seen in a certain light and context. Alongside the performances, shot over two nights in San Francisco as The Band call it a day and perform their final shows,

---

[11] Ironic, given Dylan's predilection for the same in his own career.
[12] Personally, I think *Rolling Thunder Revue* is the best 'Dylan film' and Scorsese's best music film.

there are interviews conducted latterly with the band members that recall the shows and The Band's career together. As well as this there are performances by The Band shot latterly on a soundstage in a style recalling Scorsese's musical *New York, New York* (1977), which he made concurrently with *The Last Waltz*. These formal and temporal extensions of the concerts create a cinematic myth around the shows and by connection, The Band. This, and the well-documented fact that Scorsese's insisted the shows be filmed on 35mm as opposed to the standard 16mm of the era, elevate the film to the realm of the magical.

Scorsese doesn't approach the music film with the dismissal that they are 'just' music documentaries or concert films in the way discussed in the introduction to this book.[13] He is a filmmaker first and almost equally an avid music lover. In *The Last Waltz* he frames the concert footage in a way that celebrates what made the event so special without excluding people not able to be there. His decision to include so much material that extends beyond the concert privileges the cinema audience as opposed to the concert audience, who are also included in this experience with so much material they haven't seen. As Scorsese himself said in a 1978 interview with the *Village Voice*, 'after *Woodstock, who wants* to see the audience anymore?' (1999: 81). And what of the concert footage? Well, it is incredible. The shows see a plethora of guests coming on stage to sing The Band's songs with them. This highlights how special The Band were as songwriters but also captures what an incredible backing band they were. I re-watched this film when writing this book in a double bill with *Eat the Document*, where The Band largely make up the band that back Dylan on his 'Judas' tour, then known as The Hawks. Side by side these cinematic objects chart an incredible decade for this group of musicians, from possibly the best live rock 'n' roll backing band of all time to one of the foremost bands of the 1970s. To say goodbye, performers including Neil Diamond, Dr John, a memorably coked up and out of time Neil Young,[14] and Bob Dylan himself, join them onstage. Dylan's appearance in the film is given an extended run. At the time it was seen as taking the shine from The Band somewhat. Re-viewed, following the release of *Rolling Thunder Revue*, it serves

---

[13] In a piece in the *Village Voice in* 1978, Curtis Fox makes the outrageous claim that before *The Last Waltz* 'only hacks were supposed to do rock-concert films' (1999: 79–80). I wonder how the likes of Pennebaker, Lester and Godard would respond to that?

[14] The producer recalled the difficulty of trying to edit out a cocaine crystal from Young's nostril in an interview with Peter Biskind in 1991 for *Premiere* magazine (1999: 193).

as a further reminder of what a great performer Dylan was in the 1970s, countering the narrative that his best days were behind him.[15]

Scorsese's use of songs by The Rolling Stones in his narrative work has led to two of cinema's most iconic music-driven sequences: Robert DeNiro's entrance in 1973's *Mean Streets* to the strains of 'Jumping Jack Flash' and Ray Liotta's celebration of the epoch of the Wise-guy life in *Goodfellas* (1990) to the thump of 'Gimme Shelter'. It could be said that Scorsese falls on the side of the Stones in the 'Beatles vs Stones' argument, bolstered by his concert film of the band discussed shortly. However, in 2011, he directed an epic ode to the life of Beatle George Harrison, in *George Harrison: Living in the Material World*.[16] Nestled within this work, thanks to the contributions of Paul McCartney and Ringo Starr, is a lovely Beatles documentary, with both the still-living Beatles recounting their experiences of George before, during and after their time in the band. Scorsese's ability to respond to material is on display in a very different way to a film like *The Last Waltz*, showcasing his ability to master context. There's much less sense when watching *Material World* of a directorial hand framing the footage and material. He seems more content to sit back and let the material and the contributions speak for themselves. He presents the archive and interview footage quietly, with purpose, echoing the perception of George, in the film and from lore, as a quiet and spiritual man. This presentation is radically different to the Dylan presented in *Rolling Thunder Revue,* another reminder of Scorsese's understanding of the people behind the music he, and audiences, love, as well as his devotion to presenting each artist in a way that reveals their uniqueness each time.[17]

1970 – *Gimme Shelter* and the Rolling Stones

If the 1960s commonplace idea was that The Beatles and The Rolling Stones were polar, binary opposites musically and in terms of image and tone, two

---

[15] Admittedly, of the three songs Dylan performs in the film, none of them by The Band. Two are Dylan songs and one is the traditional folk song 'Baby Let Me Follow You Down'.
[16] There's a legend that his path crossed with another Beatle in an interesting way, from the Phil Spector documentary *The Agony and Ecstasy of Phil Spector* (dir. Jayanti, 2009). Available at: www.nytimes.com/2010/06/27/movies/27spector.html.
[17] Though, as discussed in the next section, the 2008 film *Shine a Light* focused on The Rolling Stones fails to reveal much at all.

major films featuring Jagger, Richards et al. certainly bore this out. 1968's *The Rolling Stones: Sympathy for the Devil* [originally titled *One + One*] was directed by Jean-Luc Godard and there is nothing light or cheeky about either the band or the filmmaking, though the filmmaking is formally playful, and this film is discussed in the next chapter in terms of the process of making music. The film the Stones are most commonly associated with is a similarly dark and brooding work. 1970's *Gimme Shelter,* the account of their American tour that ended in 1969 with tragedy at Altamont, directed by the Maysles Brothers and Charlotte Zwerin, feels starkly oppositional to the whimsy of the majority of Beatles cinema. *Gimme Shelter* is a powerful film, both in the murky horror of the murder of Black concert-goer Meredith Hunter by Hells Angels and the foreboding sense of tragedy and naïveté that builds to the event. Hunter is, in the words of Hanif Abdurraqib, 'the victim of that concert's logical conclusion' (2021: 199). There is power also in the formal construction of this and other events depicted and their juxtaposition. Editor Charlotte Zwerin's input on the framing of the film's component parts and her suggestion that the band were filmed in the editing suite responding to footage captured at Altamont and prior rightly elevated her to the credit of co-director, a fact overlooked in many sexist references to the film's authorship since. Altamont and the death of Meredith Hunter dominate the film and its reputation, meaning that other aspects have been somewhat overlooked.

Largely, this is because of how the film is pieced together to show the factors that led to the tragic occurrence, from the lax logistical planning of the event on all sides, to a hubristic ignorance on the part of the band and how they saw themselves culturally. At a press conference early in the film, Jagger appears brazen about how the event they are headlining will be a celebratory culmination. It is a hubris chipped away at in scenes where the location changes at the last minute, where security is a constant concern and where the stage is put up fast and late. Amanda Howell writes that 'Jagger's countercultural rock masculinity [...] appears as a failed experiment in the transformative power of youth and music cultures' (2012). The film captures Jagger's face as he is confronted in the edit suite by the moment that shows Hunter's fatal stabbing.[18]

---

[18] James, in *Rock 'N' Film* (2016), writes of how the film was responsible for the [greater] understanding of what had happened to Hunter, due to the event being captured on film.

Zwerin and the Maysles put Jagger in between the cinema audience and the footage, and his face reveals his own sense of culpability and sadness at what occurred. It's remarkable, given the Stones' track record of squashing or limiting releases, that they allowed the film to go out as is, given how the band are made to look so disconnected from the reality of the event and situation throughout. Much of the film's overall power, however, stems from how this material is juxtaposed with material of the band onstage during their American tour and recording songs at the legendary Muscle Shoals studio, as they zigzag across states to the West Coast and disaster.

Footage from the band recording at Muscle Shoals in *Gimme Shelter* appears in a later documentary about the studio entitled *Muscle Shoals* (2013). Benjamin Harbert writes about the *Gimme Shelter* sequence in the film at length in his book *American Music Documentary* (2018). Harbert claims that the cinematography and editing 'encourage us to view and, more importantly, listen [...] in a particular way' (2018: 34) as the band listen to the playback of 'Wild Horses'. The sequence is fascinating in what it reveals about the band at a considerable peak. The hubris of the press conference is repackaged here as confidence in craft as the band piece together their song 'Wild Horses' with an ease that feels jarring when compared to the film-length account of their writing and recording of 'Sympathy for the Devil' in Godard's film of the same name. Harbert writes that in this sequence in *Gimme Shelter,* as we watch and listen to drummer Charlie Watts, 'a slight expression of approval and a head nod keeps us listening, perhaps wondering: 'What's it like for Watts to listen to himself?' (2018: 41). The slowness, the lack of cutting and the camera up close makes the viewer privy to a private creative moment, one that celebrates the artistry of the musicians being filmed. However, while the film honours and respects live and studio craft it also captures the opposite. Like *Let it Be,* it could be accused of skewing the reality, or facts, of the event being filmed. *Gimme Shelter* ends early in the Stones' Altamont set, not long after Hunter's death, suggesting that the event resulted in the end of the show or a truncated set.

One of the striking things, still, about *Gimme Shelter* is how much negative chaos and disorder there is in the film. The early part of the film, featuring the band launching the Altamont show with a pre-emptive celebratory press conference, explodes with footage of a sell-out indoor show in New York. The band look and sound fantastic and the fans are on board. As the film progresses, darkness descends, not only in the austere images of the band watching the Altamont footage but also in the desperate (lack of) organization preceding it. A disaster feels almost inevitable given the haphazard logistical preparations. The film is a wrenching document of a dark event, as so much time is spent relaying the stop-start nature of the Altamont performance. The bad vibes and antagonism are dwelt upon. The band try and play but they don't do it that well and the sound is poor. They are clearly on edge at what is unfolding. And this is the last third of the film. It doesn't cut dramatically to the tragic death moment, but forensically builds a sense of dread and inevitability. Indeed, knowledge of the murder is revealed earlier in the film. It's gruesome but compelling and the result is a very specific version of events, one that at no point tries to persuade that this was a fairly decent Stones show with a freakish tragic interlude, which by all accounts it was; indeed, little was known of the murder until footage shot for the film emerged. The general cultural (if apocryphal) consensus that Altamont was one of the twin events in 1969 that signified the symbolic end of the 1960s project of free love and peace is cemented, cinematically, in this film that presents a band's astonishing slide from hallowed adoration and slick professionalism to murky, uncontrolled anarchy and despair in the time it takes to fly across America and play a few songs along the way.

If *Gimme Shelter* has emerged as the pre-eminent Stones' film, it wasn't the first. It was preceded by the now-largely-forgotten tour film *Charlie Is My Darling* (1966), directed by Peter Whitehead. It's strange how this film isn't as well-known as other Stones films, as it contains some of the best footage of the band live. It also captures them at a pivotal stage where they are naively curious and exaggeratedly reflective about the future of pop music and their role in it, as well as clearly unnerved by the force of adulation directed at them. The film follows them across Ireland on tour and one show is curtailed almost as soon as it begins by a stage invasion which foreshadows the chaos and disruption of *Gimme Shelter*. In one brilliant moment Jagger is frank and honest about the sexual power of performance and the sexual dynamics between performer and audience that recalls the frankness of Paul Anka in *Lonely Boy* (1962), as discussed in the introduction. By the time of 1968's long-unaired TV special, *The Rolling Stones Rock and Roll Circus* (eventually released in 1996), the band, Jagger in particular, assert a control over proceedings that attempts whimsy and tongue-in-cheek charm but, in the words of James, is instead 'sluggish' or 'noticeably less propulsive than usual' (2016: 273). Maybe the reason for the delay in release is that the Stones, even though they are the main attraction, just don't play as well as their undercard which included superb turns from The Who and the John Lennon-fronted supergroup The Dirty Mac.

Post *Gimme Shelter,* the Stones' films flatter to deceive in a similar fashion to the *Rock and Roll Circus.* The casual missing off of Zwerin's name in conversation about the directors of *Gimme Shelter* is sadly not the only example of sexism in connection with the film, or other Stones' cinematic objects. Scintillating footage in *Gimme Shelter* of tour support act Tina Turner, then performing with husband and abuser Ike, is uncomfortably offset by a leering Jagger, clearly smitten by her beauty and presence. 1972's *Cocksucker Blues,* directed by iconic photographer Robert Frank, and documenting the band on tour and in the studio, is full of moments where women are treated poorly and presented as objects for the pleasure of the band's entourage and crew. Even though the band are not overtly present or responsible for some of the onscreen humiliation, it is clear why they wouldn't want to be associated with the film. They issued a diktat that it could only be shown with director Frank or the band in attendance.[19] The band and Frank have said very little on the record about the film and as it is only viewable via bootleg copies uploaded to the internet and rarely screened in other forms, legends and myths emerge in place of statements of record. Alongside some truly distasteful footage such as women being coerced to strip on private planes and one sequence where a woman is at the mercy of the crew's sexual desire on camera in a hotel room, the film does include moments where Frank's photographic eye for detail, Americana and composition shine through.

The myriad ways Frank has been described as an artist – a distanced, curious, unsympathetic but ultimately interested observer – are present in the film. It's messy and uncontrolled, with Frank as director responding to the carnage and the quiet, the famous people and the banal drives with equal cinematic interest. Mulholland writes that 'offscreen sounds, of music, of dialogue, constantly interrupt or obscure the conversation or onscreen music, leading to an eerie, drugged feeling of dislocation' (2011: 121). It's hard to know if what is available to view is the film as

---

[19] Robert Frank died in 2019 and any update to the viewing restrictions of the film has yet to be issued.

finished or intended, and this is somewhat thrilling given the control the band exerted in audio/visual representations following this film. As with even the least-interesting Beatles films, the performances of songs by the band shine through. As discussed earlier in this chapter, filmmaker Martin Scorsese often repurposes and reframes pre-existing film footage in his music films and in *Shine A Light,* his 2008 concert film of the Rolling Stones live in New York, he includes snippets that first turned up in *Cocksucker Blues.* Footage of the Stones meeting Dick Cavett forms a contextual archive that wraps around straightforward footage of the band performing an intimate (for them) show at New York's Beacon Theatre. Nearly forty years on from *Gimme Shelter* the band are comparably energetic but slicker, more controlled and less prone to frenzy. It's consummately professional and not very interesting because of that. The most engaging moments are those focused on Scorsese trying to direct the filming of the live event. Famously nervy, the film shows him tearing his hair out at the band's laissez faire attitude to the show.

All Scorsese wants is a set list so he can ensure the lights are in the right place at the right time. 'We cannot burn Mick Jagger', he exclaims. What is conjured is a reminder of Jagger the naive, the supremely confident, from *Gimme Shelter,* assuming nothing could happen that would leave him *burned.* Even though the whole enterprise feels controlled to within an inch of its life, it is still a good example of how often artists are not good judges when it comes to how their on-screen behaviour is captured and understood. Part of the pitch of *Shine A Light* is the guest roster of artists sharing the stage with the band including Buddy Guy, Jack White and Christina Aguilera. The former two artists are respectfully allowed to perform their guitar and voice work unobstructed, unbothered. Aguilera, however, is subject to close contact grinding from Jagger throughout her guest slot that lets some of the sexism that was so rife in the earlier films seep through here. It's awkward and uncomfortable and one wonders if, from the cultural vantage point of 2024, Jagger would have liked to have behaved differently, or would now cut this sequence out of the film.

1981 – *The Decline of Western Civilization*

Penelope Spheeris' trilogy of films centring on Californian music and culture in the 1980s and 1990s, built mainly around punk and its legacies, are unique for several reasons. Unlike the films about Bob Dylan previously discussed, there is very little lag time between production and release, meaning that they capture a cultural moment and also enter the cinematic culture while that moment is still ongoing to some degree, or at the very least in the immediate past. Spheeris is one of several filmmakers – others including Julien Temple and Don Letts are discussed elsewhere in this chapter and the book – who saw the moment of punk as an opportunity, as permission, to pick up a camera and make a film with ideas around experience, entitlement and hierarchies, jettisoned. *The Decline of Western Civilization Part I*, as it became known upon release of *Part II* in 1988, stands as one of the great punk films and unquestionably the greatest punk film of the punk era.[20] Don Letts' *Punk Rock Movie* (1978) came earlier but was hampered by poor post-production, most notably in its sound. Julien Temple, possibly punk's greatest documentarian, only came of age cinematically regards music film with 2000's *The Filth and the Fury,* discussed later in this chapter. His contemporary punk work, 1980's *The Great Rock 'n Roll Swindle,* is valuable only as a time capsule curio, its cinematic qualities negligible. Lech Kowalski's *DOA* from 1980 has some interesting visual footage of American punk fans (or rather in some cases concert attendees as they don't seem to like being there) captures something of the atmosphere on both sides of the Atlantic. Ivan Král and Amos Poe's *The Blank Generation* (1976) stands as the earliest full-length document of the American punk and nascent post-punk/new wave scene, but with grainy footage and non-sync sound it rarely moves beyond being a curio. Even if those films were better, Spheeris' document would likely still tower over them because, despite not being much more experienced than her peers, if at all, her focus and filmmaking ability are exceptional.

There is no archive material in *Civilization Part I*, no interviews conducted latterly to frame or reframe recorded footage. The film is a document of its time, wholly. It also incorporates its making in an overt way that is only hinted at in the music films that preceded it. Amidst the chaos of shows and parties in squats, Spheeris can be heard shouting questions above the chaos, trying to

---

[20] A case could be made here for Derek Jarman's *Jubilee* (1979) but its experimental narrative sensibilities, despite its aesthetic closeness to the feel of the era, make it seem like an outlier to the focus here.

capture a reflection on the moment[21] in the moment. The result is an exhilarating energy that reveals the oft-quoted chaotic energy of the punk scene in a delightfully indirect way. Elsewhere, stage managers read out a notice about the filming taking place to audiences before shows commence. This is repeated throughout the film, moving the inclusion from a mere aside that recalls the filmmaking process to something that captures the weirdness of the venture, of filming the likes of Black Flag and the Germs and their fans engaging in the act of a punk show. Throughout, the film focuses on performances by bands who were key to the hard-core punk scene of the late 1970s and early 1980s. There is as little editorial intervention as possible by the filmmaker. The bands who played a role are all allowed similar screen time and their views and personalities allowed the same amount of space. The difference between the cathartic, emotionally driven performance of a band such as Circle Jerks stands in sharp contrast to the homophobic, violent words and actions of a band such as Fear. Neither are judged. Spheeris' confidence in the audience is remarkable.

That confidence and reluctance to judge is present in *The Decline of Western Civilization Part II: The Metal Years,* from 1988. Spheeris as a filmmaker is associated with punk due to the power and legacy of her first film, but the second instalment shows her as a respectful and curious documentarian, someone willing to meet a scene on its terms and try to figure out something about it. The decades since 1988 have not been kind, critically, to the sub-genre of heavy metal known as 'hair metal' that Spheeris captures some of the rise of, but the film is not exploitative or unkind. As with *Part I*, the filmmaking is respectful, allowing space for its participants to reveal themselves without judgement. For the most part. The sexism of the scene and its blatant objectification of women draws Spheeris out somewhat. As with *Part I,* she is a constant if quiet presence. However, there are moments where her opinion breaks through. There is a delightful elongated 'Okaaaay' in response to some braggadocio about drugs and money from Aerosmith that is followed by a critical piece of editing that questions Steven Tyler's claims of originality, using his scarf as a semiotic framing

---

[21] In *The Last Waltz* there is extended coverage of Scorsese interviewing Robbie Robertson on screen but it was rare for the filmmakers to be so overtly present in the films, something that is part of the legacy of Direct Cinema.

device. Elsewhere, the band London present themselves in such a ludicrous manner as if they think *This is Spinal Tap* (1984) is a documentary without Spheeris' film having to do anything but present them being themselves for the band to expose their hollow core. They are clearly trying to shock and unsettle Spheeris and she, mostly, lets the footage speak for itself.

Part II is not a repeat, formally, of *Part I*, which is a testament to Spheeris and her approach to documentary making. Whereas the first film is a direct document of the bands involved in the scene and all the material captured includes those seen in the film performing and attending the shows that make up the bulk of the footage, *Part II* extends its reach to include the voices of fans more predominantly but also, via interviews, the figures that sit atop the sub-genre's hierarchy of value. The observational elements follow bands on the fringes of popularity and acclaim. This results in a much more layered film and experience as the gaps between fans, bands on the fringes such as London, Faster Pussycat and WASP and the likes of Alice Cooper, Lemmy and Aerosmith are stark. There is very little need for editorial manipulation. Even at the time the film was made, the fame, popularity and influence of Cooper, Motörhead and Steven Tyler and Joe Perry on Heavy Metal was clear. What links the films, is Spheeris' interest in how this scene emerges from the context of Southern California and Los Angeles in particular. These three films emerge as geographically clustered portraits by a filmmaker looking at their environment at a particular time, through the lens of music.

The vacuous proclamations of *Part II*, such as 'I'm in it for the money', how the joy of touring comes down to meeting and sleeping with women, or the neo-liberal, entitled conviction of 'making it' against the backdrop of Reagan-era America, have deeply melancholic echoes and resonances in *The Decline of Western Civilization Part III* (1998). In *Part II,* participants claim they don't want to end up on 'skid row', that seemingly mythical gutter space where dreams go to die. *Part III* reveals skid row to be a reality for many young people who identify either aesthetically or ideologically with the punk movement as it is mythologized and (re)presented. Openly the most personal film of the three for the filmmaker, it follows young people living on the margins of society.[22] They

---

[22] I had the privilege of interviewing Spheeris on the occasion of the trilogy arriving remastered on DVD and Blu-ray for Directors Notes in 2015. Available at: https://directorsnotes.com/2015/09/01/penelope-spheeris-the-decline-of-western-civilization/

are predominantly not musicians but fans, unable to make a shift to more amenable, sustainable or commercial forms of music or careers as did many who Spheeris and her peers chronicled in the early 1980s. They are bound to the ideals of punk and living outside the capitalist system to the degree that they are crushed by it. Many not even born when Black Flag were performing for Spheeris' first instalment (heck *Part I* captures Black Flag before Henry Rollins had joined) are still seduced by its (illusory) ideals. Yet, Spheeris is curious and empathetic and gives them time and space, so their stories are elevated to the same level as the now icons captured by her previous works. Their sadness, at one point a participant says to Spheeris and her crew off camera 'you guys won't miss us', represents a moment where those involved speak indirectly to the audience, through the filmmaker, returning punk to its pre-music connotation of referencing young people who cannot live in the society that awaits them.

1984 – *Stop Making Sense* and Jonathan Demme

The film consistently regarded as the greatest concert film ever made is not regarded as a concert film by the filmmaker who made it. Jonathan Demme described 1984's *Stop Making Sense* as a 'performance' film[23] and this claim isn't a way of devaluing the genre – of the 'I didn't want to *just* make a concert film' variety – but of placing the filmmaking and its viewing in a particular mode. The audience present at the Talking Heads shows in Los Angeles that make up the footage in *Stop Making Sense* are largely peripheral, heard via rapturous applause but rarely seen, glimpsed as background, fuzzy beyond the clarity of Tina Weymouth's hands in close-up doing bass runs, and other such performance details. The audience emerge in clarity towards the film's end when Demme and his collaborators open up the construction of the film and the performance for appraisal.[24] The film presents a band at their performance

---

[23] A film released a couple of years later, Laurie Anderson's *Home of the Brave* (1986), is much more easily recognized as a 'performance film', capturing the Talking Heads contemporary in a variety of modes – singer, dancer, orator.
[24] Demme and David Byrne's decision to largely exclude the audience in shot marks the film out and makes a strong case for it as a 'performance film'. It has remained uncommon to do it to this degree ever since, with filmmakers generally more comfortable trying to represent the feel of the live audience present, engaging with the artist.

peak. Tensions in the band are apparent in the fabric and subtexts of the film and would fray and split apart in numerous ways following this tour and the record they were promoting at the time, *Remain in Light*. Regarded by some as the band's musical pinnacle, the film would come to be acknowledged as a cinematic pinnacle too, one that still has hold now, nearly 40 years on. Pauline Kael, in her *New Yorker* review declared it 'close to perfection' and 'a dose of happiness from beginning to end' (1984). Hard to beat.

When directing *David Byrne's American Utopia* (2020), a concert film of the Broadway show of the former Talking Heads main creative voice, filmmaker Spike Lee wisely didn't try to beat or ignore Demme's film, but instead incorporated similar elements. This is most notable in terms of capturing movement and the stark simplicity of how Byrne incorporates the 'backstage' into the stage show – meaning the film is in dialogue with *Stop Making Sense*, rather than trying to usurp it. Not content to try and capture performance in a way that captures what it was like to 'be there', in *Stop Making Sense* Demme clearly understands the futility of attempting such an impossible task. The goal instead is to draw attention to how a live performance is put together, piece by piece, to create an engaging, transcendental experience for audiences. Saffle writes that the film is 'subjective', embodying the director's 'point of view as well as his production methods and techniques' (2013: 42). The result is a film that is deeply cinematic and transcends its live event origins.[25] The cinematic experience is enhanced by the band's postmodern approach to live performance, deconstructing the entirety at the same time as presenting the construction, in a way that invites the filmmaker to do the same. Both artist and director are challenged to move beyond this distancing, self-aware starting position, to reach a moment or moments where the artifice drops away and only physical, emotional connection to the music remains. It is, in many ways, a self-challenge, a response to the growing artifice of the live concert event and the concert film, where the idea of transcendence and an organic, natural relationship between music and ears and eyes is assumed as given. Across Demme's music film work there is a constant visual referral to those responsible for performing and

---

[25] I wrote about the film for the Quietus when it was released on Blu-ray in 2015. Available at: https://thequietus.com/articles/19381-stop-making-sense-article - and struggled then, as here, to really articulate why it's so good without resorting to banalities and generalities.

staging live music; not just the stars, but session players, dancers, backing vocalists and stage crew.

Stop Making Sense reminds us that audiences finding meaning in a performance is not a given, but something that requires significant work and construction on the part of those creating the performance. Similarly, for most cinema audiences merely presenting a live concert event doesn't guarantee connection, even though they may like the music going in. There needs to be a cinematic approach. Demme's cinematic approach is clear from the first few frames of the film. The crowd are heard before anything is seen. What is first seen are feet, in close up, moving across a stage. Bits of white tape whose importance will be revealed later are glimpsed. There is a slow track up after a boom box is placed on the stage. 'There's a tape I wanna play'. A version of 'Psycho Killer' starts. David Byrne strums and struts in place. He sings. A close-up of his eyes captures him gazing at the unseen audience. The camera pulls back to reveal him alone on an empty stage, glitches in the tape's playback matched by glitches in his movement. Is this real? Is this live? The stage is completely bare, save for the tape on the floor. The backstage area clearly visible, brickwork, cables and pipes exposed, no pretence to it being a 'show', one that just magically happens as so much live performance would suggest. And what's this? While Byrne is singing one of the band's most iconic songs, in a manner devoid of much of the musicality that made it so, road crew wheel equipment on to the stage, placing it where the small white tape tells them to do so.

For the second song Byrne is joined by bassist Tina Weymouth. Backing vocals are heard, but not seen. The curtains are still open and during the song the drum riser is wheeled on by road crew. It is only during the fifth song, 'Slippery People', that the 'show' comes together with all the musical pieces complete – backing vocalists now visible etc. – and the previous backstage area is replaced as a visual backdrop by a simple black curtain, turning the space into a more traditional 'black box'. Here, the performance of the group hits and magically maintains a level of quality and intensity and focus for the remainder of the performance. Even when Byrne leaves the stage to Weymouth and drummer Chris Frantz's side project The Tom Tom Club to change into the iconic 'big suit', the momentum doesn't drop. The pre-planning of how the music would be captured and, as a result, how the film would be edited, ensures this. The gleeful postmodern deconstruction of the whole experience extends beyond the music as Byrne asks the crowd, rhetorically, if they have any questions, to beyond the film and the strange promotional video for the film where David Byrne interviews himself. Dressed as a female presenter he asks himself about the motive for the big suit and Byrne, while wearing the big suit, declares in response 'I wanted my head to look smaller and the easiest way to do that was to make my body bigger'.[26] It's a reminder that music films are not definitive documents, but often paratexts that illuminate or demystify something deeper about musicians.

Towards the end of *Stop Making Sense* the camera crew are visible on the stage and in the crowd, arms around each other, dancing along. This capturing of the people responsible for the film and the event being filmed, not limited to stars, is a feature of Demme's music films. He collaborated with Neil Young on films such as *Journeys* (2011) and *Heart of Gold* (2006). The latter film is the best example of their collaboration and the perfect partner to Jim Jarmusch's punk mélange *Year of the Horse* (1997), representing so well the opposite side of Young – the acoustic, solo-driven work – in contrast to the noise and jam-band persona he inhabits with Crazy Horse. That is a simplistic description of Young and a simplistic appraisal of Demme's film. Demme is interested in Young, sharing with the participants a level of awe that he is playing the shows at the famous Nashville Ryman Auditorium the film is capturing, mere months after suffering a brain aneurism, and he spends time talking to Young about his illness and his career. However, he is also interested in the other musicians Young has chosen to share the stage with. At one point, Young says 'I just want to play well and share the stage with my friends' and Demme takes this as permission to dedicate so much of the film to visual portraits and conversations with those friends. There is an ease to the background filmmaking that is matched by the ease of the musicians onstage, resulting in a film that has a grace and ease that feels rare, and so is perfect for its subject. There is a similar focus in Demme's final concert film, *Justin Timberlake + The Tennessee Kids* (2016), on the lesser known and seen hands that go into making live performances memorable.

In addition to a, by now customary in concert films, time lapse of the performance stage being set up, Demme includes visual portraits of the session players, dancers, stagehands and backstage crew that artistically and practically

---

[26] This interview can be found on the DVD/Blu-ray of the film.

construct the spectacular and frankly jaw-dropping show led by popstar Timberlake. Demme's interest in this film feels largely rooted in an almost teenage glee at the scale and spectacle of the live show space and how Timberlake inhabits that space and moves throughout it with command as a performer. Thirty years on from *Stop Making Sense* and he is not phoning it in. Instead, he seeks out new angles, new ways of capturing performance and musicality. Demme utilizes the budget and opportunity afforded by making a Netflix film for a superstar to the fullest. There are roaming shots from the venue's rafters that match in their audacity and scope the spectacular show unfolding below them. Timberlake puts on an incredible show and Demme wants to share the sense of how incredible it is with the film's audience. The perspective shifts from a God-like omnipotence to an insect-eye view from inside the stage and the banks of musical equipment. A genuine thrill is palpable in the live performance footage, which is understood further when compared with the footage of Timberlake offstage. Demme doesn't seem to find him that interesting as a person compared to, say, Neil Young, and the footage doesn't present Timberlake as particularly worth spending time with. Either that, or he is just more interested, as with Talking Heads, in presenting the art as opposed to the artist, marvelling at the work and inviting the cinema audience to do the same. And to dance and sing along, of course.

1984 – *This is Spinal Tap* and the Narrative Legacies of Music Films

At one stage, narrative fiction films that utilize the aesthetics and conventions of non-fiction music films were going to have a more prominent focus in this book. The reality is that this area could form its own book. There are so many examples, and they are uniquely interesting, at their best, in terms of how they capture the essence of music and its ephemera, delivering a coherent, rewarding narrative. In 1984, the same year as *Stop Making Sense,* the film that sits at the centre of this particular cinematic universe, *This is Spinal Tap,* was released. While not the first 'mockumentary',[27] it established a set of conventions and

---

[27] Peter Watkins' savage satirical mockumentary about the pop music world and 1960s culture *Privilege* (1967) predates it by 15plus years and the Rutles film by a decade, but the fact that *Tap* is a comedy is why there's so much focus on it here.

undoubtedly a standard for them, certainly regarding music films. The 'mockumentary' takes the codes and conventions of the documentary and parodies them, sending up the subject but also the form. They are most rewarding when they blend a love, or at least an appreciation, for their subject alongside a healthy dose of self-awareness and gentle cynicism. Before *Spinal Tap* came, in terms of comedic innovation and prominence, *The Rutles: All You Need is Cash* (1978), a parody of the Beatles' story conceived by Eric Idle with Neil Innes providing the uncanny soundalike songs. The story of The Rutles hues to that of the Beatles tightly with chronology, characters and song names barely an inch removed. 'A Hard Day's Rut', 'Yellow Submarine Sandwich'. Bill Murray as Bill Murray the K (based on the American radio DJ Murray the K who played a prominent role in the Beatles' early US success). Jeffrey Roessner argues that the film undermines 'documentary filmic conventions' as well as offering 'a direct assault on the Beatles' musical prowess' (2013: 166), capturing the sharper edge of the satire in mockumentary. Often there is love and respect but often there is something else at play.

Murray the K appears in *What's Happening: the Beatles in the USA,* mentioned earlier in this chapter, and *The Rutles* takes moments that appeared in that film, plus other Beatles' cinematic works, as starting points for its parody. Some of the comedy is spoof-adjacent, particularly the moment, lifted from *A Hard Day's Night,* where they dart in and out of several cars and vehicles to escape fans outside a venue. While undoubtedly funny, the film is a litany of easy pickings in terms of its humour. The documentary aesthetics and behind-the-scenes scenarios, familiar from *A Hard Day's Night* and, latterly, *Let It Be,* provide an accessible template and framework for the film and a jumping-off point. *The Rutles,* while including 'archive' material in the form of film, photo, interviews, performance and news material, all painstakingly created for the purpose of the film, is framed, aesthetically, as a television documentary. Eric Idle, in addition to portraying one member of the band, appears as the host of the documentary, traversing locations associated with the band, to tell the story of what happened. The on-screen and voiceover narration feels televisual, rather than cinematic, which is not a bad thing, but another way it differs from *This is Spinal Tap. Spinal Tap* takes the work started by *The Rutles* and creates a more nuanced, cinematic and long-standing work in terms of influence and legacy.

This is Spinal Tap is a largely observational mockumentary, following the band as their tour a new album at the stage of their career where their star is diminishing. Interspersed with interviews and archive material, as with *The Rutles,* painstakingly created for a feeling of verisimilitude, the film captures a band on the decline. Unlike *The Rutles, Spinal Tap* are not a stand-in for a particular band. They are an amalgam of a number of heavy metal bands, but their story is one familiar to many rock groups from the 1960s and 1970s who found the limelight spinning away from them to focus elsewhere. It's this distance from the particular, in terms of single point of identification, coupled with a specificity about the rituals, idiosyncrasies and vagaries of the music business that make the film so influential.[28] And also, so funny. Despite seeing the film many, many times (it's a favourite shared film for me and my brother), the line that struck me this time, as I rewatched for the book, is when one of the band's tour dates is cancelled due to poor ticket sales. The date in question is in Boston and the band's manager, Ian Faith, played by Tony Hendra, says 'Boston's not a big college town'. It's a hilarious moment that captures both his complete ineptness but also a desire to be kind to and protect the artists under his care. *Spinal Tap* consistently provides laughs rooted in the absurdity of professional music and critiquing the business. However, it never veers into pastiche or cruelty, because of the richness of the central characters.

Spinal Tap consists of Nigel Tufnel (lead guitar/vocals), David St Hubbins (guitar/vocals) and Derek Smalls (bass/vocals).[29] They are the creations of Christopher Guest, Michael McKean and Harry Shearer respectively. Guest, McKean and Shearer created their characters for the film in a way that became standard for films directed by Guest following *Spinal Tap,* including the folk mockumentary *A Mighty Wind* (2003), through in-depth research and character development to the point where the character can live on camera, providing a naturalism and authenticity that carries the work. The love the performers have for their characters is deep, resulting in performances that are

---

[28] There's a beautiful, possibly apocryphal, story about Liam Gallagher not realizing they weren't a real band – see www.contactmusic.com/liam-gallagher/news/gallagher-thought-spinal-tap-were-real-band. In his defence, they have released music and toured as the band and the documentary nature of the film is very convincing.

[29] The drummers for the band are many and frequent, due to a series of unfortunate mishaps resulting in their deaths.

nuanced and complex. Guest didn't direct *Spinal Tap* however, Rob Reiner did. Reiner appears in the film as the director character Marty DiBergi, introducing the film and appearing throughout, prompting questions for the band in formal and non-formal interview settings. Di Bergi's presence draws attention to the filmmaking in the way Scorsese does in *The Last Waltz*, a clear influence on this film, and the film crew presence is always felt, despite Pennebaker's intentions, in *Dont Look Back*. A love of the cinematic genre, as well as a fondness for heavy metal and classic rock, drives the film. The filmmakers clearly think the music and the surrounding pageantry is hilarious but, as with *The Rutles*, the songs that echo the original compositions are both authentic recreations and really, really good. You can't achieve that if being snarky about something is the only goal.

The film follows the band as their career slowly turns to dust. They argue, split up at one point, go in new directions and plot long-gestating moves into musical theatre. Still, they keep playing live, for ever-dwindling audience numbers, and it's here that the film's respect for musicians comes through. There is a respect for those that keep going, a belief that it's an honourable life, that underpins the film, regardless of how silly some of the moments are. The influence of the film is not just traceable formally, as will be discussed shortly, but in its blend of ridiculousness and earnestness. In the Oasis documentary *Lord Don't Slow Me Down* (2007), also discussed later in this book, Noel Gallagher and some of the band's entourage try to open a giant, celebratory, post-show bottle of champagne in a venue dressing room. The clip starts as Gallagher grapples with the cork, the expectation being that its popping is imminent. It isn't. Gallagher fails, as do a few others. The clip ends. No champagne popped. The film returns to this moment later and it's farcical how long it takes. There's a charm to the sequence, though, as it punctures the pomposity of the rock-star life, a reminder of how so much of what audiences perceive as the glamourous reality is a construct and that famous rock stars sometimes struggle to pop corks.

If watching *Lord Don't Slow Me Down* evokes *Spinal Tap*, its legacy can be felt in films that have followed in its wake in other, potentially less direct, ways. *Spinal Tap*, even more than *The Rutles*, almost gave permission to filmmakers to use the mockumentary form to honour, homage and prick the bubble of other musical genres. If none of the successors quite scale *Tap*'s heights, some get close. There are many fine examples of films that capture the essence of different genres and the personalities and machinery that drive them. Hip Hop has *CB4*, directed by Tamra Davis and starring Chris Rock, and *Fear of a Black Hat,* both from 1993, and both tapping into that moment's gangster rap zenith, though the latter's title comes from the non-gangster rap Public Enemy's album *Fear of a Black Planet,* released in 1990. Both films capture their immediate scene plus wider Hip Hop culture and add that era's MTV aesthetic and output into the mix. Folk has the previously mentioned *A Mighty Wind* (2003), which follows a variety of folk musicians reuniting to pay tribute to a recently deceased beloved promoter, four years before Led Zeppelin did the same to pay tribute to their former label boss Ahmet Ertegun of Atlantic Records, in 2007. The film is a more refined, less rambunctious film than *Spinal Tap,* in keeping with the folk focus, but is also reminiscent of the gentle, pastoral air of Guest's other mockumentaries looking at amateur theatre, *Waiting for Guffman* (1996) and dog shows, *Best in Show* (2000). All Guest's films also follow an ensemble of equally weighted characters, whereas in *Tap,* it's all about the central band.

Contemporary(ish, at time of writing) pop music has *Popstar: Never Stop Never Stopping* (2016) featuring Andy Samberg as successful solo artist Conner 4 Real embarking on the 'difficult second album' and reflecting on the break-up and inevitable reunion of his former boy band The Style Boyz. Despite coming nearly 30 years after *Spinal Tap,* it utilizes the same format of struggle, acceptance and reconciliation and, like all the films mentioned, the verisimilitude of the songs is uncanny. They are funny sendups, but also superb sonic renditions of the source genre. Country music has *Walk Hard: The Dewey Cox Story* (2007), which is where the formal influence of *Spinal Tap* feels most stretched. *Walk Hard,* starring John C Reilly as the country music 'star' of the title, is in many ways not a mockumentary, instead taking its cues (and a bit of its title) from films such as *Walk the Line* (2005), a Johnny Cash biopic and *Ray* (2004), a film about the life of Ray Charles. Where *Walk Hard* feels indebted to *Spinal Tap* is in its dedication to authenticity of sound and event. The film, like *Tap,* follows a redemption arc but, more interestingly, it dips into cultural and cinematic history for comic effect. While ostensibly telling the story of a Johnny Cash-like figure, Dewey Cox goes through a 'Dylan goes electric' phase, presented to the audience via a press conference pulled straight from the images of *Dont Look Back* as well as a sequence that imagines Cox meeting The Beatles in India on a spiritual retreat.[30]

Walk Hard plays fast and loose with the narrative expectations of the audience based on its root musical genre but it relies on their cinematic and audiovisual intertextual knowledge to work. This postmodern bricolage approach brings humour to the fore but also reminds audiences of the similar trajectories of musicians of diverse genres and backgrounds, and of a time when the decisions and choices of musicians were held in different regard. *Walk Hard*'s reliance on its audience's intertextual knowledge of other cinematic works is not unique. Indeed, many narrative music films utilize documentary and non-fiction techniques and conventions to create a dialogue with audiences that enhances work and creates links to the non-fictional figures that drive the fictional narratives. This is most apparent in Todd Haynes' film about Bob Dylan, *I'm Not There* (2007), where a variety of actors portray Dylan. These portrayals are not of the 'real' Dylan, but of various personas that Dylan has held throughout his career. Cate Blanchett plays 'Dylan' as he goes electric and, as with *Walk Hard,* a familiarity with *Dont Look Back* pays dividends as Blanchett defends her art against a sea of press, utilizing the handheld monochrome sharpness of Pennebaker's work for referential impact.[31] Todd Haynes' documentary *The Velvet Underground* (2021) is discussed later in this chapter, but *I'm Not There* is not his only foray into narrative music films. One of his earliest works was the infamous *Superstar: The Karen Carpenter Story* (1987), a 45-minute docudrama in which he recounted the singer's life using barbie dolls.

In 1998 Haynes made another narrative music film, exploring the world of 1970s glam rock, with *Velvet Goldmine.* The film was inspired by the stories of Bowie, Iggy Pop, Lou Reed and others and tapped into the late-era Britpop milieu for performers to portray the era and proxy figures. While not drawing on non-fiction music film aesthetics or conventions, there are moments that spend time backstage and offstage with performers, in scenes common from

---

[30] Country music also has, of course, Robert Altman's *Nashville* (1975). The film, unlike others discussed here, is a not a comedy and though its visual aesthetic feels quasi-documentary in the way it observes the unfolding action, its kinship is rooted in the way that Altman focuses on the studio, live performance, the business and logistic of the music business and how it is entwined with politics.

[31] As well as tapping into the energy of Lester's *A Hard Day's Night*.

documentary. The live performance footage in the film, that so spellbinds the protagonist played by Christian Bale as he follows his idols into their world, also has a rawness and directness that feels akin to the best concert film footage. Pennebaker's kinetic and fuzzy film of Bowie's final Ziggy Stardust performance, *Ziggy Stardust and the Spiders from Mars* (1979) – discussed later in the book – feels like a very strong influence. *Velvet Goldmine* is set partly in Manchester, a very important music city in the late 1970s and beyond. The ultimate portrait of the influence and impact of the city on pop music is Michael Winterbottom's sublime *24 Hour Party People* (2002), telling the story of Tony Wilson and Factory Records.[32] The film is gloriously postmodern, both in its formal approach of Wilson breaking the fourth wall and directly addressing the camera, and in how cinematographer Robby Müller manages to make the televisual cinematic, but also in content, in that so much of what he says and what is shown is unreliable and in service of myth and mystery.

The film, while narrative, utilizes hand-held camerawork and fast-paced editing familiar from non-fiction music films to create a sense of authenticity and verisimilitude undercut by Steve Coogan's Tony Wilson and his hubristic and hazy proclamations.[33] Like Haynes, this is not Winterbottom's only foray into music film territory. His polarizing *9 Songs* (2004) tells the story of a young couple's relationship and sexual encounters. It is sexually explicit and again, like *24 Hour Party People,* shot with a documentary aesthetic for a sense of realness and rawness. Ostensibly, the film follows a young couple, played by Margo Stilley and Kieran O'Brien, as they have sex and go to see bands. What marks the film out is that the bands they go to see are 'real' bands, not bands created for the film. Winterbottom places his actors at concerts by bands including Black Rebel Motorcycle Club, Primal Scream and others and shoots the live concert material beautifully. Critics at the time argued that the live music is more engaging and exciting than the sex scenes, which kind of misses the point of the film, but the footage is great and makes me wonder why he's only made one non-fiction music film to date – 2016's *On the Road,* following the rock band Wolf Alice on tour. A final note should go out to Fred Armisen

---

[32] I wrote about both *Velvet Goldmine* and *24 Hour Party People* for a chapter on Manchester films in the *Directory of World Cinema: Britain 2* (Intellect, 2015).
[33] The film has a grimy beauty thanks to being shot by the great Robby Müller for his final feature film credit.

and Bill Hader's television series *Documentary Now!* (2016–2022), which creates a fictional documentary film showcase to present loving, eerily authentic spoof-homage short works, in the style of classic documentaries. Clips from *Dont Look Back* and *20 Feet from Stardom* (2013) appear in the show's opening credits and. across the show's first three series. the music film is tackled several times. It's clear that Armisen and Hader are inspired by Pennebaker, Demme and others but the humour and verisimilitude shows that the spirit of *Tap* is still going strong.

1989 – *Depeche Mode: 101* and the Importance of DA Pennebaker

To conclude this section before moving on to films that represent more contemporary, at the time of writing, innovations in the form, there is a further mention for a filmmaker whose work is vital when considering the trajectory that the form of the music film has taken. Indeed, the work under discussion here opened an avenue for music films, regarding how they incorporate the music fan, that Penelope Spheeris pounced on with the final part of her *Decline* trilogy. Admittedly, this incorporation, where fan input is not merely filler or captured to provide context of an event such as a concert that roots that event in time, isn't always utilized in imaginative ways in music film.[34] Also, as is discussed later in the book in the chapter on concert films and Pennebaker's *Monterey Pop* (1968), Pennebaker's interest in fans is long-standing. They are always present in his work and never as mere asides, but as a way of seeking to understand the meaning and value of a moment or a musician. Through his work on *Dont Look Back* and *Monterey Pop* Pennebaker had already established himself as a pioneer of the music film by the late 1960s and his 1989 film, *Depeche Mode: 101*, stands as a reinvention prompted by the filmmaker himself when looking at his track record in the field as well as part of the evolving filmmaking partnership he established with Chris Hedegus in the mid-1970s.[35]

[34] The same can, of course, be said for most conventions.
[35] The biography of the filmmaking pair on their official website blends all their films into one career, with works ostensibly directed by Pennebaker not separated from the works co-directed with Hedegus, which says how highly he regarded their collaboration and also how sexist so many attributions to their collaborative work as 'Pennebaker films' remains Available at: https://phfilms.com/history/

Pennebaker admitted that the decision to focus on the fans so much in *Depeche Mode: 101* stemmed from an anxiety as to how they were going to make the film interesting.[36] This was down both to a desire to not repeat themselves artistically as well as what they felt were limitations in the on-stage and on-screen presentation of the band in question. Indeed, part of their self-set challenge for the film was to find ways to make the somewhat static presentation of Depeche Mode's electronic music exciting and engaging. Frontman Dave Gahan does some of the heavy lifting on stage in that regard, but offstage there is little of the dynamism he reaches when singing. The contrast between his on and offstage personas is striking. He is often captured just sitting or standing around. The whole concept of being a hugely successful touring band – the film follows a giant US arena tour that starts in New York and culminates in a huge open-air show in Pasadena – baffles him; indeed, at one point, he says that he had 'more fun in the supermarket' where he worked growing up, where there was 'less pressure too'.[37] This curmudgeonly modesty portrays a normality that sits in stark contrast with the electronic textures of the band and giant performances Gahan conjures on stage, representing the fascinations the filmmakers have in juxtapositions. If the film strives to capture some of the disconnect – and discontent – between the band and their music, it also acts as one of the most poignant and revealing documents of music fans ever filmed.

As the band wends their way across America on tour, they are followed by the filmmakers who simultaneously follow a group of fans who have won the chance to join the band on tour under the proviso of being filmed for the documentary. *Depeche Mode: 101* stands as an early example of reality television convention that has become such a part of the media landscape in the twenty-first century. The fans on the bus are a diverse bunch, or as diverse as Depeche Mode fans got in the 1980s, and, by giving them so much screen time, some of their human complexities, contradictions and desires are revealed. This, by virtue of time spent, reveals how fans in music films prior to this (and of course still in some cases) are utilized as mouthpieces for the music, included to

---

[36] Due to the fact the filmmaking is split between following the band and a discreet set of fans the film is co-directed by David Dawkins, whose contribution should not be overlooked and isn't by Pennebaker and Hedegus – see https://phfilms.com/films/depeche-mode-101/
[37] There is another excellent Depeche Mode documentary, that *also* focuses on their fans, this time in pretty much its entirety, Jeremy Deller and Nick Abrahams' *Our Hobby is Depeche Mode* (2006).

further sell the idea of a band or a singer or a concert. There is often, due to time constraints admittedly, very little interest in the idea of a fan. This film feels like a big influence on the empathetic work of a filmmaker discussed throughout the book, Jeanie Finlay. *Depeche Mode: 101* sees the group of fans bond, get romantic, do stupid stuff, fall out with each other and debate the meaning of art in pretty rudimentary and uninteresting terms. At one stage their trajectory is held-up by the need to search for some of the party who have stormed off after a row. There is very little evidence of or interest in what the band means to them. The fact that the music is meaningful is taken for granted by the fact they won a competition about the band to come on the tour in the first place.

The fans' love for the band is made clear as the film comes to a climax with the Pasadena show. Upon entering the giant arena, they lose themselves in the moment, dancing and singing with abandon. It is touching, and superb filmmaking, to carry the limited knowledge of them as people garnered throughout the film into that space and see them so in tune with the music that caused them to take the trip in the first place. Here, the connection between the music and what it means to these people is clearer than ever. The construction of the film also makes a strong case for the relationship between fans and music as far greater than that of fans and musicians. Here, more than in maybe any other music film, the musicians are clearly vessels for something greater. That something greater is presented as something profoundly beautiful artistically but the filmmakers are astute enough to ensure that this is not a naive and utopian presentation. The staging of the Pasadena show is given significant screen time, the organization and efficiency of the production possibly acting as a dig at how the Rolling Stones' team organized the Altamont concert captured in *Gimme Shelter*. Also, significantly, the film is keen to present how lucrative and capitalistic popular music can be. As the band perform, the tour team backstage look at the night's takings and the line 'we're getting a load of money' cuts through the idealism presented elsewhere. Proof, if more were needed, of Pennebaker's life-long ability to be present for moments that capture the contradictions and complexities of popular music as an art form and business. The film is a perfect example of Hutcheon's idea, discussed in the introduction, of complicity and critique. Or, as Harbert puts it so beautifully when writing about the film, 'perhaps authenticity lingers somewhere within the commodity' (2018: 171).

'Why form a band? I dunno. Why not?'[38] – Twenty-first Century Innovations

Here we take a jump from 1989 to 2000. This is not to say that the 1990s had no innovations in form or content. Following this chapter, the book looks at significant works from that decade. However, one of the key aims of this book is to consider seriously the radical and innovative approaches that have emerged since the turn of the twenty-first century. It makes sense, therefore, to pick up again in 2000, with the release of a film that turns up frequently on 'best of' lists but also on the list of key influences for filmmakers including Paul Sng, co-director of *Poly Styrene: I Am A Cliché* (2020) and Edgar Wright, director of *The Sparks Brothers* (2020). The film in question takes the form of the music film and does some brilliant things with it. It's a creative peak in the career of a filmmaker who is one of the best music film makers of all time and finds said filmmaker peeking back into the cinematic past to great effect. The film is Julien Temple's *The Filth and the Fury* and discussion of that film is followed by a look more broadly at his body of work, followed by films that have come in its wake and continued to push the boundaries of the music film outwards.

2000 – *The Filth and the Fury* and Julien Temple

While the original punk era was the first that saw members of the scene take up film cameras to document it as it was happening in a concerted way, the films of the era that manage to transcend mere curio document of the time are slim pickings. As mentioned earlier, Penelope Spheeris' *The Decline of Western Civilization* stands apart in this regard. Filmmaker Julien Temple has latterly emerged as the UK punk chronicler par excellence due to his films on the Sex Pistols and Joe Strummer, but his only contemporary contribution in the original punk era was the lamentable *The Great Rock 'n' Roll Swindle* (1980). In 2000, Temple released his second film about the Sex Pistols, *The Filth and the Fury* and with it addressed not only the myths and legends that had built up around the band, but also addressed his own culpability in that myth-making

---

[38] Kevin Rowland in *Dexys: Nowhere Is Home* (2014)

as a young, inexperienced filmmaker. The Temple who directed *The Filth and the Fury* is not the same filmmaker who directed *Swindle*. In *Fury,* Temple sets out to present another side of the story, most notably John Lydon's, who is absent from *Swindle* bar in animated form, but also to formally show his growth as a filmmaker. *Fury* is tightly edited, conceptually daring and contains all the energy and vitriol associated with punk shot through with a reflective, melancholy air.

In the twenty-first century, the use of contextual archive to illustrate the past and the social world around a music or musician is commonplace. Here's some footage of New York in the 1960s, Berlin in the 1980s, London in the 1970s. Here's the world this music came from. It's an easy and useful way of setting a scene. Temple's approach in 2000 took this idea and exploded it, crafting a bricolage of ideas to illustrate the context from which the Sex Pistols emerged but also how they could be read and understood. Alongside the customary images of rubbish piled high on the streets due to bin men being on strike there is footage from Laurence Olivier's *Richard III* (1955) and clips of comedian Tommy Cooper, smashed next to images of sexual pleasure, jutting up against images of racist Britain. It's a chaotic swell of images delivered with such brio that when Lydon talks about the links between the Pistols and British comedy traditions and Shakespeare's hunchback king it is hard to shake the sense he is responding to Temple's suggestive stimuli. In his later work Temple returns again and again to establishing narrative context using images and ideas from existing cinematic works as will be discussed elsewhere in this section, but in *Fury* the idea takes hold and becomes a tool that music filmmakers will utilize in his wake. Though, rarely with the same degree of verve and clarity. Temple seems to have responded to the clarion call by Adrian Wootton writing in the book *Celluloid Jukebox* when he says 'it's not that rock documentaries should always try to contextualize their subject into historical reality; but there is a case to be made for thinking about this much more imaginatively' (1995: 103).

The film is an angry and moving look back at the past by the filmmaker and the band, in particular Lydon. The latter, missing from *Swindle* and rarely seen discussing his past in the band, uses the film to address some of the myths that surrounded his involvement in the band's demise, some of which is part of the narrative in and around *Swindle*. *Fury* can be read in large part as Temple addressing his culpability in how Lydon was implicated. Lydon and Temple also use the film to address Sid Vicious. The film reframes Sid's life and personality. It is not a simple glossing over of his troubles or flaws but a definite reclamation of him as a complex personality, that complexity having been robbed from him as he has become a symbolic figure, devoid of layers. Archive footage of Sid in a park, desperate, seeking a way out of his situation, aware he had already become a symbol, a cypher, is met with Lydon's tears as he recounts his friend's fall into addiction and death. The audience are reminded that Temple is not just a witness after the fact, but a friend, a contemporary, a participant in the whole story. Ailsa Grant Ferguson claims the film 'transgresses, flouts, and even parodies established [. . .] forms' and the film should be taken as 'counterhistorical' not historical (2013: 142). Temple's decision to conduct the interviews in the film with the remaining Pistols without showing their faces, placing them in shadow, has been rightly declared a way of keeping their image rooted in the past, their iconic period, but it is also a way of allowing them space and privacy to reveal more, differently, than they might have otherwise.

The kind of filmmaking maturity and approach Temple displays in *Fury* is missing from *The Great Rock 'n' Roll Swindle*, but that is largely to be expected. It was his debut feature film, coming off the back of a few music videos for the Pistols, a cobbled together short collection of Pistols TV appearances, *Sex Pistols Number 1* (1977) and the short promo/mockumentary for the band UK Subs, *Punk Can Take It* (1979).[39] *Swindle* was led by the Pistols manager Malcolm McLaren who used it as propaganda for both telling the world how to 'make' a successful punk band and how he did it with the Pistols. John Lydon wanted nothing to do with it, and even though the remaining band members Sid Vicious, Paul Cook and Steve Jones do appear, their enthusiasm for the project differs and veers wildly. The best moments of live footage and behind the scenes material are re-used and re-contextualized in *The Filth and the Fury*. This echoes how, as discussed earlier, Martin Scorsese has worked. However, there are moments where Temple brings his interest and imagination to bear in ways that elevate the material and put in place the conventions he returns to

---

[39] Temple truly is a music film pioneer, making imaginative work across boundaries just at the time of MTV emerging and just a year out from *The Rutles: All You Need Is Cash* (1978).

later in his career.[40] For example, the film starts with a prologue that establishes, cinematically rather than necessarily factually, how the 1780 Gordon Riots invented the idea of 'anarchy in the UK'. It is a cheeky, curious approach to history and context that feels appropriate through sheer will and confidence on the part of Temple who loves to suggest these lineages and connections across time in his films. Although, the less said about the sequence with Ronnie Biggs in Brazil or Steve Jones getting fellatio in a seedy London cinema, the better.

In the 1980s and 1990s Temple focused on music videos, narrative feature films and television documentaries before *The Filth and the Fury* set him on a run of cinematic music films that form an incredible body of work. Key amongst them is a duo of films focusing on the band Dr Feelgood and their enigmatic guitarist Wilko Johnson. 2009's *Oil City Confidential* tells the story of the band, while 2015's *The Ecstasy of Wilko Johnson* tells the story of the musician's diagnosis with terminal pancreatic cancer. *Oil City Confidential* is the perfect example for illustrating the ideal in music films that a film should *feel* like the music and band it is documenting. The way that Temple blends live and photographic archive of the band, with contextual archive of Canvey Island in Essex where they came from, with interviews, and the speed at which the film moves through the story to the speed of the music that the band made, means that the seams between each element are invisible and the audience experiences a sense of seeing the music. In many ways the film is the ultimate example of that utopian ideal of being a film that captures cinematically the essence of the band at its heart. Temple does this by cranking up the elements that he has become known for by this point, with old British crime films replacing *Fury*'s *Richard III* as the cinematic counterpoint, and introducing new ones, such as projecting those crime films and the band's live archive onto the power stations and amusement arcades of Canvey Island. It's aesthetically thrilling and captures the incongruity of the band's music, that doesn't sound like it could come from this place but couldn't come from anywhere else.

Temple's second collaboration with Wilko Johnson is a more contemplative affair than the first, given that it follows Johnson after he is diagnosed with

---

[40] The sequence where Sid Vicious sings 'My Way' and kills the audience also acted as the music video for that single, a device that is now also commonplace: music video segments. Rewatching that sequence reveals its clear influence on the film *Joker* (2019).

terminal pancreatic cancer and given 12 months to live.[41] The contextual cinematic references in *The Ecstasy of Wilko Johnson* are Ingmar Bergman's *The Seventh Seal* (1957), Powell and Pressburger's *A Matter of Life and Death* (1946) and the films of Andrei Tarkovsky. This offers further proof of Temple's cinephillic reach and of the development of this unique strain of contextual imagery that links his films to cinema as a medium in a way that other music filmmakers don't do, instead preferring to limit their subject to music and the social world around the music makers. *Ecstasy* is a rumination on impending death and finding acceptance, as well as how that impending death frames the past and a life lived in a particular way. Temple adapts his tone and approach to suit his subject without losing what makes his work unique such as his contextual bricolage and his binding of person and place, music and time. As the film moves on, Johnson's diagnosis changes, miraculously; the closeness between him and the filmmaker allows for a positive, hopeful climax that is one of the most beautiful sequences in Temple's filmography.[42] For all his technical flair and formal dexterity, at the heart of Temple's films are his interest in and love of people.

Prior to the Wilko works, Temple directed a 2007 film in remembrance of punk legend and his friend,[43] Joe Strummer, who died suddenly in 2002. Temple's love of music and how he understands its power is present in the opening frames of this film. It starts softly and slowly, with a campfire and people gathering around it, listening to Joe's shows for the BBC World Service, which form an audio backbone in the film, listening to news of Joe's death and sharing some tributes, before it cuts to audio of Joe being interviewed on the radio, asking to be referred to as a 'punk rock warlord'. Simon Reynolds says of the campfire device, that it 'honours the spirit of the man while providing the movie with an attractive visual thread' (2007). After the introduction of the campfire, the film cuts to a recording studio in the late 1970s. No music, just Joe shouting the opening lyrics to 'White Riot'.[44] Then the

---

[41] Wilko's main Dr Feelgood collaborator Lee Brilleaux died in 1994 and only appears in *Oil City Confidential* in archive.
[42] Johnson died shortly before the typescript of this book was submitted, on 21 November 2022.
[43] ...and Somerset neighbour. The thought of those two ageing punks roaming the South-West countryside never gets old in my mind. I talked to Temple at length about this film and his career for my podcast, The Cinematologists, in 2018. Available at: www.cinematologists.com/podcastarchive/2018/11/13/ep72-joe-strummer-the-future-is-unwritten-w-director-julien-temple.
[44] Footage of singers in vocal booths are common in music films, however few instances are as visceral or compelling as the footage of Strummer here, particularly how Temple cuts it into the finished recording for maximum impact. The power and hoarse urgency of Strummer's vocal become a pure sonic symbol of punk in one distilled moment.

music kicks in. Loud – the music is always mixed Loud in Temple's films – and the film explodes. From there it covers possibly the most traditional biography trajectory of any Temple film. It follows Joe from a child, through his time in The Clash – carefully not treading on the toes of his punk peer Don Letts' excellent documentary *Westway to the World* (2000) – through the post-Clash 'wilderness'[45] years, his comeback with the Mescaleros and shock early death aged just 50. Even though it follows familiar music film structures and conventions it is replete with little touches that set it apart, such as archive photos being held up by those who keep them, as opposed to those photos being scanned and manipulated. And when setting the context for punk's emergence in the late 1970s Temple can't help but throw in a few frames from the animated *Animal Farm* (1954).

The Future Is Unwritten, like all of Temple's work, is a celebration of music and artists, but not a hagiography. His films are never shy about confronting the mess of punk, or its bands and artists. The film confronts Joe's flaws, particularly a cowardice that stood in direct contrast to some of his fiery moral declarations. Because the film is itself a moment in time there are also absences and factors that contribute to the negative legacies of the subject, something Temple is happy to allow to simmer. Mick Jones is present in the film, past hostilities with Joe clearly resolved as his laugh when recollecting stories suggests, as much as the archive of the pair performing not long before Joe died. Fellow band member Paul Simonon, who stuck with Joe to the terribly messy and ignominious end of The Clash, is absent from the film. Drummer Topper Headon is there. His heroin addiction was a major factor in The Clash coming apart at the seams. He looks better here than he did in Don Letts *Westway to the World* in 2000, but not as good as he does in Rubika Shah's *White Riot* (2019). These films provide a visual record of his recovery. At the centre Joe is presented as charismatic, interesting and flawed. In other words, a great cinematic subject. One of Temple's great strengths is his ability to grasp not only what makes a subject interesting but also how that subject needs to be translated cinematically for audiences to be able to engage, dynamically, with them. He sees his subjects as human but also as characters in a narrative.

---

[45] I curated a Joe Strummer film festival in London in 2005, where I first encountered Julien. The festival took the view that Joe's so-called 'wilderness' years were instead a fascinating period of acting and film music work for him, something touched on in Temple's film when discussing Joe's influential score for Alex Cox's *Walker* (1987).

Sometimes this is a whole band, sometimes a single person, sometimes a place and sometimes an event.

Temple's other music films include, but are not limited to, his film about the Glastonbury festival, *Glastonbury* (2006), *Ibiza: The Silent Movie* (2019) and *Crock of Gold: A Few Rounds With Shane McGowan* (2020), which gives a feature length treatment to the story of the musician who as a young man was a punk devotee and famously appears in so much of the live footage of the Pistols and the Clash shot by Temple and Don Letts at the time. The former films, *Glastonbury* and *Ibiza* are both combination archive and observational films, experiments in the past and reckoning with ideas around change and progress. They both celebrate the cultures and unique geographical properties of the locations on which they focus. The films explore how Ibiza and Glastonbury draw revellers to them, while acknowledging the negative impacts of capitalism, greed and exploitation of the natural and the cultural world on those same spaces. The film where Temple does this to most devastating, beautiful and focused effect is 2010's *Requiem for Detroit?* Utilizing the technique from *Oil City Confidential,* of projecting a place's past onto its – in this case, decaying – present, Temple crafts a poetic essay about the changes Detroit has undergone which weaves in its profound musical history, including Motown and Garage Rock, as integral to the story and not merely ephemeral. As an account of the relationship between time, place and music it's an extraordinary work, enhanced possibly by Temple being freed from a single or group narrative perspective and allowed to let his interest in history and the collage and collision of ideas and events to roam freer. What better place to capture Temple's melancholic urges for a more bucolic and possibly imagined past than the motor city.

2003 – *Finisterre* and Saint Etienne

It is tempting, in a romanticizing way, to see *The Filth and the Fury* as a moment of awakening in music film, a freeing of the form from the established conventions, permission to poke and prod at, to rethink, ignore or parody them in ever more dynamic ways. This is the narrative for which this chapter makes the case. If it wasn't true, does that matter? Does it matter if it was? These kinds of questions about fact and the provable truth, as well as the notion

Figure 1.1 Finisterre (dir. Evans and Kelly, 2003) © Evans / Kelly / Saint Etienne / CC Lab.

of attaching romantic narrative meaning to disparate texts and experiences are present in the poetic, associative *Finisterre* (2003), and subsequent films attached to the band Saint Etienne. *Finisterre* is directed by Kieran Evans and Paul Kelly – two filmmakers whose work is discussed throughout this book – and is a film that accompanies a Saint Etienne album of the same name, commissioned or approved or provoked by the band in lieu of traditional music videos and to try and capture cinematically the nebulous London which influenced the record. The film is a poetic, psychogeographic portrait of the city, replete with interviews with cultural figures and musicians, some associated with the band, some not, all trying to share what the city means to them. Kelly said in 2014 he wanted the film to be slow because 'the influence of TV had really taken hold in films […] in documentaries at the time. We wanted to slow things down a bit'. It is a documentary, in part. It's also a paean to (an idea of) place, that is scored by the music of the band from the album of the same name, that changes the music as the film is watched. The marrying of image to sound cannot help but do so. The audience is invited to make connection and meaning, while gliding through the meeting points of filmmaker, place, participant, band and record.

The influence of the film can be found in other tales of London and music including *Elephant Days* (2015), discussed in the chapter about making music, which focuses on the Maccabees' final record and their relationship to Elephant & Castle in South London. In that film, the band are a recurring visual presence, in the studio and beyond, whereas here Saint Etienne are ephemeral participants. Present consistently through their music but otherwise elusive. The freedom to make a film like this is grasped by Paul Kelly and Kieran Evans, the latter's love of political slogans represented by images of 'support striking library workers' graffiti. The film is a portrait of London as seen by and crafted by the filmmakers, their choices showcasing their beliefs and politics, working in solidarity with the beliefs and politics of the musicians even if the music is only indirectly political. In addition to the graffiti there are abandoned and derelict spaces – 'nobody lives here now' – as well as portraits of London youth in their football and polo shirts. A street art sequence recalls the important Hip Hop film *Style Wars* (1983), and Evans' relationship with the Manic Street Preachers – he is their filmmaker in residence – is represented by a montage of NatWest, Barclays, Midlands and Lloyds banks in direct reference to their song of that name. The music feels simultaneously connected to and apart from the images and the lingering, stark images of the old and the new, mingled with snippets of voice, image and sound from the band and other participants lends a hauntological[46] air to the film that lingers long after its finished.

Following *Finisterre,* Kelly would work on more films with the band, completing their *London Trilogy,* with the shorter but no less poetic and enigmatic *What Have You Done Today Mervyn Day?* (2007) and *This Is Tomorrow* (2007). The former film stretches out to London's extreme fringes around the Lea Valley, and the latter springs back to take a macro look at the textures of some of London's modernist art buildings. The formal influence of Patrick Keiller's *London* (1994) is clear, but all the films Kelly made with the band share an optimism and hope amidst the melancholy and cynicism that perfectly suits the music that forms the sonic foundation of each piece. Rampant capitalism and a behemoth such as the looming 2012 London Olympics are treated as both cause for hope and wariness in the contributions of the participants but also the compositions and the juxtapositions Kelly

---

[46] 'Hauntology' is a term associated primarily with Jacques Derrida who coined the term in 1993's *Specters of Marx*. As an idea it has most recently been used and understood in conjunction with the work of Mark Fisher and is essentially 'the accumulation of ghost-like traces of the past as we move further in the future'. Available at: https://rhizome.org/editorial/2011/may/18/hauntology/

finds.[47] *This Is Tomorrow* finds beauty in the nooks and cubby holes of the Barbican or the South Bank[48] and *Mervyn Day* follows a paperboy across a wasteland, returning ideas of youth to the Saint Etienne cinematic narrative. In 2021, for the release of their record *I've Been Trying to Tell You,* the band enlisted Alasdair McLellan to craft a film to accompany the album. His film gravitates around youth again but moves out beyond London and the South-East on a road trip that takes in places such as Blackpool and Portmeirion. It's a poetic, melancholy film that continues the tradition of Kelly's collaborations, refracts the core philosophies and textures of the music but also serves as a portrait of the moment in colours and images and movements that are McLellan's own.

2004 – *Metallica: Some Kind of Monster*

One of the ways that Joe Berlinger and Bruce Sinofsky's film about heavy metal band Metallica, particularly in the film's extended cut, exceeds the potential limitations and pitfalls of spending time watching an obscenely successful rock act going through group therapy, is through a mixture of empathy and a superb editing structure. There's a delightful moment afforded by cinema's potential when a very anxious Lars Ulrich says of the recording of a song 'Can we fast forward to that right now?' And the film obliges him, showing a vast crowd of Metallica fans head banging to a live performance of the very song causing Ulrich such stress. Elsewhere, the use of archive material around the three-pronged structure of a band dealing with tremendous personal and interpersonal stress via group therapy, recording a new record and recruiting a new bassist is deft and used to punctuate moments, contextually, where questions around why they are doing this to themselves float to the surface. In this regard the film also allows the band to pay loving cinematic tribute to original bassist Cliff Burton who died in a tour bus crash in 1984. Empathy is also found in the editing and in how the filmmakers choose to make sure that the band never, entirely, come across as parodies or as the stereotypical 'metallers' that audiences and critics may take them to be. The sense of

---

[47] Kelly's work with the band shares more than a superficial kinship with the work of Andrew Kötting.
[48] This film in particular feels like a real influence on Alex Barrett's *London Symphony* (2017)

ludicrousness associated with heavy metal is present. In their individual portraits the band come across as pretentious, vacuous and naive when talking about art, surfing and drugs.

The film presents the expected and some of it is very funny, recalling *Spinal Tap* (obviously), and in the closing tour montage that focuses on the fans, the cult 1986 short documentary *Heavy Metal Parking Lot* with its images of drunken Metallica fans in stadium car parks the world over. The film doesn't pretend that some of the cliché images and ideas associated with the metal genre don't have real roots but takes steps to ensure that this is not the only side presented. The other side, that of three men who have recorded some of the heaviest, angriest and most forceful music ever made, being vulnerable and talking about their feelings also comes across. The process of therapy in the film is not a gimmick. The band are genuinely committed to sorting out their issues. They discuss on camera the impact of the film on the process, both in terms of what it is asking of them personally and emotionally and how it might lead them to be disingenuous. The scene where Lars visits former bandmate Dave Mustaine, unceremoniously ousted just as the band was breaking big in the early 1980s. Mustaine telling him how that event impacted him, that 'people hate me because of you' is genuinely moving because of its unexpected honesty. At the end of the film, with the album eventually recorded and the band heading back out on tour following a three-year hiatus, Ulrich comments how they made 'aggressive music without negative energy', in the process opening up the idea of heavy metal beyond stereotypes had held for two decades at that point.[49]

2004 – *Dig!*

While *Some Kind of Monster* attempts to address the damaging association between trauma and emotional struggle in the creation of art, a film from the same year roots itself in the age-old idea that damaged artists make the best art, though often aren't rewarded for that in their life time. Ondi Timoner's *Dig!* (2004) is a film that, along with the following year's *The Devil and Daniel*

---

[49] *St Anger*, the album they record in the film, received the worst reviews of Metallica's career to date, which potentially undermines the positive elements of Ulrich's realization.

Johnston (2005), shifted perceptions around who the subjects of music films that broached a wide audience could be. The fact that one of the artists, indeed the main protagonist of the film really, Anton Newcombe of the band the Brian Jonestown Massacre, was virtually unknown outside indie music circles mattered not as the film found success at film festivals and on cinema release. Even though the other band featured in the film, the Dandy Warhols, were more successful at that point, they still weren't a huge band despite one very popular song, 'Bohemian Like You'. One of the reasons for the film's success, however, is that its portrayal of Newcombe as a troubled savant, a wayward and self-destructive genius, feeds into mythical and romantic ideas of the struggling artist fighting the system, and themselves. This may be accurate. Newcombe spends the film at war with everyone around him and himself. Meanwhile Newcombe's friend and self-appointed nemesis Courtney Taylor of the Dandy Warhols declares his own band 'the most well-adjusted band in America'. Benjamin Halligan writes that '*Dig!* could be analysed in terms of psychiatric matters [...] as much as an exemplar exposé of neoliberal modes of music promotion' (2021).

A dichotomy between adjustment and dysfunction sits at the heart of the film and though it presents itself ostensibly as a film about two bands whose friendship turned to rivalry, it knows that this is a device. The film is ultimately more revealing about the music industry and ideas of independence and 'selling out', as well as how complicated simple narratives about making art and the devils of commerce can turn out to be. Twenty years on from release, at the time of writing, what is most striking in retrospect is Courtney Taylor, who emerges as a very complicated figure. He is a huge fan of Newcombe and his band and it's not lip service. His fandom reveals an internal sense of self-critique and vulnerability about his own value and worth. Many of the decisions he makes for his band in the film are foolish, but understandable given the culture of the music industry then and now. When he says: 'if only I'd been just a little bit smarter', it feels honest to a degree that jars. Meanwhile, the portrayal of Newcombe, all flailing limbs and vitriol and breakdown – while recording brilliant records in a week with no money – smacks of myth in a way that would soon become problematic. The film undoubtedly opens up questions about mental and emotional health in music making and the industry, even if at the time it was not equipped to really tackle them. As the credits roll,

Anton sits on the ground in a car park on his own and defiantly declares: 'I'm sure I'm not through'. Thankfully he wasn't. Though he is still largely unheard of – something the film couldn't change – *Dig's* success showed that audiences are more interested in witnessing danger and derangement than buying the music that grows from it.

2005 – *The Devil and Daniel Johnston*

Jeff Feuerzeig's *The Devil and Daniel Johnston* (2005) took the mantle from *Dig!* and ran with it, further changing the cultural perception of subject value in music films that reached outside niche music fan circles and taking the representation of mental health and illness in music films even further. Both films followed cult, virtually unknown, protagonists both with severe mental illnesses and/or addictions, making music that was not 'forgotten', but contemporary and never in danger of breaking out and storming the pop charts.[50] Both films played film festivals, cinemas and found strong audiences on DVD. However, unlike *Dig!*, *The Devil and Johnston* is a quiet film, one that follows the most unlikely of stars, the deeply troubled singer/songwriter Daniel Johnston. Feuerzeig's film follows the established conventions of the music film at this point in terms of use of archive and contemporary interviews with family, collaborators and friends and fans of Johnston's music. It knows the key moments of the story, such as when Kurt Cobain wore a *Hi! How Are You?* T-shirt, thus alerting most of the pop music world to Johnston's existence. It is one of the earliest and most successful films at deploying the 'lost and found' convention, where the film joins the artist in the contemporary moment of the film's production, following an opening section that lays out the historical context to that moment.

Unlike a film such as *Searching for Sugar Man* (2012), there is no sense when watching the film that Feuerzeig is claiming credit for 'finding' Johnston or that he wants to be acknowledged for making a film that will garner more attention for the artist. Daniel, at the time of the film's production, is glimpsed throughout, but is not seen in any depth until an hour and twenty minutes into the film's

---

[50] Though this is, of course, what happened to a certain extent to the 'other' band in *Dig!* the Dandy Warhols, thanks to a mobile phone advert.

hour and fifty-minute running time. The resulting half hour spent in his company comes off the momentum of a collection of sequences that celebrate both his unique music and art practice, his outsider artist status, and shares and analyses some of the many terrifying and debilitating mental health episodes involving violence and hallucination that have left him needing constant care and medication. The film's decision to hold off on spending time with Johnston means it never feels exploitative, seeking easy sympathy. The music and art are allowed to speak for themselves, to a degree, and the film avoids lingering on a cheap long-standing romanticized idea of trauma and suffering begetting great art. The device of waiting to reveal the artist the film's about, to avoid voyeuristic lingering on suffering, influences the Edwyn Collins film *The Possibilities Are Endless* (2014) to great effect. That film and another which is clearly indebted, Jesse Vile's *Jason Becker: Not Dead Yet* (2012), are unimaginable without the empathetic approach deployed here by Feuerzeig. These films are discussed later in the book in the chapter on myth and authenticity.

2006 – *Awesome; I Fuckin' Shot That!*

The Beastie Boys' 2006 concert film of their Madison Square Garden, New York, show, was described by the band (band leader Adam Yauch directed the film under his filmmaking pseudonym Nathanial Hörnblowér) as an 'authorized bootleg'. The band took the risky – or as risky as it can be for a band of that size and stature – choice of handing the filming of their huge hometown show over to the audience by providing 50 audience members with Hi-8 cameras and telling them to shoot whatever they wanted but to 'just keep shooting'. The risk in terms of making a film was that, aside from these cameras, there was only a handful of 'professional' cameras capturing the show, one roving and a few on stage that transmitted on the in-venue jumbo screens. The results of this act were multiple. Aesthetically it took the grainy, fuzzy, low-grade 'what it's like to be there' aesthetic familiar from the White Stripes recent capturing of a show on Super 8 cameras for *The White Stripes: Under Blackpool Lights* (2004) and added in the element of surprise that came from the cameras being wielded by amateurs, fans, with the freedom to film whatever they wanted and which they embraced. The film includes footage of fans wandering the venue concourse, ordering beer, moving the camera around the audience capturing some fans visibly bored during the group's instrumental, full-band funk song performances, awaiting the return of the party Hip Hop they paid to see. One of the fans with cameras is constantly encouraging those around him to make more noise and show more enthusiasm, iterating the truth of live events that not everyone has a great time all the time, and that often the live event experienced can be hampered by well-meaning but annoying fellow fans.

The Beastie Boys are happy throughout the film – from their comfortable cultural position – to shatter the cinematic illusion that concert films capture nothing but sustained joy and awe from attendant crowds. They reveal some of the banalities of the show's mechanics, seeking to hint at some previously hidden realities. In addition to the footage of this from the fan's cameras, the band and their roving pro cameras get in on the act too. For the encore, the camera captures the band heading from the main stage, via lifts (replete with elevator muzak) and an empty concourse, to various entrances into the audience seating areas, surprising the fans within with a performance of 'Intergalactic' in amongst them. This performance is captured by the roving 'professional' camera mingled with the startled, struggling-to-keep-up fan cameras, before the band repeat the banal, perfunctory return trip to the main stage. Possibly the most radical aspect of the film, however, is that it prefigures how live concerts would be filmed in the not-too-distant future following this concert. Yauch's embracing of the evolving technology of video foresees the time when most audience members will carry video capture devices in their pockets and will shoot hours and hours of footage of shows they attend, as is their consumer right, though much to the chagrin of some artists and fellow audience members. The Beastie Boys were ahead of the curve cinematically and, while the mobile phone aesthetic hasn't become a key component of music documentaries, it is there, celebratory in the case of *All Tomorrow's Parties* (2009) or invasive in the case of *Amy* (2015). By embracing the coming wave, the band crafted a concert film that feels truly unique and a true collaboration between artists and their audience.[51]

---

[51] I wrote about the collaborative and participatory nature of the film for a chapter in *The Arena Concert: Music, Media and Mass Entertainment* (Bloomsbury, 2015)

2011 – *The Black Power Mixtape 1967–1975*

Göran Olsson's *The Black Power Mixtape 1967–1975* takes footage from 1967–1975 that was shot by Swedish filmmakers researching and documenting the American Black Power movement and edits it so that it may be reflected on and used as a lens to discuss the Black American experience of 2011, when the film was made. What makes the film dynamic and vital in addition to the incredible archive material it reveals is that Olsson doesn't try to contextualize the material from a Swedish, or a White person's perspective but invites an array of contemporary Black musicians, poets and activists to provide historical, personal and contemporary context. The film uses audio recorded of the participants, including Angela Davis, watching the clips and responding to them. This audio-visual approach allows the footage to play out as originally shot without the visual interruption of contemporary interviews, resulting in an audio commentary that is never solely interested in just stating what is shown or happening, but what it means to the viewer of the footage, in the context of the film's production, and what its legacies might be for the cinema audience watching the finished film. There's a remarkable musical layering, with contemporary musicians including Talib Kweli, Questlove[52] and Erykah Badu providing commentary, while chapters and footage are scored with Black music of the period.

The result is a linking of the past and the present, a filling out of Black musical heritage and legacy, and the relationship between Black music and Black personhood. It would not have been remotely as powerful had Olsson not opened up the narration and narrative control of the film to Black artists and thinkers. The original footage is unflinching, taking in police brutality, the heroin epidemic tearing through Harlem and Black America – including a particularly difficult sequence involving a heroin addicted baby – ending with the 'end' of the Vietnam war in 1975. The footage captures, through the filmmakers sustained interest in the Black Power movement in the period, an emotional journey from hope in revolution at the outset to the despair of the drug epidemic and the exhaustion of constant oppression of Black

---

[52] Questlove took the approach of filming participants responding to archive footage into his directorial debut *Summer of Soul: Or When the Revolution Could Not Be Televised* (2021) but chose to show their reactions rather than just hearing them.

rights and personhood at the close. Musician Erykah Badu exclaims at the film's end that 'we have to write and document our history'. The final words are from poet and academic Sonia Sanchez who reminds us that the work of telling the story of Black life and struggle 'is a lifetime job' and *The Black Power Mixtape* is a unique addition to that work, one that understands the politics of representation, agency and who should tell whose stories. It also provides an innovative blueprint for how White artists can support and engage in the work of Black narrative reclamation without taking space that is not theirs to claim.

2013 – *Mistaken for Strangers*

The question of who gets to tell whose stories finds an odd answer in this strange film that is partly about the band The National, partly about one member of the band The National, lead singer and lyricist Matt Berninger, and partly about the relationship between Berninger and his brother Tom. The reason the film is largely about the relationship between Matt and Tom is that Tom directed the film and couldn't reach any reasonable level of objectivity and make it not about him and his brother. Unlike films where the filmmakers insert themselves into the narrative to remind the audience of their cool cache and responsibility for bringing a certain story to the screen, here the filmmaker uses the filmmaking process, which follows The National on tour and in and out of the studio, to address long-standing issues in himself that his brother's success manifests. It's a strong if prickly relationship, Matt reminding Tom 'you *are* here because you're my brother', but also showing support by inviting Tom into his home to finish the film. The film captures the fractious side of the relationship, when Tom oversteps or his lack of experience causes issues, but there is also some superb live footage and the fact that Tom is not an experienced documentarian, or even that interested in The National's music, results in refreshingly novel questions such as 'How famous do you think you are?' and 'How fast can you play?', the latter to guitarist Aaron Dessner. The film balances the family story with the music and, while it is not an approach that would work for many subjects, somehow The National's music sits well with this kind of cinematic self-examination resulting in a film that extended the scope of the music film in an interesting direction.

2019 – *Everybody in the Place: An Incomplete History of Britain 1984–1992*

Artist Jeremy Deller's film about rave culture at points feels completely unique, as if it might be reinventing the music film whilst also paying tribute to films including John Akomfrah's *The Last Angel of History* (1996) and *The Black Power Mixtape 1967–1975*. Similar to films such as Kieran Evans and Paul Kelly's 2013 film *Dexys: Nowhere Is Home*, it takes existing conventions from mainstream and less well-known music films and performs a recalibration, but it does so in ways that feel radical. The most radical aspect is that the first audience for Deller's 'incomplete' history is a group of London schoolchildren, born long after the era on which Deller is delivering a lesson. The film watches these schoolchildren partaking in a lesson about the emergence and short-lived life of rave culture in the UK. It runs the risk of coming across as gimmicky but instead, brings together the music and the social context in a way that attempts to move the historical moment into a more prominent position in conversations about British culture and about the criminalization of particular activities and communities. It also brings to the fore fascinating conversations around technology and its impact. The schoolchildren can't believe that people used to go out all night and dance without phones clasped to their hands always recording, communicating. The class ends with school kids' hands gliding through lasers. The film captures the reality that, while it may feel like recent history, the pre-digital age is a distant past in many ways, though one that can still have resonance years on. As one of the children says, beautifully, of the scene 'I'm happy that I live on a planet where that happened once.'[53]

2020 – *Delia Derbyshire: The Myths and Legendary Tapes*

The introduction of this book, and the chapter later surrounding myth and authenticity, wrestles with the notion that music films, can only ever be representative or suggestive, because the subjects are performers, therefore the films are a performance, an extension of persona. Caroline Catz's daring 2020

---

[53] For maximum impact, pair with Mark Leckey's nostalgic, hauntological short poetic essay film, *Fiorucci Made Me Hardcore* (1999).

Figure 1.2 Delia Derbyshire: The Myths and Legendary Tapes (dir. Catz, 2020) © Catz / Hickson.

film *Delia Derbyshire: The Myths and Legendary Tapes,* about the life and work of the electronic music pioneer and *Dr Who* theme composer, approaches that inherent challenge by embodying the film's subject, literally, as a means to tell her story. Catz 'stars' as Derbyshire in stylized, dramatic reconstructions that recall films as diverse as *Berberian Sound Studio* (2012) and *Synechdoche, New York* (2004). Catz 'plays' Derbyshire in scenes that dramatize the musician's humiliating job interview to be a composer at Decca records and the stimulating and frustrating time she spent as a member of the BBC's landmark Radiophonic Workshop. Orbiting these reconstructions, literally in some cases by sharing adjacent studio space, is composer Cosey Fanny Tutti who is responding to the tapes that form the title and communing with Derbyshire as a ghostly influence. The innovations in the film are myriad and combine beautifully, honouring Derbyshire cinematically in ways that echo her own pioneering sonic achievements.[54] The careful use of traditional conventions such as interview and archive material only enhance the storytelling, allowing Derbyshire's importance to British musical culture to be felt as much as directly told. It

---

[54] A companion film is Lisa Rovner's film *Sisters with Transistors* (2020), released around the same time as Catz's film, which tells the story of female electronic pioneers including Derbyshire, her peers and those she inspired.

helps that Catz is a strong performer. Not many could take this approach, and the result is enthralling as audiences watch an actress perform a life, and simultaneously watch a filmmaker bring a story to screen and understand a subject all at once.

2021 – The Velvet Underground

Todd Haynes' remarkable film about *The Velvet Underground* is a bold statement in support of the idea that music films should not be taken as definitive but viewed as one take, one view of the lives and works of the musicians and the music that they bring to cinematic life. It is also a strong example of how cinema can be used to reclaim music and musicians from readings that have built up over time and removed the music and its makers from original contexts. It takes a while for The Velvet Underground to emerge in the film. There is significant emphasis on the art and experimental film world that they were borne from, and significant time spent on the background of the key figures in making the music, the 'degenerate' Lou Reed and the 'classical' John Cale and how that blend is so important to understanding the music. AO Scott (*Popcast*, 2021) argues that Haynes is a filmmaker 'steeped' in the experimental and Avant-Garde contexts of the time, 'establishing links' between art, film and the band's music. When the music arrives – from the combined influences of artists and filmmakers such as Andy Warhol, Stan Brakhage, Kenneth Anger and La Monte Young[55] whose works are presented in split screen throughout the film – the power and difference it evokes is returned to it. The music is dark, violent, strange, queer and yet, since attaining cultural power, has become somewhat removed from these contexts through the reproduction of the iconic Warhol-designed debut album sleeve on t-shirts sold in shopping centres the world over. The film returns the music to its origins, placing it back into a messy, experimental, New York context through interviews with surviving members and limited archive video and audio.[56] There is also an exciting reframing of the

---

[55] These filmmakers (and musician Young) are key figures in experimental and underground cinema (and music/sound) that emerged primarily from New York in the 1950s and 1960s – though Anger was outside of this geographically, being primarily based on the West Coast of the US.

[56] This film was shot by Todd Haynes' long-time collaborator who directed the wonderful performance film *Songs for Drella* (1990), featuring Lou Reed and John Cale performing the album they wrote in honour of the death of Andy Warhol. Some footage from this work is included in *The Velvet Underground*.

band's appearances in Warhol's famed *Screen Tests*, which is how the band are introduced in the film. Their individual dark power is retained forever on stark, unflinching celluloid.

As the book moves from here into more thematically defined sections, the introduction and this chapter have sought to situate the music film as a genre with established conventions, inherent tensions and an ever-evolving palette of attributes, permutations and combinations. Whilst some films depend on established conventions, others explore ways of critiquing, exploding or playfully addressing the limitations of cinema as a form of representation, finding new, different and evolving ways of capturing music, musicians, biography and history that are artistic works in their own right. The films that feature in this book show (there are obvious exceptions that will become clear), a respect for the music and musicians they document and engage with, alongside a desire to not allow that respect, or their fandom, to reduce the films they make to fawning hagiography. All the films here know that their story is not the whole story, and that 'fact' and 'reality' may not even be present, but that certain truths about music, musicians, and lives lived in pursuit of creativity may be reached when cinematic techniques and innovative approaches are embraced where music meets film. While music films continue to change, that essence has remained steadfast from the form's earliest days.

2

'We'll try for a groove'[1] – Music Making and the Careers of Musicians

While making music is, of course, central to music films – if there's no music made there's no film to make – the capturing and discussion of writing and recording music normally forms part of the narrative alongside, often in equal portions, live performance, biography, and cultural context. This chapter looks at films that place the writing and recording of music at the forefront of the narrative in different ways. There are films that seek to (re)address who gets credit for making popular music popular, focusing on session and studio musicians and backing singers. There are films that are documents of the recording of specific records by artists and in one case, a single song. Finally, there is analysis of films that focus, primarily, on the careers of those struggling to gain or retain careers as independent artists, to stay together due to artistic difference and/or for financial reasons, what happens when you never quite make it to a sustainable financial, economic and recognition level and how these things and others impact the running of a small independent record label. One thing most of the films have in common is a desire to celebrate all the different facets of writing and recording music, the defiance of those on the fringes of sustained success, the magic of being in a room and bringing a record to life and the constant assessment and reassessment of why people dedicate their lives to pop music, against odds that often seem insurmountable, or for often slim return in terms of acknowledgement, recognition or sustainability.

---

[1] *Sympathy for the Devil* (1968).

'You never know when you're making history'[2] – 'In the Background' of Popular Music Recording

The early twenty-first century has seen a slew of music films that seek to bring to light key contributions to twentieth-century popular music that have gone largely overlooked. Some of these films, including the Oscar-winning *20 Feet from Stardom* (2013), are discussed in this section. This trend kicked off with 2002's *Standing in the Shadows of Motown*. The film tells the story of Motown session band 'The Funk Brothers', a fluid group of musicians who played on all the key hits that emerged from Berry Gordy's Detroit-based record label in the 1960s. The film sets out its agenda straight from the off, with the audiences being alerted to how 'unheralded' this group of musicians is and members of the Funk Brothers lamenting being 'left out of the dream', asking 'will anyone ever know?' about their contribution. What stops the film being a simple exercise in settling grudges is the structure. It revolves around a celebration concert and tour reuniting the remaining Funk Brothers – thankfully a significant number were alive and playing when the film was made – for performances where the hits they played on are sung by contemporary artists. Similarly, the concept is elevated by being shot on 35mm film,[3] giving the performances and interviews a gravitas that aligns the form with the content's ambition of presenting these musicians and their contribution as valid, vital. There are other narrative devices that make the experience charming and inclusive. The Funk Brothers discuss their careers and lives – the latter being inseparable from the former with the film eloquently capturing issues of race and place through poetic, evocative recreations, and use of contextual archive – in informal settings such as diners and the Motown recording studios. These sessions often feature the group talking to each other and sometimes with guest vocalists from the celebration show such as Joan Osborne and Ben Harper.

One of the poetic reconstructions revolves around an infamous incident while the group were, literally, on the road with Berry Gordy's '1962 Motown Revue'. This section is presented like a standalone short film. It is a funny

---

[2] *Muscle Shoals* (2013).
[3] Even though Scorsese used 35mm beautifully for *The Last Waltz,* it was and remained uncommon in music film prior to the arrival of digital, with 16mm the favoured format.

sequence, made more charming by the warmth of the older Funk Brothers remembering the event, and the knowledge that such a potentially endangering scenario as leaving a Black man on the side of the road in the middle of nowhere in the 1960s ended without tragedy. What emerges from the conversations, rooted in collective and individual memory, is the community the musicians shared with each other and, remarkably, how little conflict and ego there was between them all at the time. This feels rare and makes the work they did feel even more remarkable. When the film spends time on this aspect, their contribution, for example in their demonstration of how they built a song, 'Ain't Too Proud to Beg, by The Temptations, from the drums, it achieves its aim of showcasing the pivotal role these musicians played in some of the most famous pop songs of all time, even if their sometimes grandiose assertions that without them there would be no Motown feel a little exaggerated, particularly given the people they were working with included figures such as Marvin Gaye and Stevie Wonder. Ultimately, as Garry Mulholland contends, this is a 'vital historical document with a serious political subtext about the exploitation of workers' (2011: 371).

The Wrecking Crew! (2008) takes the *Standing in the Shadows of Motown* template and essentially copies it in form and content. It tells the story of another group of backing and session musicians – this time the crew of the title. Based in Los Angeles, they played on hit records by The Beach Boys, Nancy Sinatra, and hundreds more. The film also takes the conversational remembrance approach, with members of the group in different configurations sat around remembering the process, labour and joy, that went into working with figures such as Brian Wilson and Frank Sinatra as well as the impact on their home lives. The family and home life context are key in this film because it is directed – and narrated – by Denny Tedesco, son of one of the crew's key figures, Tommy Tedesco. As director, Denny Tedesco is clear about his intention to try and set the record straight regarding his father and his father's peers and ensure they receive due attention for their contribution. It's an admirable intent but one undermined by a lack of filmmaking flair and rigour, making it feel less focused and thematically coherent than its Motown predecessor. For example, Tedesco's assertion that his father is unknown is undermined by archive footage of him leading seminars for aspiring guitar players with them in rapt attention, suggesting that he was at least well-known within this not insignificant circle.

Elsewhere there's a lack of visual imagination, though the calibre of contributor testifying to the group's importance often makes up for this formal lack. Similarly, the filmmaker tries to push his father and the group into serious conversational territory as regards rights, hours, contracts and visibility, but more often than not the responses barely scratch the political surface. Where the film does do well is in the role played by bassist Carol Kaye, a rare example of a woman allowed to play a pivotal role in terms of instrumentation in these kinds of recording studio and record label environments. She is celebrated throughout the film and when discussion turns to gender, the men around her are thoughtful and delightfully awkward in engaging with this aspect of the story. *Standing in the Shadows of Motown* has a similar moment, with Funk Brothers bass player Bob Babbitt – an interesting parallel – talking, movingly, of being accepted as a White man in an all-Black space and how the terrors his friends and peers faced taught him about race and privilege. Also akin to *Motown's* breaking down of 'Ain't Too Proud to Beg', *The Wrecking Crew!* devotes time to highlighting Carol Kaye's role in the opening of Glen Campbell's – another crew member before becoming a successful solo artist – iconic 'Wichita Lineman'. This small section, focusing on one part of one song, becomes a signifier for the larger thesis of these films, that without these musicians in the background, these hits loved by audiences may not have been so successful, because so many special pop moments came from the minds and hands of these players.

There are several ways in which *20 Feet from Stardom* differs from the earlier films discussed. The film opens with Bruce Springsteen talking about the difference between being at the front and at the back, the conceptual '20 feet', and what separates a star from a good technician or craftsperson. Next, the film is not merely a celebration of, in Springsteen's words that echo *Motown*, 'unheralded' voices, but a document about how the role of the backing singer has endured and changed by looking at some contemporary performers, including some (still) looking to traverse that 20-foot distance. In addition to Springsteen the film includes testimonials from artists including Stevie Wonder, Bette Midler and Mick Jagger, the latter coming across somewhat patronizing and naïve when considering why someone would be a backing singer for so long without wanting to make the step up to the front of the stage given the race and gender of the majority of backing singers. The film allows this narrow perspective to sit alongside examples of why some singers may not make that step, including a sequence focusing on how Darlene Love was creatively exploited by Phil Spector despite being the lead vocalist on one of his first hit songs. Assured of being presented to the world by her own name, the finished record of 'There's No Other (Like My Baby)' bore no trace of her identity and was instead packaged as a release by 'The Crystals'.

Love's work forms the emotional core of the film, with tributes paid by both artists and fellow backing singers as to her place in the hierarchy. In addition, the film tells of how she ended up cleaning houses, having been excluded by Spector, and only returned to singing upon hearing a Christmas record she had made with him playing on the radio in a house she was cleaning. The film is a combination of honest, complex testimony, glowing tribute, contemporary struggle and, since the role of backing singer is overwhelmingly taken by women, a comment on historical and still-standing gender biases existing in the pop music industry. The structure of the film and the choice of participant stories to follow, replete with some fascinating insights into famous moments in background vocals such as Merry Clayton's performance on the Rolling Stones' 'Gimme Shelter', means that the personal and the political remain well-balanced throughout.

Released the same year as *20 Feet from Stardom, Muscle Shoals* (2013) tells the story of the session musicians responsible for playing on the hit songs recorded at the famous recording studio Muscle Shoals Sound Studios in Alabama, on the banks of the Tennessee River. The film is very much about place, seeking to locate the story within a context, described early in the film as 'magnetic' by Keith Richards and an 'enigma' by Steve Winwood, with the former describing hearing music recorded there and thinking 'we gotta go'. Bono enigmatically says that 'the songs come out of the mud' and is surprisingly eloquent in arguing for the relationship between rivers and popular music. The film sensibly doesn't try and answer the question of why this place brought such a specific sound to mid-century popular music, particularly working with artists from the Stax label such as Otis Redding; instead it seeks to celebrate the 'magic' of the locale alongside the labour and ability of the group of mostly White musicians who created a unique sound within the Black music forms of Soul and R&B. The film argues that the music made by these people resulted in a 'specific form of R&B' but also goes into the reasons why they may never have received the credit for this. The film covers the difficulties faced by studio founder Rick Hall in working with record companies and musicians, resulting in losing the recording of Aretha Franklin's breakthrough album to New York and a group of musicians splitting off to form a rival studio across town.

The film deals with the political and racial contexts surrounding the story reasonably well, highlighting where Rick's judgement was lacking, resulting in big, missed opportunities – around not seeing the career potential in Lynyrd Skynyrd, for example – and also in the White musicians' recollections of being on the road and seeing the reality of life for the Black musicians and performers they worked with in the studio. However, like the other films in this section, it excels when detailing the contribution of the artists in question to the story behind legendary music from which they have previously been excluded. The sequences in which the musicians recall the recording of Percy Sledge's 'When a Man Loves a Woman', and Spooner Oldham 'finding' the way to play *I Never Loved a Man (the way I Love You)* by Aretha Franklin so that she could sing it as it deserved and needed to be sung are beautifully observed testimonies. In the case of the latter, it's an excellent example of a film stating the role of previously overshadowed personnel in something iconic, but one that doesn't seek praise beyond what's deserved. It's clear from the interviews with the Muscle Shoals musicians that they relish not only the chance to share their contribution but also to praise the icons they worked with and for, with Dan Penn's admiration for 'special' Aretha and her unique 'aura' a case in point.

'I never want to listen to it again'[4] – Recording the Recording of Music

Most films discussed in this section focus on artists and the recording of a single album; however, one of the most (in)famous examples of a film tracking the recording process focuses on the writing, development and recording of a single song. In truth, Jean-Luc Godard's *Sympathy for the Devil* from 1968, also known as *One Plus One* in a slightly different version, only half focuses on the recording of a single, legendary song. The other half is a commentary on

---

[4] *Scott Walker: 30 Century Man* (2006).

life and culture in 1968 in the form of slogans and visual provocations that Godard was starting to blend into his work around this time.[5] There are not many songs whose inceptions deserve or withstand being scrutinized in this way, but 'Sympathy for the Devil' (song) and *Sympathy for the Devil* (film) are representative of the cultural moment that was 1968, which sparked subsequent youth uprisings across the world, as well as the dark days that marked the end of the 1960s and the early 1970s as illustrated by the Vietnam War (explicitly referenced by Godard), the Manson murders and the Rolling Stones' own darkest hour at Altamont in 1969, captured in the later concert film *Gimme Shelter* and discussed in the previous chapter. The film evokes the fascinating banality of how a song that has such powerful weight attached to it comes into being. Godard captures the slow, unremarkable trial-and-error process beautifully and is interested in the process, of both art and protest. The story goes that the final released version of *Sympathy for the Devil* had the finished version of the song added to the end of the credits without Godard's approval (he was so disapproving that he apparently punched the film's producer at the première).

The camera tracks slowly around a rehearsal room cum studio as the Rolling Stones play with different instruments, pacing and approaches, slowly finding the song through a series of improvisations. These improvisations are intercut with staged performances of speeches about resistance and cultural decay set in junkyards and porn shops. It's a jarring visual juxtaposition and in hindsight shows prescience on the part of Godard for how this song would capture the darkness he saw in the world in 1968.[6] Agitprop graffiti is daubed all round London by young militants and in one moment the exterior and interior are linked with the sight of a paint can on the piano in the Stones' makeshift studio space. Workmen – studio technicians and those responsible for making the studio space – stand around and a central idea of the film emerges. This is all work, labour. The work of activism and resistance, the work of recording music and creating recording spaces, and the work of writing and recording songs as a band. This is not a glamorous film. It is, if anything, a statement about the

---

[5] Wim Wenders describes it as a 'science-fiction film' (1991: 10).
[6] It captures growing darkness within the band too, with Brian Jones repeatedly ostracised, physically separated by temporary sound-proofing panels, throughout the recording session.

poisonous notion of reducing art to something glamorous that doesn't involve labour and process, to the ethereal and mysterious. David E James writes that the film is striving to undermine any 'myths of rock 'n' roll spontaneity' and demystify 'the primal inevitability of the finished record' (2016: 268). Godard's version, *One Plus One,* minus the finished version of the song (the wilful withholding of a commercialist artefact) attests even more to this reading of the film, though in terms of being a document of the complete artistic process, the commercially driven version alas works best.

Another film that is riven into tonally and ideologically divergent parts is *A Dog Called Money* (2019).[7] The film documents the creation of PJ Harvey's 2016 album *The Hope Six Demolition Project,* the making of which the public were invited to witness via the building of a special recording space at London's Somerset House where the public were able to gaze on Harvey and her band as they recorded, with the artists positioned inside a sound-proofed makeshift studio. When the film is capturing the recording of the music it feels like a valuable addition to the canon of films that are testaments to the music-making process. There's a particular sequence that captures the stages of development acutely as film audiences see a choir leader played a demo of what his choir needs to sing, on a phone in his office. This leads to the film audience seeing the choir taking the demo and making it soar, which leads in turn to the film audience hearing this soaring accompaniment become part of the final version of the song back in the studio with Harvey. It is a beautifully constructed sequence whereby the film audience understands and witnesses the practical, logistical stages of a song's creation, but where the editing reminds us that what links those stages is craft and artistry, on all sides. Where the film undermines the creative process, and inadvertently makes the argument that maybe the artistic process should remain mysterious and enigmatic, is in the other threads of the storytelling.

The film is a collaboration between director Seamus Murphy, also a renowned photojournalist, and Harvey. The film tracks Harvey as she follows Murphy on assignment to Kosovo, Afghanistan and Washington DC, using the

---

[7] I reviewed this film on its release in 2020, for the Quietus. See https://thequietus.com/articles/26090-pj-harvey-a-dog-called-money-film-review – I struggled with it then, and I still struggle with it now.

trips as inspiration for *The Hope Six Demolition Project*. Whereas the result, and the creation of it, manages to convey a deft relationship between music and cultural context, the sequences that follow Harvey trying to source the inspiration come across as patronizing and woefully naïve, on both their parts. The opening shot, of a poor child with their face pressed up against the filmmakers' car window, and a late moment at a Trump rally featuring a Black man yelling 'build that wall' are two examples where the film presents images and sounds that should have formed part of a collage of images and sounds that fed into Harvey's album, but instead just feel preachy, and overbearing in their smugness. The impact isn't helped by Harvey's voiceover, which never manages to bridge the gap between raw encounter and eventual artistic transformation. It's hard to gauge the audience the filmmakers are conceiving of. It's too brusque and unsubtle to affect much audience engagement beyond recognition that the world is a terrible place, and the feeling remains, sadly, that an audience coming to the film who listen to PJ Harvey in the first place, would know all this already and, if reminded, would want to be so in a more creative and less infantilizing way.

The lines between inspiration, environment and output aren't direct. In *A Dog Called Money* the impression is given that they are, which results in a flattening of the artistic process and much of what is noble about it is lost. A film that takes a similar, associative approach in terms of its storytelling but to a more successful degree artistically is *Elephant Days* (2015). The film's tagline is 'stories from South London' and that's what it is. In essence, the film is a

Figure 2.1 Elephant Days (dir. Caddick and Cronin, 2015) © Fiction Records.

collection of stories of some of the people who live in the London borough of Elephant and Castle, just south of the River Thames. One of the stories is that of local residents The Maccabees, documenting the recording of their fourth record, 2015's *Marks to Prove It*. The film places their story alongside those of other residents including a pie-shop owner, a young family running a community garden, a tailor and his swing-band-leading best customer, and a basketball team en route to the national finals. The film is given extra poignancy by the fact that the record was the band's last and, in the final images of the film, one of the area's physical landmarks is torn down. Regeneration, and the loss of character and individual identity that goes with that term and process, is on its way. This film is a time capsule of the people who lived and worked there before its homogenisation.

The work of the band on the album tracks several stages from 'an empty slot in front of us . . . exciting' through 'politeness has gone' to 'gentle relief is kicking in. It's only what it is' and ends with the band performing one of the new songs live at an intimate show. These stages are echoed in the recollections of the other people whose stories are told in terms of the stages of life in Elephant and Castle across the years. The old: tailor George and his main customer Natty (a Charlie Chaplin impersonator, Chaplin was a local too) and the pie-shop owners, staff and customers. The younger: Richard and Lila who create the urban garden, and the Peckham Pride basketball team. Their stories, delivered as oral histories over beautifully photographed sequences, create a roving portrait of place and community, taking in race, class, faith, community and economics. The band and their music – the band scored the film in addition to it showcasing the songs from the album being recorded – may sit at the centre of the narrative but the filmmakers ensure they don't dominate (their contributions in snatched interviews throughout suggest this was a strategy they agreed with the filmmakers) and by being borne from a place of interest and curiosity the film manages to be insightful about so many things, including the creation of a particular record in a particular place at a particular time.

One of the qualities that comes through in *Elephant Days* is curiosity about people and place. It's a quality that also flows through *Junun* (2015), directed by Paul Thomas Anderson and focusing on the recording of an album by his friend and collaborator Jonny Greenwood with Israeli musician Shye Ben Tzur. Anderson simply goes with his camera (he mostly shot the film himself) where his curiosity takes him. This curiosity is not limited to the music being recorded in front of him but the location of the recording. All the rooms of the makeshift studio and the external surrounding area of the Mehrangarh Fort in Rajasthan, India. He's interested in its entirety and doesn't know what to privilege, which makes the capturing of this artistic moment refreshing. His instinct and this display of curiosity in humanity recalls his idol and mentor Jonathan Demme. Images of a nonchalant and defiant cat, a pesky pigeon in the rafters being cajoled to leave by producer Nigel Godrich with a mic stand, musicians lying around relaxing as they wait for power to come back on, their shoes collected outside the recording space. The film's images flow together to create a portrait of recording that eschews all the stereotypes of art needing stress and conflict to be memorable. Nick Shager (2015) writes that the film 'functions as an experiential documentary, one in which all meaning and emotion is derived from being wholly submerged in the music on display', which captures much of the film's essence. Elsewhere, Anderson follows one of the musicians as they go waistcoat shopping ahead of a performance, takes a moped ride through the city to get a Harmonium tuned and keeps in a backing singer's bored yawn as a reminder of the labour of recording music.

One of the facets of the *Junun* project (it provides the film and the album being recorded with their title) that Anderson understands is that this is a collaboration that is not hierarchical, ergo one that would put the westerner Greenwood at its centre. Greenwood doesn't put himself into the centre of the recording process and Anderson doesn't put Greenwood in the centre of the film. In fact, at some points, it's hard to find him in the frame as he crouches over his guitar and effects pedal, obscured by cables and stands, blending into the walls of the recording room. Similarly, Anderson himself is barely heard, instead spending his time watching the players through his camera and heading out with drones over the surrounding area creating a visual collage of locations that echo the way the album is being recorded – live with musicians in a circle – with sounds from instruments, voices, the room, and the city outside all becoming part of the recorded experience. Anderson's intimate distance, giving over space to the performers and their craft, spending long takes recording sections of vocal and instrumental performance, ensures the film never feels like a signalled presentation of access in the way that the more famous and lauded *Buena Vista Social Club* (1999) does with its positioning of Ry Cooder in relation to the Cuban musicians in that film, as discussed later in this book. At 54 minutes long there's no sense that a film was ever really the goal. The scant snatches of interview suggest this also, and this lack of a pre-ordained plan results in a film that feels spontaneous, natural and insightful.

Heinz Emigholz's *2+2=22: The Alphabet* (2017) conjures memories of both *Junun* and *Sympathy for the Devil* in different ways. The distanced intimacy is reminiscent of *Junun,* as is the way it links the recording space to the geographical space outside the studio walls. The studio space in which the recording takes place looks and feels like the big room studio space in Godard's film. However, Emigholz's camera is not as roving, preferring instead to remain mostly still and at a remove from the action of recording. One significant way it differs from *Junun* is how it uses structure to create a portrait of the recording process but also, through essayistic association, a city symphony with elements of bricolage. At the centre of the film sits a fascinating observation of the band Kreidler recording their album *ABC* over five days in 2013. Long, static shots of equipment being set up and musicians and technicians pottering about are intercut with streetscapes of Tbilisi – the film forms part of Emigholz's *Streetscapes 1* series – and scanned pages from the filmmaker's journals. Extracts from the latter also form the film's voiceover leading to an associative feel akin to *Sympathy for the Devil* where the music being recorded acts as both a catalyst for and response to other contexts and stimuli. The streetscapes are divided into chapters derived from letters of the alphabet[8] and the voiceover comprises Emigholz's philosophy of the city streets.

One of the pleasures of both *Junun* and *2+2=22* is the films' interest in the music being made directly in front of the camera. From the perspective of an English-speaking audience, there may also be a relative inexperience, and lack of expectation, around the music being made. This is different in the case of *Scott Walker: 30 Century Man* (2006). Walker was a huge star in the 1960s as the iconic central figure of pop group The Walker Brothers, before shunning a potential life of fame and fortune trotting out the same swooning ballads for a life of sonic exploration that involved dropping breeze blocks to get a particular sound and proclaiming 'we love that, we're having that'. *30 Century Man*

---

[8] Does the film's title make sense yet? It took this author a minute.

captures Walker in the studio, working, which at the various times of filming involve hitting a huge wooden box or punching a side of meat. As he says, 'I'm not making groove records'. The film knows and honours this; it is interested in the process of this revered artist and wants to know how he gets the sounds that haunt and terrify listeners. There is a practical smartness to this approach, because as Walker feels genuine interest in his contemporary work from the filmmakers he candidly talks about his life, career and philosophies of music, fame and art.

As a pop artist early in his career, Walker was renowned for his immaculate, silken voice, so it's jarring to hear him stretching and twisting it into new shapes to find something that is as far away from 'The Sun Ain't Gonna Shine Anymore' as it is possible to conceive. The film closes with an incredible sequence, centred on amazing footage of him singing, before the image dissolves into abstraction following Walker stating: 'I fail lots of times but at least I'm trying.' Around Walker's reminisces, self-analysis and self-deprecation the film builds a tribute to his work as both a modern avant-garde master and by delving into the process that led from The Walker Brothers to his seminal album *Tilt* (1996) and beyond. It draws out where his work is trying to find avant-garde fissures in the pop space, for example on the Walker Brothers 1978 'comeback' album *Nite Flite*. As Brian Eno says in the film of that moment in pop history, 'it's humiliating to hear this, we haven't got any further'. The film pulls out a thread in Walker's art that runs from his increased interest in song and sonics during the first Walker Brothers records, through his initial solo records – a period culminating in the initially disastrous and later reclaimed as masterpiece *Scott4* – to the now of the film, with meat being punched and orchestras being invited to enter terrifying and violent sonic terrain. The intelligence of the film, however, is to acknowledge the gulf between this now and the bucolic (for older audiences) then. The image of Lulu, a contemporary of the Walker Brothers, listening, confused, to the nightmarish *Tilt*, lingers, as does early Walker devotee Marc Almond's declaration, 'I hate *Tilt*'. *30 Century Man* is a rare example of a film that gives copious access to artistic process and biographical information and exhilaratingly leaves audiences as flummoxed as when the film started.

In many ways, Sam Jones's film about the band Wilco, *I Am Trying to Break Your Heart* (2002), is the ultimate example of the 'studio' film as it captures a seismic moment for a band in their artistic and commercial journey. Shot in black and white (on 16mm film), there is a gravitas to the aesthetic, one that suggests an artistic importance to what is being captured. The look and feel of the film are distinct, but it also feels related to other films in this section. In terms of how the film captures a seminal moment in a band's life, it is closest to *Sympathy for The Devil*. However, here the driving creative and professional factors are laid bare up front by the band's manager who declares both 'this is their moment' and how the album needs to be the band's 'big one'. The film not only documents the creative process of writing and recording their iconic record *Yankee Hotel Foxtrot* from 2001 (the detail and care given over to this aspect is beautifully rendered) but also captures the breakdown of the band's creative core of Jeff Tweedy and Jay Bennett, providing a document of Tweedy's increasing influence on all things Wilco. It also captures the early stages of Tweedy's addiction to painkillers that would plague his next few years. The film captures evidence of Tweedy's migraines, brought on it suggests by the stress of recording a major work.[9]

There's a sense that the band themselves conceive of the moment as pivotal for them. As one member says early on, 'it's ours to destroy'. This recalls the sentiments expressed in *Elephant Days* by The Maccabees around the potential of recording, one that is a positive but also contains a negative. In an interview for *Filter* magazine, Tweedy said that he felt the film made him and the band seem miserable and the process arduous and that 'the part that was really fun for me wasn't in the movie' (2007: 56). Though the film contains tough elements in terms of relationships – the breakdown between Bennett and Tweedy is captured with some brilliant whip pans as they argue over a single, tiny, moment in the song 'Heavy Metal Drummer' – it also captures a band at a pivotal moment creating their best known and most critically lauded work.

The practical and symbolic role of the studio, in particular the mixing desk, as a site of potential and power in success or failure in recording music comes up visually across music films. In *Sympathy for the Devil* there's a fascinating juxtaposition between the band in the studio and the lab-coated

---

[9] There's also the little factor of being dropped by the label on completion of the album only to sell it back to a subsidiary of the same company.

technicians behind the glass pushing faders and emerging occasionally to reposition mics. Mostly music films show the band or artist sat alongside the producer and/or engineer at the desk[10] seeking perfection in a mix or idea. This is felt keenly in *Elephant Days* and at its most intense in *I Am Trying to Break Your Heart* where Tweedy and Bennett almost come to physical blows as each seeks to assert dominance by deciding the final level of a single fader on the studio desk. The desk as a site of artistic war feels powerfully captured here.

Admittedly, the film leans into the idea that great art is borne from struggle. However, it doesn't exclude the band at peace. They enjoy playing together in rehearsal and on stage as they road test new songs and 'find' the songs in their rehearsal space through a series of extended sequences as the music comes together. The sequence of the band working through the song 'Reservations' is a particularly strong moment where the audience feels privileged to be witnessing the birth of a song. The film opens like a road movie, with the credits appearing over images of driving round the band's hometown of Chicago. It unfolds with journalists providing context on the band and the American music industry at that moment. There are insights into the solace and awkwardness of live shows as Tweedy takes time out from recording to play some lone shows. As the band and the film head towards the unknown, the unforeseen, the fact that any sort of album was recorded given some of the context feels remarkable. That a modern classic was the result feels like magic.

'I'm not gonna sweeten it'[11] – Struggle, Failure and the Battle for a Career

Wilco's struggle to achieve something creatively rewarding and commercially sustainable, documented in *I Am Trying to Break Your Heart,* has a happy ending, an almost unbelievable one. The level of success and sustainability achieved by Wilco rarely happens and, as the twentieth century has given way

---

[10] The bassist is often slouched on a couch in the background.
[11] *Kate Nash: Underestimate the Girl* (2018).

to the twenty first, the battles are harder to fight, the rewards slimmer and the casualties greater. The 2018 film about singer/songwriter Kate Nash, *Kate Nash: Underestimate the Girl*, captures similar creative battles, as the musician seeks to break out from the image aligned with her initial success, achieved when she was a teenager and captured in the bittersweet admission that 'I'm into punk music and rock music but I need to make a pop record because I have no money'. The film tracks the period of trying to make a new record as a solo artist and deals openly with the difficulties of being a woman in the music industry and the difficulties of achieving major success at a young age. Also, at the centre of the film, beyond the existential struggles of gender, identity, trauma and the rapidly diminishing buffers of the record industry, Nash must deal with the personal ignominy and hardship of having her manager steal her money, leaving her pretty much destitute, exhausted and miserable. As she sells her clothes and downsizes her apartment it's hard to not agree wholeheartedly when Nash's friend exclaims that this is 'a business where the bad guy definitely succeeds'. In echoes of Kathleen Hanna in *The Punk Singer*,[12] Nash declares 'music keeps me alive, the music industry nearly killed me a bunch of times', and the film expertly captures the resilience required by solo artists to maintain any level of a viable career.

After being dropped by her label, Nash self-funded the record *Girl Talk* (2013) and the film, including the subsequent tour, follows Nash in the period following that investment and exertion, while drawing on Nash's archive material from her youth and diarizing activity. She performs for music industry insiders at their office, on their lunch break, she writes songs for others and jingles and commercials and travels solo to the industry showcase CMJ in the hopes of reigniting her career. The film is a delicate blend of self-shot testimony and retrospective interviews that captures the highs and lows, immediacies and reflections of Nash and her life, and it keeps returning to the music, the songs and the live performances. Director Amy Goldstein believes in Nash as an artist, displaying her lyrics on screen wherever possible and ensuring that she is given time and space to showcase her abilities as a writer and performer but also as a person in interactions with her bandmates, and as a woman.

---

[12] Discussed in a later chapter.

There's a defiance in Nash that suggests she will always fight for the right to be a performer, regardless of external validation and this film constantly challenges the trivialization of female pop performance. One of the most moving sequences is seeing the work Nash did in schools when she first broke through aged 20 with her song 'Foundations'. This archive material captures the profundity of her life experience and how she cherished this moment, proud of how she reached out to girls younger than her at that frenzied moment and took her responsibility seriously. Because, as she says, 'there's nothing silly about being a teenage girl'.

Silliness is at the core of early noughties nearly-rans The Parkinsons' appeal and Caroline Richards' film about the band, *The Parkinsons: A Long Way to Nowhere* (2016), is a heartfelt exploration of why a band doesn't quite break through to the point where they even have one huge single, something like 'Foundations' by Kate Nash.[13] There is an increasing number of films dedicated to cult bands and those who never quite make it to a recognized level of fame or maintainable level of security. The most famous is *Anvil: The Story of Anvil* (2008), discussed in a later chapter. Often it is the case that the films remain rooted in a narrow field of interest, for the few diehard fans of the band and can resemble pained yells on the part of the filmmaker that the band or artist should be more well known when all evidence is to the contrary. What makes *The Parkinsons: A Long Way to Nowhere* different is that even while it's clear that Richards has a fondness for the band, the filmmaking interest is in exploring why this band never 'made it' even though most of the ingredients were there for them to do so. They had the requisite word-of-mouth hook – they liked to get naked at their shows – to get people to come and see them and they managed to snag some high-profile support and headline slots as their reputation and momentum grew. However, the reputation outpaced the musical development, and they soon became expected to misbehave on stage with gigs becoming debauched spectacles rather than musical events.

The film explores several factors that impacted the band's ability to break through, which ensures it's not a simple retread of their infamy and as a result the complexities of success become clearer than in most films with a similar

---

[13] Richards is commonly known as an editor for Julien Temple, working with him from *Oil City Confidential* (2009) onwards.

focus. Seeing via archive material and hearing via the band's recollections, it becomes apparent [again] how London-centric the music industry was and is, and how a reputation there doesn't necessarily travel. What fans like in the capital doesn't necessarily travel either. Even in London, it's a very short window where the band can do what they like. There's also a moment where the film argues for the role of luck in making or breaking a band. At a high-profile mini-festival at London's ICA to coincide with the Queen's Golden Jubilee, an event itself echoing the Sex Pistols' Silver Jubilee Thames protest, fate intervenes and cuts The Parkinsons' headline set short due to the venue being evacuated when an alarm is triggered. By the time the event restarts most of the crowd have gone and the momentum, that word again, has fizzled out. The next evening, the headliners are not interrupted, and it's seen as the gig where The Libertines cemented their rising reputation and became a band that would break through. Thankfully, the film doesn't proclaim injustice on the part of this one moment; instead recognizing that maybe the band don't have the songs to succeed and maybe lead singer Afonso 'Al' Pinto doesn't have a voice that will carry the songs they do have over the line. As the film ends, all scuffles and breakups have been mended and the band are simply playing, for fun, for the devoted few, and it becomes what it always should have been, something where, as Al states, 'there's no destination'.[14] A film that makes a lovely double bill with this film is Fred Burns's 2013 ode to punk nearly-men Johnny Moped, *Basically, Johnny Moped*. The film is charming and makes great use of animation in displaying the family tree of the band's iterations which at various points contained Chrissie Hynde and Captain Sensible.

Much of *We Jam Econo: The Story of the Minutemen* is spent driving round San Pedro with Mike Watt, one of the band's leaders, telling the story of the band and their relationship with their hometown. It's shot on video, very lo-fi, and Watt seems to be humouring Irwin in the sense that, while very forthcoming about the band's history, he isn't sure why anyone would care to see a film about it. This humility, coupled with a reserve rooted in the tragic death of Watt's friend and co-band leader D Boon in 1985, with the band still very much operational, is both charming and at odds with the intense intelligence of their hard, minimalist punk music.

---

[14] I had the privilege of talking to Richards on the release of her film, for Directors Notes in 2018. See https://directorsnotes.com/2018/04/27/caroline-richards-the-parkinsons-a-long-way-to-nowhere/

The interview set-ups are shoddy (meant as a compliment) and the form of the film direct and stripped back. The live archive footage is smartly taken from a small variety of shows, with each one showcasing several song performances. This articulates the essence of those individual shows at individual times in the band's short career. One approach of many music films is to show a broad array of live footage to convey importance. The alternate approach here is equally, if not more, powerful. As the images of flyers and live shows fill the screen and testimonies from all the key players in the independent punk scene of the early 1980s – Ian Mackaye, Jello Biafra, Henry Rollins – tell of the Minutemen's importance and as the audience learns of D Boon's working-class ethic regarding when shows should take place for people who had work the next day, the shoddy approach that belies a real heart and intelligence melds perfectly with the music the Minutemen made. What emerges is a belief that this film had to be made this way, on video, intimately, quietly, or else it couldn't really be a film about the Minutemen.

Instrument (1999) is a collaboration between filmmaker Jem Cohen and the band Fugazi. Collaboration is an apt word here as both filmmaker and band are credited as directing and editing the work. Harbert writes that 'the film stands out within [Cohen's] body of work as an 'intensely collaborative film' and that 'Fugazi's and Cohen's shared principles of art, audience, and market emerge obliquely, through a provocative aesthetic experience' (2018: 202). Defiant in its approach, one that represents the ethos and aesthetic of the band and their music, as with the other films discussed here, *Instrument* is a cinematic and poetic piece of work. The film documents the band from 1987 to 1996 but, similarly to Jarmusch's *Year of the Horse* (1997), it does so by creating a portrait across time, allowing that time to reveal changes in the band's musical approach, their physicality and their fans, while simultaneously reinforcing their ideological approach to the commerce and economics of the music industry. A poetic feel is further attained by the films both being shot on a variety of formats and the matching of contextual footage of cities and skies shot by the filmmakers 'on the road' with the music of the artists.

In parallel with *We Jam Econo* (*Instrument* is dedicated in part to D Boon, and in part to John Cassavetes) the live footage archive is also curated to showcase how a Fugazi show might have felt, its movement and energy, something the film really captures in its pacing as a whole. Within that archive are moments that play out as part of a narrative that is incredible to witness, if not overly dramatic. In one sequence, the band play a show at a prison in 1990 (many of the shows featured are benefits of kind or another), with a few inmates looking on and dancing in a leisurely, bemused mode at odds with the band's intense performance. In another, singer and guitarist Ian Mackaye marches an unapologetic spitter from the stage in a headlock. Two electrifying examples of how Fugazi were maybe both the most punk and anti-punk band simultaneously. There is a tension at the heart of the film, with band and filmmaker working through so much as they create the work, from a deeply invested place. As Harbert frames it: 'Can rock still be political if mediated?' (2018: 207) and, as Cohen says in Harbert's book, 'How do you make a music film that *embodies music* [author emphasis] rather than discusses music?' (2018: 216). The film allows many complexities to sit side by side, in tension. John Cassavetes would have approved.

Towards the end of Niall McCann's[15] *Lost in France* (2016), Stewart Henderson, of the band The Delgados and head of record label Chemikal Underground, says to camera 'I don't know why you're making this film' and in one sense the question is valid as the focus is on a mildly successful independent record label from Scotland, one with a roster of bands that are well-loved but none who are massive. The only real connection to the 'big leagues' is Alex Kapranos of the band Franz Ferdinand. Kapranos is in the film as his old band Karelia were on Chemikal Underground and played the event that forms the impetus for the narrative here, a tiny festival celebrating the label that took place in a small town in central France in 1997. However, despite the potentially narrow interest in bands such as Mogwai, Arab Strap and The Delgados (comparatively and not disparagingly speaking) the film succeeds in being illuminating as to what makes those bands and other artists tied to the label so special and draws out valuable lessons and insights about the music business and its changing (and ever-present natures). It is a celebration of independence, friendship and art that cleverly uses a historical event as a moment of reflection to base the narrative on. This reflection, using interviews and archives, is accompanied by a road movie element as the key participants from the 1997

---

[15] McCann's next film, *The Science of Ghosts* (2018) is a warm portrait of Irish musician Adrian Cowley that is a worthy addition to any music film watchlist.

festival head back to the town of Mauron to relive the event, play some new shows, and make a film celebrating independent music.

At one point Henderson declares that 'we're at the end of one epoch and the start of another' and as the participants discuss the key factors on making their careers sustainable – John Peel's radio show, an Evening Session booking, a good review in a music paper such as the NME, or the importance of the dole[16] as a way of supporting emerging creative practitioners including musicians[17] – it's hard to disagree that the business of popular music has undergone fundamental change. Even so, the vagaries of who makes it and who doesn't remain. Kapranos talks of finding success with Franz Ferdinand and asks 'Why not them as well?' in reference to his peers and friends in bands and *Lost in France* captures so much of the magic and mystery of being a professional musician. While it covers the negative aspects it never dwells on this side of things, preferring instead to celebrate. Stuart Braithwaite of Mogwai says at one point, of music, that it 'has an effect on people that can't be quantified' and *Lost in France* works because it's not trying to quantify anything. It is a curious and caring work. In 1997 the bands went to the middle of France for a tiny festival because they were asked. For the film, they went back because they had a blast and Henderson's acknowledgment that 'it was about the trip, it wasn't about the gig' can be read as the ethos behind the whole Chemikal Underground enterprise.

Braithwaite's philosophical insight into music as something that results in unquantifiable effects can be related to the enterprise of writing this book, which explores the feelings and effects of these films and how they capture, fleetingly or otherwise, the ineffable qualities of the music their narratives are centred around. The films discussed in this chapter centre on music-making as craft, labour and career. They offer insight into shared experiences and obstacles amongst musicians of different eras, styles and genders. The struggle is real, as the musicians featured say. This book aims to draw a picture of the music film as a discrete cinematic genre or style, that has reflected music as performed, recorded, and industrialized since its inception in the 1950s. In this chapter, the

---

[16] I wrote about this film when it was released and one of the most powerful aspects was and remains Kapranos' eloquent defence of the dole as a societal mechanism for good and how those that felt its benefit and went on to achieve success paid back that investment to a significant degree.

[17] The dole was unemployment benefit, which from the early 1980s to early 1990s in the UK, when these bands solidified their success, was largely free from the bureaucratic demands that came to dominate it.

focus has been on the recording of music and the subsequent labour of getting that music in front of audiences whilst earning a living at the same time. Rather than look extensively at individual films, here I have sought to trace thematic relationships by focusing on a wide variety of works that examine the challenges of the music industry, the role of chance, the importance of structural inequalities and the motivations of musicians. To close this chapter, there is a short discussion of a film that, whilst exploring all these facets in its manifestation of the music film, also raises questions about what it means to be a musician and how it might be possible to achieve a different kind of success: one that is problematic, not especially desirable, and highly conditional.

The Man from Mo'Wax (2016) documents the career of James Lavelle. At its heart it is a story of an against-the-odds comeback, a startlingly honest portrayal of the creative process and a cautionary tale of excess at the height of unimaginable fame and stardom. The amount of confessional home movie footage shot by Lavelle and subsequently shared, is remarkable.

What sets this film apart from others discussed, however, is Lavelle and his (and the film's) inability to identify what his talent is, beyond his capacity to see an idea and bring it to life. The idea that drives the narrative and drove Lavelle to fame and stardom was the UNKLE project but, as the film displays, this idea emerged from a variety of components in Lavelle's life including his work as an influential DJ and record label boss. His Mo'Wax label released records including DJ Shadow's legendary debut *Endtroducing . . .* (1996). Lavelle was also a music journalist and taste maker. The UNKLE project was Lavelle's move into making music following a period of success releasing or spinning it. The term 'making' is key but slippery here because, as the film shows, Lavelle's role in writing, performing and producing the music UNKLE made was non-existent to begin with. The first record, *Psyence Fiction* (1998), is clearly the result of the imagination and labour of DJ Shadow and the album's roster of guest vocalists including Thom Yorke and the Beastie Boys' Mike D.

Lavelle's refusal to acknowledge this creative imbalance and his unwillingness to engage with the business and labour of music making – as one contributor puts it, 'he made a career out of being a perpetual adolescent' – results in Lavelle becoming estranged from his collaborators and friends and drowning under gargantuan amounts of debt that force him back to the 'nocturnal narcotic lifestyle' of being a DJ just to stay financially afloat. Lavelle's comeback doesn't hit the same heights he was experiencing pre-crash but, by learning to write songs and sing and engaging in serious reflection on his life and failures, he gains dignified success of a different kind. The film builds to a tense finale as Lavelle returns to the spotlight curating the esteemed Meltdown Festival on London's South Bank and even though previous collaborator 3D from Massive Attack doesn't grab the olive branch, DJ Shadow does and the pair perform together live for the first time. It's a touching moment and a signifier of how perseverance and determination, married with luck, can result in success in a film that shows that ideas are great, but what lasts is often the application of those ideas, and the hard-worn scars that are recognised as sacrifice by both audiences and peers.

Part Two

Politics and Place

3

'Secret Black Technologies'[1] – Black Music

One of the troublesome things about writing about the commonalities across a series of films about Black popular music in the twentieth and early twenty-first centuries is that the commonalities are often sad and tragic, resulting in accounts that end up dwelling on sadness, oppression, exclusion and death. These themes are so bound up in the lives of Black people, particularly Black Americans, that hardly any story can escape touching on tragedy profoundly, even in minor doses. This chapter struggles with not making these negative commonalities the central motif, wrestling with how to balance these with other equally important aspects such as talent and artistry, innovation, joy and impact. Hanif Abdurraqib writes of how Black music of the middle of the twentieth century 'acted as both a call for people to take to the streets and a reprieve after a long day of protest, marching, or working some despised job' (2021: 13). The conclusion I draw is that these negative commonalities – those that look closely at the struggles of Black artists – be discussed mostly in relation to films in the Soul, R&B and Blues section.[2] This means that the focus in other areas won't touch as deeply on these aspects, though rest assured they are there. Of course, space is given over in each of the films to moments of joy, light and transcendence. Because, for example, how could a film about Nina Simone not be joyful? So, while this chapter contains analysis and discussion of how the films discussed have provided access points to issues of race, social injustice and systemic oppression that contribute to the music but also its exceptionalness, time is also spent focusing on how they are vehicles for philosophies of Blackness, Black life and life more broadly. This chapter also

---

[1] *The Last Angel of History* (1996).
[2] For good or ill, for ease of categorization, for admittance of failure on my part regards the nuance of these matters.

acts as a record of how cinema has captured the innovation and unique abilities and visions that have contributed to twentieth century popular music's most enduring and original forms; Blues, Jazz, Soul and R 'n B and Hip Hop. Before moving into discussing films grouped by musical genre, there is discussion of two films that set the tone for the political and philosophical themes that run through so much Black music and films about Black music. They are John Akomfrah's *The Last Angel of History* (1996) and first, Herbert Danska's *Right On!* (1971) featuring The Last Poets.

Herbert Danska's film captures a performance by The Last Poets of their stage work, *Right On!* While there is a deep performativity and theatrical staging to the film, it is also an ebulliently exterior work. The Last Poets perform their works on a Lower East Side rooftop, Manhattan spreading out behind. The sound of the city constantly bleeding in, jostling with vocal performance, adding to the film's sonic texture. Melissa Anderson (2013) writes that the performances 'go beyond mere bulletins, expanding into brutal diagnoses and blunt imperatives'. The film is structured as though it takes place over the course of a single day though time is fractured through jump cuts that reveal different costumes, and locations such as alleyways behind derelict buildings. The film cuts from their electric proto-Hip Hop being performed 'live' with conga drum accompaniment to the disorientating experience of suddenly seeing them lip-synching, intentionally slipping out of time, to a non-diegetic recording. The cinematic construction of the film is drawn attention to repeatedly in inventive ways.

The band's direct address of their poetry – to the camera, to people in their apartments, to those strutting past them in the street – is powerful and fidgety. The group are always moving and so is the camera and the cutting. When the film leaves the group, it does so to cut away to contextual images that relate to the songs but also to abstract images of New York that recall the work of William Klein. There's a relentlessness to the film's pacing and the group's performance that leads to the sensation that there is a pressing need to capture these sounds and these words, these ideas, before time runs out. One softer excursion accompanies 'Black Woman', a beautiful sequence that finds a Black Mother and Son naked, bonding skin-to-skin in a softly lit bedroom. Its slow juxtaposition to the frenetic exteriority of so much of the film adds to the poignancy. Later, as the performance nears its end, Danska's camera captures the group halo'd by the setting sun, the Empire State Building in the background. It's a serendipitous moment that frames The Last Poets as angels of Black conscience and creates an iconic image of a band that were trailblazers of the New York birthed art-form of Hip Hop.

John Akomfrah and the Black Audio Film Collective's *The Last Angel of History* is a poetic essay film about Black Consciousness and how that relates to and is borne from Art. Angels and aliens abound as a data thief from 200 years in the future finds himself in the 1990s tracing the Black experience from the drums of Africa to the drum and bass of Jungle by way of science fiction and science fact. The data thief draws a line from Robert Johnson to Sun Ra to George Clinton to Lee 'Scratch' Perry to Derrick May and Carl Craig and Detroit Techno and ends up at Goldie and A Guy Called Gerald. Along the way he drags Nichelle Nichols, Octavia Butler, Samuel R Delany and the first Black astronaut Bernard Harris into the slipstream of the thesis that revolves around the Black experience – 'we're like aliens trying to explain our experience to people on earth' says Ishmael Reed at one point – and the profound reasoning that slavery was akin to alien abduction. The interviewees address the audience as the data thief is seen traversing, in the words of Kodwo Eshun (a contributor in the film), 'entirely posthuman scenographies that paralleled the posthuman compositions of British drum 'n' bass' (2007: 97).

There's a fierce intelligence at play in a film that lasts a mere 45 minutes and it is not merely Akomfrah's as a filmmaker. The gathered artistic and critical voices speak to the thesis of the film from lived and learned experience[3] that, coupled with the alignment of the visionary artists in such close sonic and visual proximity, results in the overwhelming sense of the data thief digging up 'techno fossils' of a history that lay in plain sight for a long time. Jean Fisher writes of the film that 'we could not have a clearer demonstration of the philosophical conundrum of the human as historical being – that the past is not something that has happened to us, but is what afflicts us as a haunting from the future' (2007: 28). This haunting effect is in form as well as content. The film was shot on video, which adds to its purpose as an artefact, particularly as time goes on. The ultra-degraded versions that pop up on YouTube enhance

---

[3] As an aside, it is thrilling to see so many Black critical voices such as Kodwo Eshun and Greg Tate talking so beautifully about Black music and culture. Too often music films exclude the voices of critics who share race and gender with the music and artists being discussed. One such example, sadly, is *Chasing Trane* from 2016, about John Coltrane.

the fossilized aesthetic and give greater potency to the ideas contained within. The speed with which the film deals with its subjects, and in parallel with how quickly the data thief learns of these extraordinary, what Kodwo Eshun calls in the film, 'impossible imaginary musics', lends the film a hope that the future of Black Music will continue this angelic, alien trajectory and forever speak of the uniqueness of the Black experience as lived on earth.

'We work on the other side of Time'[4] – Jazz

One of the key Black messenger figures in *The Last Angel of History* is legendary jazz musician and band leader Sun Ra. *The Last Angel of History* contains short moments culled from the 1974 film about Ra called *Space Is the Place*. On the DVD release of the film, director John Coney talks about how he wanted to make a film with Ra that was also an homage to the cheap 1950s science-fiction cinema he so loved. 1974 was also the commercial height of the Blaxploitation[5] genre and *Space Is the Place* is a Sci-Fi Blaxploitation performance movie, which sees Ra as a cosmic traveller setting up a new planet for Black people and playing a game of the fates to ensure safe passage for Black travellers. However, the film is also a vehicle for the unique philosophies of Sun Ra and gives space to his ideas about the relationship of Black people to space and time and life on earth. Jamie Sexton describes it as a 'cult film by proxy', which he defines as 'a film that has gained its cult status primarily through its relation to other media, in this case music' (2006: 198). This idea of the 'cult film by proxy' resounds with the music documentary as a form, one where music is often the gateway to the cinematic.

Space is the Place has music at its heart, but also the musician. At various points Ra bypasses the conventions of acting in a scene with professional actors or staying in character to issue his philosophy directly to the audience, to declare that 'Black people are myths' or to say:

---

[4] *Space is the Place* (1974)
[5] A wave of 1970's American pulp cinema that provided leading role opportunities for Black actors in a mostly narrow range of roles including pimps, criminals and avengers. Famous for providing careers to stars including Pam Grier and Richard Roundtree, and for funk soundtracks by artists including Curtis Mayfield, James Brown and Marvin Gaye.

'My kingdom is darkness and Blackness. The people have no music that is in coordination with their spirits. They are out of tune with the Universe'.

It is a reminder that the cosmic philosophies of Black Art that the data thief finds in *The Last Angel of History* are not buried deep but resting on the surface of culture. The finale of *Space* is at once a plea to Planet Earth, a Utopian vision for Black people, and a moment that places Ra directly in a lineage of Black leaders such as Dr Martin Luther King Jr and Malcolm X. What miraculously grounds these ideas together is the music, played by Sun Ra and his Arkestra in a rare portion of the film that lets the band fly, an opportunity they duly take up by taking off into space sonically and literally. Time has not dimmed the activity or power of the Arkestra, as Ephram Asili's 2009 documentary *Points on a Space Age* attests. The film follows the continuing journey of the group under the stewardship of Marshall Allen following the physical passing of Ra in 1993.

Connections to Space and ideas around the earthly Black experience and its forced limitations recur in Shirley Clarke's dynamic *Ornette: Made in America* (1985). Clarke's portrait of her friend Ornette Coleman is one that seeks to ensure the cinematic experience is akin to the experience of listening to Coleman's music. Engulfing, disorienting, overwhelming. Completely disinterested in linear biography, this is a film that is experimental, associative, temporally fluid and formally jarring. At the heart of the narrative, ostensibly, is the premiere of Coleman's symphony *Skies of America,* performed in his hometown of Fort Worth in 1983. The film takes in rehearsals, a club performance in the arts centre's adjacent bar, the premiere performance, Coleman's recollections of growing up in the city and his early days in New York, revealed in footage captured back then by Clarke. However, the order that things play out reinforces that it's in the associative relationship between sequences that the film's intent lies.

It's a heady mixture and the construction of the material, which also includes poetic reconstructions featuring a 'young Ornette' walking Coleman's childhood street and sometimes gazing upon 'older Ornette', is free and driven by an emotional impulse rather than a logical or chronological one. For this reason alone, it stands as possibly the greatest jazz film. It plays around with motifs, repetition and outer movement, while always moving around the central idea or note of the artist and their way of life. As the film goes on and the different ideas and time periods collide, it gets progressively weirder. Clarke relies more on more on stroboscopic visuals to accompany the music, NASA comes into play as do the Buckminster Fuller domes in Texas, with Coleman's band performing in one. Clarke is urging viewers to feel their way through the film. It is a film that, like a lot of jazz, reveals more of its nature upon repeat engagements. One theme that stands out prominently, that feels merely biographical upon first watch, is the relationship of Coleman to his son. Seen as a young man being taught the principles of the drums in Clarke's early footage he emerges as a key collaborator and inheritor of his Father's philosophies of music and life as the jazz legend performs the premiere of his classical and jazz symphony, in sync with his offspring.

Similarly attuned to its subject and as brilliantly stubborn in its refusal to do the expected is the portrait *Milford Graves Full Mantis* (2018)[6]. The film opens with a title card:

Figure 3.1 Milford Graves Full Mantis (dir. Meginsky, 2018) © Jake Meginsky.

> Look at the room downstairs
> Look at the garden outside
> Don't try to analyse it
> Just take it in
>
> Milford Graves

---

[6] I interviewed director Jake Meginsky for the Quietus on the film's release in 2018. Available at: https://thequietus.com/articles/25007-milford-graves-full-mantis-jake-meginsky-interview.

That acts as an instruction for how to experience the film. This is followed by a slow camera crawl that pulls back from a mirror to reveal a room in Graves' house. The non-diegetic music is Graves' and over the course of the introduction we are shown elements of, and full objects in, the space that will form the focus of attention in the film: biology, plants, Africa, history, philosophy, martial arts, sound. The film tells audiences to settle in, that this is something different. After this set up, Milford is introduced. More than the subject, he is the guide for the film. He moves through ideas – such as testing his heart and the hearts of his visitors, to the development of his own martial art based on the praying mantis – that reveal more of Graves' biography than a simple retelling of facts and events could.

The film gives its subject, the guide, time to tell stories and reflect upon the philosophical underpinnings of all areas of his life. Though tonally different, it is like *Ornette: Made in America* in that the film feels like music. However far out it goes philosophically, it always returns to music as the physical expression for Graves' philosophy. Music sits at the heart of everything, and the film knows what each aspect of his story and music needs cinematically. The filmmakers are happy to let the camera sit on Milford as he tells a story, or move in time, utilize extreme close ups, manipulate and distort the film's colour, or focus on one of the plants in his garden as he talks about how all beings are connected. The film was directed by Jake Meginsky, a student of Graves, with assistance from Neil Young. Meginsky's direction showcases a belief that his teacher's lessons are worth sharing but never loses sight of the need for film technique to assist in conveying those messages. The result is that form and content are so married the result is a uniquely memorable experience if the viewer just 'takes it in'. Writing for the *New York Times* on the film's release in 2018, Glenn Kenny wrote that if it's facts you want about Graves, there's always the Internet. What this film does, like the best music films, is 'give you, well, the man's heart, and it's a beautiful one'.

Another of the great Jazz films is *I Called Him Morgan* from 2016. Director Kasper Collin imposes the structure of a mystery unfolding, being investigated. The film travels towards the answer to the question of what happened to Lee Morgan, the brilliant trumpeter. This shrewd approach works to extend the film out beyond the core Jazz audience (who may know) and also because the answer is extraordinary. He was killed by his common-law wife, shot in a New York Jazz Club. One of many remarkable decisions the film makes is to

Figure 3.2 Lee Morgan performing with Art Blakey and the Jazz Messengers, Amsterdam, 1960; featured in I Called Him Morgan (dir. Collin, 2016) © Ben van Meerendonk.

give more time to his wife Helen Morgan than to the musical artist at its heart. Part of this is fortuitous, in that she dictated her story late in her life to an evening-school teacher and Jazz fan, where she reflected on her life before and with Lee, up to his death. Despite this storytelling gift the film feels more than opportunistic. Morgan's talent and career are given a full celebration and his personal life a thorough examination; at no point is Helen seen as simply a 'Jazz wife'.

The film is also the Jazz documentary that most deeply delves into the world of photography that accompanied the classic eras of the music in the 1950s and 1960s. Many Jazz documentaries include incredible, particularly black-and-white, archive photos but *I Called Him Morgan* pauses to revel and reflect in that art form and its role in capturing the music and musicians. They have a tactile presence in the film, the beauty and power of the images allowed to tell part of the story of this music and its cultural impact. The film is never derailed by this or other diversions because of its central formal premise. This is a poetic piece of, in the words of José Teodoro in 2016, 'jazz history meets true crime' fusion. Collin uses the passing of time as told through the rotations of a cassette in a tape player to excavate a life, career and a relationship and frees them all from myth, cliché and prejudice. The film is not Collin's first Jazz documentary. He first engaged cinematically with the little-seen portrait *My Name Is Albert Ayler* (2005), which adopted a similar approach using old audio recordings as a foundation, but with *I Called Him Morgan,* he added a film to the canon of Jazz films that feels truly special and unique.

A striking sequence in *I Called Him Morgan* is the recounting of Morgan commissioning and recording the song 'Angela' in response to the arrest and persecution of Angela Davis. It captures a moment of artistic response to an emotional, personal and political event and is one that has a similarly affecting counterpoint in *Chasing Trane* (2016), a documentary about John Coltrane. In *Chasing Trane* time is spent recounting Coltrane's composition and recording of the song 'Alabama', his response to the murder of four girls in a church in Birmingham, Alabama, by White supremacists in September 1963. The sequence powerfully captures an artist at the height of their powers, reaching a place of pain and sublimity that feels unique and is a standout in the film.

What *Chasing Trane* lacks is a central approach to the subject that makes the previous films mentioned so remarkable. They are each so different, but each focuses on a way of telling the story that serves, through form, to bring out something other than 'fact or footage'. Each film is structured to ensure that the telling of the story reveals something that can't be expressed directly by the content. Not so with *Chasing Trane,* which skims over so much biography, cramming in so much information, to the point that the depth that audiences are told the artist contains can only be assumed, rather than experienced cinematically. The film relies on the power of Coltrane as an artist to carry it through, but it does him a disservice by not engaging in a formal dialogue with him. Despite this, almost because of it, there are some moments that do get close to the core of Coltrane though they aren't very cinematic, most notably Cornel West's description of Coltrane's 1965 magnum opus *A Love Supreme* as 'the individual expression of a musical titan, who wants to give a certain message to the world in light of his own relationship to God'. Sadly, there's little in the film that feels like individual expression or a certain message.

The lack of a central approach in *Chasing Trane* is also present in the documentary about one of his mentors and collaborators, and a similarly titanic figure. The approach in *Miles Davis: Birth of the Cool* (2019) is so broad, generic and lacking any kind of formal association with its subject that one of the strange effects of watching it is the desire to stop watching and read the work of some of the Black commentators featured in the film. Alongside the repetition of key archive photos and a – sadly commonplace in contemporary music documentary – 'flip book' approach to some of the session and live photography material there are some fantastically insightful and poetic contributions from writers and scholars such as Farah Griffin, Greg Tate, Gerald Early and Tammy L Kernodle that share intellectual and philosophical weight with Miles Davis' own reflective contributions, voiced by Carl Lumbly. However, these are at risk of being lost in a film that, like *Chasing Trane,* is so determined to cram as much biographical information in chronological order as possible that what it purports to be about, in this case how Davis was and defined 'the personification of cool', is undermined.

'I thought they needed teaching'[7] – Blues, Soul and R&B

Liz Garbus's 2015 film, *What Happened, Miss Simone?,* is a suitable bridge to move from Jazz to Soul, R&B and the Blues because Nina Simone as an artist straddled all those categories and more. Dubbed the 'High Priestess' of Soul, Simone saw herself (and trained as such) as a Black Classical pianist. This, plus the wealth of audiotaped interviews with her that make up much of the film's narration, puts her in common with Lee Morgan who saw the music he played as Black Classical music. However, the commonalities with Morgan or anyone else are slim because Simone, as the film reminds us, was a truly unique artist. Made with the support of her family, the film is a repositioning of Simone away from negative narratives and her association with the late career re-release of 'My Baby Just Cares for Me' following its use in a commercial. It is a reclamation of her as an artist and Civil Rights Activist, not merely an abused, difficult singer. In her review of the film, Manhola Dargis wrote of how important the film felt due to its messages and timing of release in the mid-2010s, a(nother) darkly tumultuous period for Black America. She wrote that she 'can't be the only American who will despair at the relevance'.

[7] *What Happened, Miss Simone?* (2015)

While making sure, à la *Chasing Trane,* to cover as much biographical ground as possible – and it doesn't sugar coat the trauma and difficulties – it is in the decision of the film's structure to linger on the shift in Simone's career when she embarks on direct activism following, like Coltrane, the Alabama church murders of 1963 and writes 'Mississippi Goddam' that the film's thesis can be found. Significant screen time is spent on this aspect of her life so that it stands out as the film's defining statement. It is picked as the moment that gives her career meaning, having been racially excluded from the possibility of training as a Classical pianist. In this long sequence there is significant contextual archive footage of the 1960s Civil Rights era and commentary from key figures including comedian and activist Dick Gregory who proclaims 'Mississippi Goddam got my attention. We all wanted to say it, she said it'.

Saying what needed to be said from Black artists' perspective, and the impact of saying it on the careers of those who did, is a recurring theme across several films under discussion here. Central to many of these films, like the Jazz films, is a focus on the political music of 'popular' artists. In many cases it's seen as a turning point or the moment that artists cannot simply perform pop hits but need to make meaningful personal statements. Syl Johnson's major

Figure 3.3 Syl Johnson: Anyway the Wind Blows (dir. Hatch-Miller, 2015) © Rob Hatch-Miller.

statement in this context was the song 'Is It Because I'm Black' and its writing, recording and legacy is a key part of Rob Hatch-Miller's *Syl Johnson: Anyway the Wind Blows* (2015). Johnson, in his late seventies when the film was made, is shown still performing, driving the film forward with his charisma but also his bitterness. He carries with him the feeling that he was owed more and has never made peace with not crossing over, as he sees it, to wider acclaim. One participant says 'Syl was supposed to be Al Green', referring to the fact that Willie Mitchell wanted to sign him over Green, which would have put his career on a different track.

However, as RZA from Wu-Tang Clan says in the film, Johnson was 'grittier' than Green and the reasons he didn't 'cross over' weren't only limited to not being signed by Mitchell. RZA's presence and that of other Hip Hop luminaries reflect the most fascinating aspect of the film, Johnson's relationship to Hip Hop. Johnson's song 'Different Strokes' provided New York Hip Hop with one of its seminal early 'breaks' and the definitive 'UH!' sample. This fact sends the film into a fascinating diversion that looks at the impact of sampling on 'classic era' artists and their compensation. Producer Prince Paul talks of the impact on those artists when they are sampled and RZA, again, talks of how he essentially kept Johnson and his 'breaks' on a retainer over the years, helping him build a house out of the dividends. The moment when RZA learns that Syl calls his home 'the house that Wu built' visibly moves him. Also, a short animation that relays all the artists Johnson has sued for royalties is mind-boggling. It's a fascinating insight into a murky area of Hip Hop history and to have the artist as a (somewhat understandably) cranky guide only adds to the experience.

Cranky and bitter are adjectives that could be applied to singer Billy Paul who, like Johnson, was alive for the film production of his story, *Am I Black Enough for You* (2009). Named after the song Paul recorded as a follow-up to his mega-hit 'Me and Mrs Jones', the film follows Paul, still performing and still married to his beloved wife Blanche who appears in the film alongside him, still unable to shake the fact that he feels the release of 'Am I Black Enough for You' following 'Me and Mrs Jones' led to his career being stymied. Davies (2009) writes how the film is built by the filmmakers as a 'whodunit', asking 'Who killed Billy Paul's career?' This makes the film a companion to both the Syl Johnson film and the soon to be discussed Teddy Pendergrass film and, as with those works, there is more at play. As Kenny Gamble of Philadelphia

International Records – Paul's label and home to the 'Philly Sound' that included Paul, Teddy Pendergrass and The O'Jays – says, lovingly to a degree, 'Billy Paul is a Madman'.

One artist for whom the reason their career didn't follow its upward trajectory is clear, is Teddy Pendergrass. Pendergrass was paralysed in a car accident in 1982 at the height of his fame and popularity. A figure from the same 'Philly Sound' school as Billy Paul, Pendergrass is the subject of Olivia Lichtenstein's 2018 *Teddy Pendergrass: If You Don't Know Me*,[8] a film that is simultaneously the story of a heroic comeback but also one that includes some less-heroic elements, with Pendergrass often at the centre of them. Beyond the sadly usual addiction demons and womanizing there is the unsolved murder of Pendergrass's lover Taaz Lang. While the film never accuses Pendergrass it also never absolves him. Teetering on the edge of conspiracy theory there's space to ponder, given what is also shown of Pendergrass's upbringing on the streets of Philadelphia, what his involvement might have been.

There's also space to ponder, because of the position of Pendergrass in relation to the police in Philadelphia, their involvement in his accident. Stopping just short of conspiracy theory again the film is open about the harassment Pendergrass suffered at the hands of police as a successful Black man. And not just successful, but openly proud of his success and lavish with his spending. The tragedy of the accident is given extra poignancy due to Pendergrass overcoming difficulties in his career from within the Black recording industry community. As the voice and undoubted star of Harold Melvin & the Blue Notes the film reveals how Melvin sidelined Pendergrass and the other Blue Notes – some of whom appear in the film – creatively and financially. The moment that ostensibly closes the film, footage of Teddy in a wheelchair performing at the Philadelphia leg of Live Aid in 1985 not long after both being told he may not sing again and contemplating suicide because of that message, feels richly earned. The fact that Queen's performance remains the most famous 'comeback' story from Live Aid is unsurprising considering how this film, and the others discussed around it, highlight the often-insidious ways Black artist's careers are at best sidelined and at worst removed from the narrative of popular music.

---

[8] I reviewed this film for the Quietus on release in 2019. Available at: https://thequietus.com/articles/26047-teddy-pendergrass-if-you-dont-know-me-olivia-lichtenstein-review.

The three films just discussed were all produced between 2009 and 2018. The 2010s proved to be a decade where a significant number of films about Black musicians were released, with the intention of claiming or reclaiming space in the narrative of twentieth-century popular music front and centre. Another example is Lily Keber's 2013 film about New Orleans piano player James Booker, *Bayou Maharajah*. This is a complicatedly structured film that tells a complicated story, but in way that doesn't feel like that. It tells the story of universal and specific Black artistic struggle and celebrates Black artistic excellence. The factors that account for James Booker not being better known are personal – his addictions and to a lesser extent possibly his sexuality, both of which are beautifully enmeshed in the film rather than given discrete sections – as well as the more universal, the career difficulties of Black musicians including no management and no representation so no access to opportunity and no fair recompense. The film blends all the reasons Booker never made it, on a level commensurate with his talent, alongside prolonged showcases of his greatness through incredible archive performances and an astonishing series of graphics laid out like bill posters listing who Booker played piano with and for.

Carine Bijlsma's 2019 documentary *Devil's Pie: D'Angelo* is told from the vantage point of soul superstar D'Angelo, who has attained a more substantial level of critical and financial success during the height of their career than some

Figure 3.4 Devil's Pie: D'Angelo (dir. Bijlsma, 2019) © Carine Bijlsma.

of the figures discussed in this chapter, yet still cannot escape the traumas and challenges faced by those artists. *Devil's Pie* is an intensely claustrophobic experience. So much of the time spent with D'Angelo is in dark or dimly lit spaces. The rehearsal room ahead of the Second Coming tour in 2015, to mark the release of the album *Black Messiah*. The tour bus. Hotel rooms. The realization builds that the audience doesn't see the artist outside in open space, The fleeting drone shots of the rivers and natural world that Bijlsma includes are so necessary to the process of the viewing experience, serving as a counterpoint to these internal spaces. Even on festival stages it's night and the point of view is from behind, on stage, close. Snatches of daylight are felt as D'Angelo steps from bus to venue, car to rehearsal room etc. It makes for a deeply personal connection with the artist and takes on extra weight and significance when one of his collaborators, Questlove, talks about the legacy of the kind of success D'Angelo achieved with his albums *Brown Sugar* and *Voodoo* in the late 1990s.

Questlove's commentary in the film contextualizes what is felt in the claustrophobic intimacy. He outlines the oftentimes result of Black success – from death or jail to chronic lateness – as symptoms of 'survivor's guilt', the price of ascending to heights where an artist is proclaimed a Black genius. The film tries, respectfully, to get into the 'lost years' where D'Angelo was a virtual recluse at least in terms of recording and performing, and one of its achievements is how this probing is thwarted by the participants. There is power here since D'Angelo, a popular living and working artist, admits, alongside his manager, knowing that the filmmaker wants and needs this information but that it's not possible currently to really open up and give it. The intimacy of Bjilsma's camera and the quietness of this moment ensures it feels genuine rather than a brush off. Elsewhere, D'Angelo is open about his addictions and the fact that, as Questlove says, 'it's a struggle for him', to bear the weight of being declared a chosen one. The film does what it can to introduce viewers to the experience of being (around) this mercurial and troubled artist. It spends time ensuring that the sincerely spiritual aspects of his life are given space and respect but also ensures that, when it can, it shows that there are parts of his past and his present that run in direct conflict with that spirituality. D'Angelo is fully aware of this. As he says at one point: 'This shit is a contact sport, so many didn't make it.'

To conclude this section, a film about a musical artist who never really 'made it', certainly not to the same level as D'Angelo, Nina Simone or even the others profiled in the films discussed here. He did, however, have his moment, albeit very late in his life. *Late Blossom Blues* (2017) is a portrait of Mississippi Blues artist Leo 'Bud' Welch. While he never really came to prominence, certainly not fame, the film captures Welch having just released his debut album at the age of 81 to critical acclaim thanks to the support of an army veteran who becomes his manager and alerts the record label Fat Possum to Welch's existence. Fat Possum were actively looking for overlooked and under-represented Blues musicians to work with, having released work by Junior Kimbrough and RL Burnside. Much of the wonder of *Late Blossom Blues* is that it exists at all and acts as a document of an artist who may well have never been discovered.

The film follows Welch and his manager/friend Vencie as they tour a series of Blues festivals and clubs in the American South, learning Welch's story along the way in a series of intimate conversations and observed moments. The largely observational style is well deployed, capturing Welch tuning up in the church where he has played every Sunday for decades. So many films about Black Soul and Blues artists, including D'Angelo, highlight the role of the Church in the formation of artists' talents and identities but *Late Blossom Blues* focuses on an artist for whom the Church was always the primary outlet for their musical expression. The film also captures some of the tension in the story of the Blues between the Church and the 'devil's music'. However, footage of Welch at 82 delivering food, in his car, to the needy suggests that he found favour in the afterlife he believed in, when he sadly passed in 2017 not long after this moving tribute to an incredible artist was finished.

'Word, sound and power'[9] – Reggae

One of many, many remarkable moments of authenticity in Steve McQueen's *Lovers Rock* (2020), part of his *Small Axe* anthology of films, a film comprised entirely of moments as opposed to plot event, is the sight of a paraffin heater in the bedroom of the film's female protagonist Martha (Amarah-Jae St. Aubyn). The significance of this object to the Black British community of the time and the symbolic, ritualistic role it played in the lives of families, in particular young

[9] *Stepping Razor: Red X* (1992)

people, and the Blues parties that provided sanctuary, space and joy, is given ample time in Menelik Shabazz's 2011 documentary *The Story of Lovers Rock*. Comprising contextual footage from his own early 1980s documentary work to shine light on the 'backdrop to the music',[10] the film is a loving, playful and intimate celebration of the particularly British-fuelled sub-genre of Reggae that finds its spiritual cousin in McQueen and co-writer Courttia Newland's narrative exploration of the textures, sounds and feelings of the music and the context it was most often experienced. Writing in 2011, Ashley Clark said that Shabazz's filmmaking shows 'deftness and lightness of touch which never lets us forget that his core subject is the joyousness of the music and a developing sense of black British identity'.

Shabazz's documentary acts as an oral history of the genre and the Black British experience that spawned and responded to it. On a darkly lit, clearly studio set, participants recount their experiences of the music, the parties, the dancing and romance and the life around it all as a Blues party hypnotically happens around them. These interviews about the rituals and reminiscences are funny and insightful conversations about Black life that add depth to the familiar sights of archive footage, contextual footage and traditional interviews with producers and songwriters such as Dennis Bovell and singers and musicians such as Janet Kay, that make up the remainder of the film's aesthetic. The film doesn't diminish the racism that drove Black communities into house parties or the racism that meant so many of the genre's figures remained 'indie' artists by necessity, but it foregrounds artistry, love of the music and community. For, as one participant notes perfectly: 'you can't have Lovers Rock with one person'.

Some of the reconstructions – hallucinatory, nightmarish and in a subjective point of view – in *Stepping Razor: Red X* (1992), about the life and death of Reggae musician Peter Tosh, recall the reconstructions in the work of Menelik Shabazz, particularly his 1996 docudrama about Paul Bogle, *Catch A Fire*. *Stepping Razor* and *Catch A Fire* both share a 1990s video aesthetic and the production values of working in forced low-budget conditions. However, in both cases, the powerful stories of Jamaican anti-authority figures overwhelm the limitations faced by the productions. Told chronologically, *Stepping Razor* deploys techniques seen elsewhere in this chapter, deploying tapes (the Red X tapes) recorded by Tosh himself as an audio source, familiar from the Teddy

---

[10] The racial and social context of Britain in the 1970s and 1980s is a core part of the film. The above comment is from musician Levi Roots.

Pendergrass and Lee Morgan films, with the investigative tone also recalling that latter work. The investigative nature brings to the fore the message that the filmmakers, like so many others around Tosh at the time and since, believe there is more to his death than the facts allow.

That said, the film honours the gaps in the story rather than donning a tinfoil hat. The idea that there was more to Tosh's death helps the film's thesis of positioning the artist as a truth teller, someone who forged their own path and who, the film makes clear, was angry at and had real problems with the Christianity and colonialism that makes up his country's history. The film gives equal space to Tosh's connection to Rastafarianism, his harassment at the hands of police and authorities, his own love of conspiracy theories and how all these elements coalesced towards the end of his life in increased paranoia, fear and talk of ghosts. Tosh's artistic life is well served by copious, charged live footage and a solid rendering of how his music was the expression of his philosophy. The film's connective tissue to wider contexts such as Rastafarianism – providing context that undermines romanticized and exoticized ideas and reframes it as a resistance movement as much as anything else – sees the film emerge as one of the most compelling and insightful films about Reggae music.

Figure 3.5 Inna De Yard (dir. Webber, 2019) © Nicolas Baghir Maslowski – Valdés.

The 2010s saw an increase in films about Reggae that broke through into wider consciousness, somewhat. Shortly after Shabazz's film was released, Kevin Macdonald (a filmmaker whose work is discussed later in the book) directed the very formulaic documentary about Bob Marley, *Marley* (2012). Later in the decade two more aesthetically and emotionally interesting films arrived. *Rudeboy: The Story of Trojan Records* (2018) tells the story of the legendary record label, Trojan and, while structurally and formally it feels like a straightforward music film, its digressions – particularly into the examination of the impact of Reggae on British White working-class males – as well as its attempt to investigate the 'tricky thing' that is money in the record business, make it stand out. As does the way it brings together so many sub-genres, cultural ideas such as the Rudeboy itself, and legendary figures such as Derrick Morgan, Toots Hibbert, Don Letts and Ken Boothe. Even better is Peter Webber's *Inna De Yard* from 2019. The film is a study of Jamaica as a place akin to *Stepping Razor* but is more closely aligned narratively to the problematic *Buena Vista Social Club*[11] in its depiction of a group of musicians responsible for incredible songwriting that are not as well regarded outside of their homeland as they deserve, or as the few signifying icons of the genre. The participants, a group of musicians seen recording and performing stunning acoustic versions of their classic works before staging a triumphant show in Paris – including Ken Boothe (again, and here captured in a beautiful sequence with his wife), Winston McAnuff and Cedric Myton – clearly trust Webber, who manages to draw out ruminations on life, career and in two particularly moving sequences, family death caused by violence, that elevate the film beyond hagiography to something truly revealing about a community scene.

'One day the world's gonna come looking for this'[12] – Black Punk

Community is commonly associated with punk music, but for one band that sense of community was not possible, that band was Death. In 1975 the band, consisting of three brothers, recorded one record at the famous United Sound

---

[11] I write about why I think it's problematic in a later chapter on geographies and place.
[12] *A Band Called Death* (2012).

Systems Recording Studio that captured their anger at the state of the world and harnessed their love for The Who and Alice Cooper into one of the most individual albums to emerge from the mid-1970s punk scene. That album was never released. One of the brothers never recovered from the album being shelved and the band side-lined, drifting into alcoholism and bitterness. The other two brothers did the best they could, eventually having mild success in a reggae band. *A Band Called Death* (2021) tells the remarkable story of how the album was rescued from obscurity thanks to music fans, including avid collector Jello Biafra of fellow punk legends the Dead Kennedys, finding some self-pressed 7-inch singles in 2008 of key track 'Politicians In My Eyes' and how, before he died of lung cancer in 2000, the band's spiritual leader David Hackney told his brother Bobby to keep the master tapes of the album safe because 'one day the world's gonna come looking for this'.

The film is straightforward in its style, choosing simple but effective graphics, interviews and archive to tell the story in a mostly linear way. The power of the film is in the story of three Black brothers and the musical racket they made that they, David most of all, believed in so much. It is a film about family. Power in the latter part of the film, where the band receives long overdue recognition through the record finally being released and being lauded critically, comes from the filmmakers being present for reunion shows as well as the death of the brothers' mother. The filming of this period, where the family deals with further loss as well as the practical burden of David's prophecy, captures both that loss and the bittersweetness of that prophecy coming true without him being around to enjoy it. Earlier in the film, when talking about why the band were rejected, strangely for the time less to do with race or the unusual context of an all-Black rock band, but because of the negativity that people saw in their name, Death, the remaining brothers discuss how they were willing to change the name but David wasn't. At the end of the film, as Bobby watches his three sons onstage performing as Rough Francis – named after one of their uncle David's side projects – the music of Death, he and his brother Dennis understand the importance of David sticking to his guns. 'David didn't waiver' the audience is told. Thanks to David and Bobby the world has the remarkable album ... *For the Whole World to See* (2009) and the film is a fitting tribute to the brothers' story, one that convincingly argues for their importance to be recognized alongside more renowned and successful peers.

Afro-Punk (2003) as can be gleaned from the title, is a film concerned with representing Blackness within the US, punk scene. It follows four people – musicians, DJs and fans – in a portrait of life in relation to punk. Within its 70-odd minute running time it features a litany of perspectives that ensures Black punk life is not conveyed as a niche. Refreshingly, there is a strong representation of Black female punk fans and participants. The sheer number of testimonials ensures a critical mass to solidify the film's thesis. One of the many illuminating aspects of the film is how the interviews capture universalities of punk awakenings that are not exclusive to Black fans and musicians, such as being drawn to the anti-capitalist ethos of Hardcore punk and being turned on to different sounds by elder family members and friends. However, there are also elements of experience unique to Black devotees, including racist aggressions, being seen as exotic objects and 'safe' in comparison to other Black people outside the punk circle. The film showcases those drawn to punk for its potentiality, framed by Rachel Garfield as 'finding a voice in [...] a disenfranchised world' (2022: 09).

What comes through most powerfully is the sense of alienation Black punk fans and musicians feel both inside the punk community – often being the only Black people at shows and the lack of other people of colour to build romantic relationships with – and within the Black community – being ostracised for being different and, in the case of female fans and musicians, being hassled on the street by groups of Black men. However, as one of the participants, Damon Locks, says towards the end of the film, 'all Black people are part of the Black community' and despite showcasing the negative and challenging aspects facing Black punks, the film also celebrates a unique perspective in a predominantly White space. Punk is presented as having the power to provide an identity to those who feel outside the system that overwhelms the challenges of belonging. There is little on Black punk musicians – though there is footage of the band Cipher[13] in the studio – with most of the attention paid to punk as a way of life. This way of life is expressed in terms of dress and physical presentation, political affiliation and expressions of politics, DIY culture and a sense of community. Participants discuss how punk can be

---

[13] It's fascinating that the film features a Black-led punk band called Cipher given the word cypher's context and role in Hip Hop. Available at: https://medium.com/collected-young-minds/the-underappreciated-cypher-in-hip-hop-music-f8356d8afd4b.

seen as a Black music due to its roots in early Rock 'n' Roll, whose pioneers were Chuck Berry and Little Richard. One performer discusses how much of punk's couture accoutrements – studs and piercings etc – could be regarded as contemporary Eurocentric versions of African and Bush customs. It's interventions like this that push the punk discourse into new territories that even expansive works like Don Letts's superb *Punk: Attitude* (2005) don't get to. Garfield writes how 'the history of punk is a history of living memory and of fandom' (2022: 01) and *Afro-Punk* is an important record of Black and female Black punk fandom, lived experience and community.

'There's no retirement in this'[14] – Hip Hop

Through its visual and participant choices *Style Wars* (1983) documents an emerging community scene, one that would become known globally as Hip Hop, and how the scene is in tension with the existing power structure of the city that birthed it. It is a remarkable document of a time, capturing the social and cultural energy that resulted in the combined music, dance, style and art that would go on to become one of, if not the most, dominant cultural forms on the planet. In the film, the city is represented by the patronizing, bemused and frustrated figures of mayor Ed Koch and other White representatives of the transit authority who cannot see the connection between past actions on behalf of the city and this new form of creative resistance by those within it that it has failed. Murray Forman writes that 'hip-hop [...] stands out for the urgency with which its creators address the urban environment around them describing, in often painstaking detail, the activities that occur there or mapping the cultural byways that delineate their localities and give space meaning' (2002: 67).

Style Wars centres on the New York subway system, a system that gives the localized, marginalized members of the communities portrayed the opportunity to be visible, to be seen and showcases their painstaking, dangerous and urgent work in great detail, spending much time with the artists and providing significant footage of their work without commentary. Berman

[14] *Beats, Rhymes & Life: The Travels of a Tribe Called Quest* (2011)

(1999) writes that graffiti artists 'knew how to be citizens, seeking a public meaning for their lives' and *Style Wars* seems to come to that conclusion following its investigation. In *Style Wars*, the resistance, visibility, freedom and mobility that comes from the work of the graffiti artists is celebrated but one of the most striking visual moments is the sequence showing pristine, new trains contained behind prison-like walls replete with barbed wire fences and patrolled by dogs. It's a chilling visual signifier of the city's response to graffiti culture, priding property over people, protecting the trains – taking these vessels that give identity and visibility to so many unseen people, and attempting to make them, once more, invisible.

The ambition to make a permanently visible mark in society is echoed somewhat by Nas in *Time Is Illmatic* (2014) when he discusses how Hip Hop gave him the opportunity to provide 'proof that I was here'. Nas is looking back past his successes and accrued wealth to the roots of his expression, from within the projects looking out to Manhattan and beyond. *Time Is Illmatic* is a film about the rise of Nas and the circumstances around, and legacy of, his seminal debut album *Illmatic* (1994) and it shares, in some respects, a similarity with *Style Wars*. Where *Style Wars* understands the importance of repetition in creating meaning through its use of the subway train, *Time Is Illmatic* builds meaning through its repetition of images of the Queensbridge projects that were home to Nas as he emerged as an artist. The film works to deconstruct mythologies around the projects and ensures that other ideas about their relevance and impact are discussed and understood.

The film takes place predominantly in the Queensbridge projects, at the time of production, with Nas's brother looking back at incidents and events that occurred in its environs as Nas was developing into the artist that would record *Illmatic*. The film also places Nas at the centre of this world when he revisits the projects. This creates a direct link between his past and his art and cements[15] the album's status in the Hip Hip canon. The idea that the film is attempting to demythologize and de-romanticize ideas surrounding the projects in Hip Hop is hard to avoid due to the repetition of the use of the stark image of the tower blocks throughout the film and the early inclusion of Cornel West being interviewed about redlining, White flight and the emergence

---

[15] Apologies. Sometimes a pun is just too good to pass up.

of the projects. This underlines another aspect of the film's thesis, to (re)assert the importance of New York in the Hip Hop story. It challenges, directly, the pivotal Hip Hop lyric by Rakim: 'it ain't where you're from, it's where you're at' (from 1987's 'I Know You Got Soul'), suggesting that actually, it *is* where you're from which matters.

Time Is Illmatic was seemingly conceived to create a cinematic marker of the relevance of Nas and his debut album in Hip Hop. This status-building or confirming is in some way part of the modus operandi of music films[16] and feasibly that was one of the reasons Michael Rapaport wanted to make a film about A Tribe Called Quest when they 'reformed' to play the Rock the Bells festival tour in 2008. However, the two primary members of the group, Q-Tip and Phife Dawg, get in the way of the film being a celebratory reunion. The film captures a group bound by incredibly close bonds, bonds that evidence the 'familial' in ways that many groups that say they are like a family never come close to achieving. The film captures bickering, rifts, anger and bitterness, confusion and the impact of long simmering and unresolved tensions. Hanif Abdurraqib writes that the film is 'largely about sacrifice, but who is doing the most sacrificing depends on which lens you view the film through' (2019: 143).

There's a pressure in music films to be joyous, positive, heroic, cathartic, triumphant, unless tragedy sits at the heart of the story. But cinema is not always these things. Sometimes it needs to be difficult, sad, unfulfilling. Like life. Tragedy in the Tribe story comes after the film was made, with Phife Dawg's death from complications with diabetes in 2016.[17] It's easy to imagine a film made in the wake of Phife's death and the release of the posthumous, and presumedly final, Tribe album *We Got It from Here. . .Thank You 4 Your Service* (2016) but it's unlikely that would be as true a film. In that film the sadness over some of the difficult to watch tensions that mark a major rift between Phife and Q-Tip would likely be an act break rather than a melancholic motif that hangs over the entire piece. Even though *Beats, Rhymes & Life* ends on somewhat of an up note with the group cordial in rehearsals and heading to

---

[16] In an interview for this book, filmmaker Tony Palmer, whose work is discussed throughout the book, claimed that his work was 'propaganda' and that he saw his job as having audiences 'whistling the tunes' as the films finished (interview, 2022).

[17] Phife's condition forms a moving, central theme of the film.

Japan to play festivals in 2010, containing much celebration of what makes the group so seminal, significant screen time is given over to difficulties. By dint of when it's made and what they are all going through, the film stands out as unusually honest, open and revealing about creative struggles and innate difference.

The tension and melancholy that marks out *Beats, Rhymes & Life* is absent from *Scratch* (2001), a film about the art of the Hip Hop DJ and turntablism, though the film acknowledges how Hip Hop evolved in ways that left the DJ behind somewhat. The Hip Hop DJ and the art of turntablism are separated in that description because the film shows that while there are connections, they are discrete from each other in key ways. The film celebrates many facets of the DJ from their emergence and role at the origin of Hip Hop to the rise of the turntablist, to crate digging and, in some moments that veer close to video essay, the art of beat making and mixing. What makes *Scratch* vital, beyond excellent high-profile interviews, live and archive material, is how it pinpoints and argues for a single moment spawning a movement. The sheer amount of contributors who recall seeing DJ DXT beat mixing for Herbie Hancock's performance of 'Rockit' at the MTV Awards in 1984 and who claim it their epiphany moment convinces of the performance's zeitgeist status.

'We Shook up the World!'[18] – Black Joy

Much of what has come before in this chapter focuses on struggle, challenge and battling racism and both external and internal forces. That could create the idea that the films don't contain some of the most exhilarating examples of musical performance committed to film or video or that they aren't also celebrations of artists and arguments of historical and committed importance in the narrative of popular music. That is not the case. Even films dealt with critically here, such as those about John Coltrane and Miles Davis, showcase moments that argue for what makes those artists mesmerizing on stage and record. They cover highs and lows, racism and creative acknowledgement, and hint at the mercurial nature of genius if never really presenting that genius in

---

[18] *Dave Chappelle's Block Party* (2005)

a way that befits the artist. However, part of the intention of the book was not to simply present films with the expected lines of commentary. So, to close this chapter, there is a focus on two moments that capture and create joy.[19] They are both to be found in the extraordinary concert film *Dave Chappelle's Block Party* from 2005, directed by Michel Gondry.

There are two moments in *Dave Chappelle's Block Party* that rank amongst the most joyous that can be found in any music film. The first is when the Central Ohio State University (OSU) marching band coach reveals to the predominantly Black band if they are going to perform at Dave's block party. The camera, hand-held, gets in close, as does Dave Chappelle, as the band gather round, and the coach tells them that Saturday's meet is off. As they will be going to New York to perform at Chappelle's block party. The instantaneous eruption of noise is overwhelming. Bodies, limbs and instruments fly as the news sinks in. The camera is buffeted around, and the mic levels peak as the noise overwhelms it. They hug each other, the coach, and Dave. Dave smiles at the camera. He knows what this means to these young Black people, and he revels in his ability to have conferred such a moment in their lives. It's a moment of mayhem, the construction of which is built on the knowledge that this information will be life-altering for the young people on the receiving end. It is a moment that relies on the expected outcome to work; the participants don't disappoint because it is a moment that captures pure, free, unbridled joy. There is a quiet manipulation in the filmmaking but not in the gesture it captures. The joy sparked carries through every appearance of the marching band throughout the remainder of the film as they talk with Wyclef Jean from The Fugees, dance a routine to Kanye West's performance of 'Jesus Walks' and generally bathe in a truly once-in-a-lifetime experience.

The other moment is a more straightforward example of live performance, where crowd and stage management by an artist is met perfectly with the cinematic capturing of the moment – in terms of composition and editing – where the film understands what is being created and how to present it. During Hip Hop Duo Dead Prez's performance of their song 'It's Bigger Than Hip Hop' the music drops out and the MCs deliver a key verse, one that speaks directly

---

[19] There is so much quiet joy to be found in Posy Dixon's *Keyboard Fantasies* (2019), a beautiful portrait of Black Trans musician Beverly Glenn-Copeland, a film I am sorry to not be able to write about more here.

of standing up against oppressive forces and not believing structural lies, and that uses Hip Hop to speak of a need for resistance by Black people, a cappella. The delivery, without music, emphasizes the liveness of the moment, the struggle to maintain lyrical flow against the adrenalized exertions of live performance, the MCs seemingly in a race to get to the end of the line in rhythm. The camera is still, waiting and watching, the audience the same. The tenterhooks of listening to the message and marvelling at the craft. The verse goes on and the realization of its nakedness becomes apparent until the question of 'Where is the music?' is emphatically answered when it crashes back in. The MCs deliver the chorus with a new lease of life, empowered by the crowd's attention to the lyrics. The MCs, the camera, the audience bounce in unison. The cutting of the film carries the song to its end. It's euphoric. The MCs on the stage craft a moment that allows the audience to be part of something singular and communal and sympathetic filmmaking allows the cinema audience to experience their own version of that moment. They are included in the power and joy and release of it, rather than simply shown that it had happened.

The film retains an increasing singularity. Chappelle got The Fugees back together, providing a positive audiovisual document of Lauryn Hill that counters the negative ones. He narrates a film that, with great subtlety, links early twentieth century Hip Hop with 90s Hip Hop, and further back, through the participants on stage, those discussed who grew up near the location of the free Bedford-Stuyvesant concert (Notorious B.I.G.) and the location itself. Bed-Stuy is a historically mixed area – pointed out by the day-care centre manager in the film – home to Black and Hispanic people. This is significant in the context of Hip Hop due to its early days and the role played by Black and Hispanic people in its development. This is something that is explicitly noted and represented in *Style Wars* through its footage and participants. In *Block Party* knowledge of this significance is more assumed.

A block party in Brooklyn serves a variety of purposes. It seeks to recreate, in spirit if not in actuality, one of the founding practices of Hip Hop in one of the most important locations for the form. The film is famously inspired by the concert film *Wattstax* (1973). Here, as with Mel Stuart's earlier film, locals watch the construction of the stage and the show itself, from their stoops or on deckchairs on the pavement. Chappelle rounds up audience members from the surrounding streets via loudhailer and buses in people from the small town in

Ohio where he lives, affirming his personal belief in that Rakim lyric that 'it's where you're at'. And, as Ali Jafaar (2006) writes 'performing in intermittent rainfall, the sheer enthusiasm of the musicians, often collaborating with each other spontaneously, lends the film a winning nostalgia'. The film features superb live footage from the aforementioned acts and Black Star, Jill Scott, Erykah Badu all underscored by The Roots as house band, but would not work without Chappelle. He is the benefactor, the MC of the event, the narrator and facilitator for knowledge and history of the area and its illustrious Hip Hop past to emerge and crucially, an excited fan. As he says of the acts he chose to perform 'before I ever met them, I was a fan'. This shows through in his interactions with them and candid footage of Chappelle backstage and in rehearsal. Rarely has celebrity benevolence been used for such joyous ends.

4

'Wherever we are, we are'[1] – Place

In Julien Temple's film about Dr Feelgood, *Oil City Confidential* (2009), discussed in Chapter 1 looking at milestones and innovations, the band's former manager Chris Fenwick remarks that 'bands all come from somewhere'.[2] Music films usually include reference at the very least to the geographical starting – or indeed end – points of the artists, labels, or scenes they are about. However, some films place more emphasis on the role that place and location play in a band's music, identity, success and legacy. In some cases, place is a backdrop. In some cases, it is integral. In some cases, it is presented as the latter but is ultimately the former. An example of this can be found in the Fela Kuti documentary *Finding Fela!* (2014). The film repeatedly returns to Lagos, Nigeria, where Kuti lived, worked and was persecuted for his outspoken political music. However, because the film has no central themes or identity, and spends a lot of time veering between ideas and points, the relationships between Kuti and Nigeria are never explored to a satisfying degree. Merely because a film spends so much time showing us a place, it does not necessarily mean that it is about that place, or about the music and that place.

This chapter discusses a series of films where place is inextricably linked to the music and musicians being documented, either directly as stated by the artists or indirectly through context. Some of the contexts under discussion involve global contextual understandings of places, for example *Buena Vista Social Club* (1999). In this film audiences are led to understand the socio-political context of Cuba through the lens of authorship. It is safe to assume that films about place made by people from that place are more sympathetic to and more nuanced about the resonances and politics of location on the lives

---

[1] *Crossing the Bridge: The Sound of Istanbul* (2005).
[2] Julien Temple's film is as much about Canvey Island, Essex, as it is anything else.

and works of musicians, though not always. This chapter includes discussions of works where this is the case, films that are empathetic and centralize the subject and their experiences. However, there are also examples where native and non-native directors have made, intentionally or not, films that fall into traps around representation of race and gender or where saviour narratives or othering and exoticized readings can come to the fore. This chapter will discuss the authorship of the films in question, and how understandings of places and their peoples are shaped.

'You need culture for a language to survive'[3] – Wales

It is worth looking at *Separado!*, *American Interior* and *Anorac* as a triptych of sorts. This is not to diminish their individual merits but because they are so similarly attuned. They are not observed or passive but participatory and deeply active. They involve journeys, quests no less, with musician Gruff Rhys in *Separado!* and *American Interior,* and DJ and promoter/label owner Huw Stephens in *Anorac,* as they seek to learn more about Welsh language and culture, Welsh language music and where they fit into their nation's musical history and legacies. They are all deeply personal films. Predominantly in Welsh with English subtitles, that do not follow musicians simply making or performing music, though they do contain those elements. Instead, the focus is on ideas and topics other than music. There are bigger questions than music at play, though all are poetic and philosophical accounts of the roles indigenous language music and culture play in national identity.

Separado! and *American Interior* are two feature-length collaborations between filmmaker Dylan Goch and musician Gruff Rhys, best known as the lead singer of the band Super Furry Animals. Both films follow Rhys as he travels from Cardiff, Wales to Central and South America in *Separado! a*nd to the United States in *American Interior.* Rhys is in search of the comfort of history and knowledge, familial and national, that will help him tie both his musical approach and national pride to something bigger than himself. Formally both

[3] *Anorac* (2019).

films follow the conventions of a road movie, with Gruff writing songs and performing these and others from his back catalogue, along the way. The objectives of the quest, to track down a distant relative Rene Griffiths, a Patagonian Gaucho troubadour who sings in Welsh, in *Separado!* and retracing the steps of explorer John Evans into the American interior in *American Interior*, throw up questions of colonisation and expatriation, both in the countries where these figures built or found legacy but also at home in Wales. The reasons why Welsh people ended up in deepest South America and the American Midwest are always bubbling under the surface. *American Interior* hinges on Evans' belief, handed down to him, that there is a tribe of Welsh-speaking Native Americans to be found and strangely, or maybe not, both films must reckon with Welsh involvement in the annexing of traditional lands in both Patagonia and North America.

The films do not shy away from acknowledging complicity in these events but also leave unspoken, in the subtext, the parallels between these oppressions and the ostracizing and terrorizing of the Welsh language and its speakers by the English in Wales. In both films Rhys meets with academics, historians, and local and native people to learn about the history of their countries. Raymond Williams writes that 'it's how past and present relate that tells in a culture' (2003: 08). Rhys acts as mediator between past and present in both films. Each one has wonderful sequences where Rhys meets community elders who talk of the struggles to maintain long-standing identities, both Welsh immigrant and Native American, again echoing the struggle for the survival of the Welsh language that Rhys is so passionate about. In both cases the sense grows that Rhys is not necessarily learning anything new but rather using the films to physically interact with people and share these untold stories with the cinema audience. In both films he performs for local audiences, using the making of the films as reasons to play gigs off the normal beaten track. Both films contain odd performances rendered as quasi-music videos, framed as interludes from the journey.

All of this could lead to the belief that the films are the same, the latter a rehash of the former. While there are many thematic and structural similarities, formally and tonally the films are very different. *Separado!* is billed as a Western, leaning into the Gaucho identity of Griffiths, the troubadour Rhys is tracking down across Patagonia to the foothills of the Andes. Rhys's travels in the film are relayed as traditional – cars and trucks – and non-traditional – teleportation. Rhys dons a helmet that fans will recognize from live performances, particularly with the Super Furry Animals, and, as the frame dissolves in visual and sonic psychedelic squalls, he moves from South Wales to South America, first Brazil and then Patagonia, and back again. It is a much looser and weirder film than its successor, recalling the energy of Alejandro Jodorowsky in parts. *American Interior* is more muted, its strangeness less pronounced. Presented mostly in black and white, the film features colourful animated sequences mapping the journey. For the physical journey, Rhys is joined by an incarnation of the never-photographed John Evans, rendered physical in the form of a small puppet imagined by frequent Rhys collaborator Pete Fowler and built by Louse Evans, also known as Felt Mistress.

Rhys is a selfless guide, eagerly engaging with the felt puppet, bringing Evans to life in a playful way. As a musician and performer Rhys is smart, funny and off-kilter; these films celebrate and showcase that, providing symbiotic audio/visual representations of his audio output. Yet, as playful as the formal approaches in the films are, they are serious projects, aimed at introducing the world to overlooked Welsh figures and addressing the pressing issue of the future of the Welsh language by engaging with little-known pasts. The serious aims of *American Interior* are encapsulated in the Transmedia nature of its emergence into the world.[4] As well as the film and corresponding album, both released in 2014, there is also a book and an app, all adding to the story and the experience of listening to the music Rhys creates alongside his work as an excavator of histories.

In a film discussed later in this chapter, *The Man Behind the Microphone*, the director/narrator says that home is 'not a place where you live, but where you are understood, where you recognise yourself'. *Separado!* and *American Interior* involve watching Rhys making music as a way of tracking an experience and creating something recognizable. Songs that maybe help him understand home. While it is common for music films to feature documentation of a band or artist in the process of making music, it is less common for so much of two films to be

---

[4] I wrote about this aspect of the project on the film's release. See https://directorsnotes.com/2014/05/08/gruff-rhys-american-interior/

given over to one artist performing music that is in the process of being written or that has just been written, in front of live audiences away from home. However, the result is that the relationship between what Gruff Rhys learns on his odysseys and the music he is making is undeniable. Music is shown as his way of processing what it means for him to confront the history of his beloved Welsh culture and language, and its possible future. Because of the artist he is, and because the director and editor Dylan Goch knows him so well, the cinematic representation of that process of learning is enjoyable and feels natural.

In his essay *Welsh Culture,* Raymond Williams writes about the problem of cultural identity:

> I wish I could see it in one of its popular forms: in a kind of emphasis on Welshness against an alien and invading culture; in a consequent emphasis on culture as tradition, and on tradition as preservation.
>
> 2003: 07

The 2019 film *Anorac* can be seen as a response to Williams' call to arms. Another road movie, this time it is a journey closer to home. However, it remains connected to the themes of investigating Welsh language music and relates the past to the present once more as a way of considering and safeguarding the future. In the film, Huw Stephens journeys around Wales, starting from Cardiff just like Rhys, to find musicians of all genres singing in Welsh. Over conversations that always seem to involve eating and drinking, Stephens debates the merits, virtues, challenges and pitfalls of singing in Welsh. In one conversation the musician Gwenno says she is often asked why she sings in a language few people understand, to which she replies: 'that's the point'. It is a tone that recurs throughout the film, swerving from point to point on the spectrum from pride to resistance and back again. The film contains a multitude of performances, often in and around the eating and drinking establishments in which the conversations take place.

The multitude of musicians featured in the film is necessary to make the point that artists singing in their native tongue are not limited to the obvious. Yes, there are folk musicians, but also Hip Hop, electronic, and a plethora of indie bands. The performers encompass a wide range of ages and genders. It's a film of celebration and statement, and one of the strongest statements is made visually. Over time, the recurring locations for conversation and performance start to reveal a deeper theme: class. The locations are those traditionally associated with the working class – working men's clubs, pubs, bus shelters and greasy spoon cafes. The film, through its locations, dispels what might be presumed, that those choosing to sing in Welsh are a privileged few from a particular demographic. Despite telling the story of a small nation, one that, as musician Gwilym Morus says in the film, has often defined itself as an 'oppressed nation', the film doesn't feel insular in its scope.

Significant screen time is given over to the national cultural tradition of Eisteddfod, a celebration of the Welsh language, in particular the Maes B stage where the youth of Wales come to sing their songs in a variety of genres. However, the film ends at another large communal celebration, Festival No 6, which takes place at the location that also gave the event its name, the Portmeirion estate that was the location for cult television show *The Prisoner* (1967–1968). The headline act are Welsh music icons the Super Furry Animals, whose album *Mwng* is the biggest-selling Welsh language record of all time. Stephens picks up a vinyl copy in nearby Cob Records in Porthmadog (though surely, he must already have a copy) before watching the band's set and talking to their frontman, Gruff Rhys. Despite difficult conversations about Welsh language music, and Welsh language struggles in general, the film is never pessimistic. It is defiant but also hopeful and practical. As Rhys says near the film's end, and echoing Williams somewhat, 'popular culture offers ways into the language' and, as *Anorac* shows, many bands and artists actively feel the same.

The fourth film about Wales under discussion is formally different but the questions at its heart, about Welshness and what it means to be Welsh, are just as prominent. *Truth & Memory* is a film compiled and edited by Kieran Evans from material filmed by the Manic Street Preachers and those around them at the time of recording and promoting the release of their 1998 album *This Is My Truth Tell Me Yours*. The footage recorded at the time, on a variety of low-grade video formats, is intercut with subtle, atmospheric visuals shot and graded by Evans to match the tone and aesthetic of the aged visuals. In addition, there are quotes and slogans that fans familiar with Manic Street Preachers' live shows or album sleeves will recognize. What works so well in the context of the film is the fact that the quotes capture the theme of the film, as narrated by bassist and lyricist Nicky Wire, of a band finding and reminding themselves of their place in the music world and their home country. Wire mentions at one point that *This Is My Truth Tell Me Yours* is the Manics' 'Welsh folk record' and the film plays with that idea in its visual relationships to poets, politicians and cultural figures.

The film, like the album it documents, expands from Welsh poet RS Thomas's work *Reflections* (1995), in which readers gaspingly 'partake of a shifting identity never your own'. The footage captures a band working on a record at a significant remove from their most infamous moment, the disappearance of co-lyricist and spiritual figurehead Richey Edwards in 1995, grappling with life after that moment and simultaneously their national identity and musical direction. The fact that the footage from the studio and on the road was shot by the band themselves, for seemingly no specific aim, adds poignancy when viewed in retrospect. When talking about the future in the film Wire comments, looking back furtively on the band's younger days, that there are 'no more Stalinist five-year plans. Since Richey disappeared it's one-day plans. Too much disaster lurking round the corner'. There's a fragility to Wire's reflective narration, which sounds like it is coming from a future, the present now, rather than the moment of recording. This is married with seeing the video format footage assembled and distributed on the Internet – the film was released via the band's YouTube channel in 2019 – and edited with filmed footage of polaroid stills from the time – the most nostalgia surfacing photographic format – that convey, visually, the sense that this is a film seeking to make sense of both the present and the past. In many senses a film about the past and memory, filmed on old formats such as Mini-DV and featuring Polaroid photos, belongs on the internet. As Simon Reynolds writes 'the Internet places the [. . .] past and [. . .] present side by side. Equally accessible, they become the same thing: far yet near . . . old yet *now*' (2011: 85).

Recording starts in two Welsh studios, Monnow Valley and Rockfield. There is footage of the album cover photo shoot at Blackrock Sands near Porthmadog (though Wire in the film says it's Harlech beach, nearby). Wire talks about writing the lyrics to the song 'Tsunami' after seeing a BBC Wales documentary about the 'silent twins', June and Jennifer Gibbons, from Haverfordwest. Wales runs through the film and the album visually and thematically. Wire is heard talking about Welsh identity and what emerges from Evans' construction of material and additional context is that the genesis of the album was bound up in evolving and returning questions of Welshness, just as so much of the Manic Street Preachers' work is.

'Where do you go from here?'⁵ – Northern England

As mentioned earlier, in *Anorac*, Huw Stephens buys a Super Furry Animals record in Porthmadog's Cob Records. Earlier in the film he buys a copy of Gwenno's first record *Y Dydd Olaf* from Spillers in Cardiff, the world's oldest-known record shop. In *Separado!* Gruff Rhys scours a record shop in Buenos Aires looking for records by his distant relative Rene Griffiths. In *The Man Behind the Microphone*, director Claire Belhassine sifts through the racks of a Tunis record shop looking for the work of her grandfather Hedi Jouini. Record shops, and vinyl, have an important place in the mythology of many musicians and artists. Records are the artefacts that offer artists, as Nas says in *Nas: Time Is Illmatic* (2014), 'proof that I was here'. They are also, perhaps more importantly, the artefacts that have historically connected artists with their fans. Since the start of the 2010s several films have sought to capture the unique, often

Figure 4.1 Sound It Out (dir. Finlay, 2011) © Jeanie Finlay.

⁵ *NG83 When We Were B Boys* (2016).

particularly male, atmosphere of record stores and the people who frequent them. One of the earliest, and the best, is Jeanie Finlay's *Sound It Out* from 2011.

Finlay's film is a portrait of Sound It Out Records, the last remaining record shop in Teesside, Northern England. It tells the story, through portraiture rather than all out biography, of owner Tom and to a lesser extent, in terms of screen time, his staff David and Kelly.[6] Equally, however, the film is a portrait of the town of Stockton-on-Tees, where the shop is located, and the people who live there and love music. The first section of the film, as audiences get acquainted with the staff and regular customers, sets the scene by showing where the shop is in the town. In a side road off the high street, near the job centre and a cheap pub. The orbit of the shop that the film does in its opening moments makes it clear the type of place Stockton is, and by extension the type of customers Tom serves. The visual theme being drawn out echoes that of *Anorac* and its choice of locations. This is a place that you don't see in the mythologies of rock music and the customers are people also excluded from narratives of musical glory. However, music is as important here as it is in London, Manchester, New York.[7]

Over the course of its short – 75 minutes – running time, the characters the film introduces audiences to run the gamut from the casual punter looking for a Dire Straits CD through to the obsessive Chris with his 2,000 plus records, framed Nick Cave lyrics and Boards of Canada t-shirt. In and around are Sam and Gareth who like 'anything suffixed by the word metal' and who proudly tout their 'battle jackets',[8] Makina DJ Big Dave ruling the internet airwaves from his shed and Shane with his unabashed Status Quo obsession. The film spends a lot of time with each of the shop's regulars, listening to them and giving them space to talk, thus building empathy. One of Finlay's skills as a documentary filmmaker is making people feel comfortable and caring for them. To merely glance at people such as those interested in the distinctly

---

[6] Between writing and publication of this book, Sound it Out owner Tom Butchart died. Filmmaker Jeanie Finlay described him as a 'bones deep friend'. See www.gazettelive.co.uk/news/teesside-news/tom-butchart-tributes-pour-after-27107890.

[7] A wonderful film about a New York record shop and community is *Other Music* (2019). The film is directed and produced by Puloma Basu and Rob Hatch-Miller whose earlier work *Syl Johnson: Any Way the Wind Blows* was discussed in the chapter on Black music.

[8] Find out how to make your own Battle Jacket here: https://toiletovhell.com/how-to-make-your-own-battle-jacket/.

regional dance music Makina would show little concern for them as people and risk adding to stereotypes of them as 'Chavs'.[9] In *Sound It Out* they emerge as complex, interesting people with a deep passion for music and a knowledge of how that passion is protecting them, to a certain degree, from an even more difficult life.

There are cutaways to the dying high street with its ubiquitous charity and pound shops or looming, smoking, industrial stacks. As one of the Makina fans says, 'it's dreadful, it's awful, but it's home. I feel safe here. The Northeast'. At the centre of all these people's universe is Tom and his shop. He knows the importance of music to wellbeing and as hard as it is to maintain a living, he knows why it matters that Teesside has a record shop. The film also highlights the importance, financially, of Record Store Day. As he says at one point 'records hold memories' and it becomes clear as the film spends time with him that his defiance is not stubbornness but an act of vital goodness for his town. The most moving moment is when the camera candidly catches Tom watching an in-store performance by Stockton-born musician done good, Saint Saviour. Leaning against the door of his shop, behind a packed crowd, all are, and him most of all, lost in the music.

Another film worth discussing is one that, similar to *Sound It Out,* seeks to acknowledge the role and impact on the opposite side from those making music. In *NG83 When We Were B Boys* (2016) the focus of fan response to music is not collecting, entirely, but dancing, mostly. The film captures through a wealth of archive material the impact of Hip Hop on the predominantly Black working-class youth of Nottingham in 1983. Through contemporary interviews the film also investigates what happened after the initial excitement and, more crucially, community support for the city's breakdancing crews dissipated. It looks at life after breaking in a place without the same cultural life that other cities impacted by Hip Hop and subcultural movements often benefit from. Much of the film's past and present revolves around the Rock City venue in Nottingham. One of the main crews in the film are the 'Rock City Crew', a name that pays tribute to their base location and pioneering New York break-dancers 'The Rock Steady Crew'. The most poignant moment of the film,

---

[9] There is a lovely short documentary about Makina that can be found here via the British Council. Available at: - https://music.britishcouncil.org/news-and-features/2020-04-30/watch-makina.

one that reveals so much about the disparate legacies of the breakdancing youths, is when, during an on-street interview, one of the film's protagonists, veteran B Boy 'Dancing' Danny, spots someone from 'back in the day' who enters the film for a moment. He is smart, confident, on a night out and went by the name of Flux when he danced for 'Supreme Force'. He is the opposite of Danny, and this chance moment is where the film most readily captures how the city holds stories and legacies in its everyday. The universe of the film and its central story is expanded, momentarily, and the melancholy truth of that fleeting couple of years in the early 1980s is most keenly felt.

The final film under discussion in this Northern England triptych is about a band who started plying their trade in the early 1980s but didn't find prominence, and later fame, until the mid-1990s. Pulp, an art-pop band from Sheffield, was one of the trinity of bands, along with Oasis and Blur, most readily associated with Britpop.[10] The film, *Pulp: A Film About Life, Death & Supermarkets,* centres around a hometown show at Sheffield's Motorpoint Arena in December 2012, which would prove the final traditional concert of a successful reunion tour. The film isn't a traditional concert film; instead, the director Florian Habicht and band leader Jarvis Cocker use the opportunity to investigate cinematically the role that Sheffield played in the band's work but also the legacy the band left, and still leaves, on its home town. Owen Hatherley writes how, for Pulp, the 'hometown becomes the subject matter – and [Sheffield] is a sexualised city, where the post-industrial landscape is suffused with carnality in its every twist, turn, alleyway and precinct' (2011: 33). The film playfully positions Pulp within the fabric of the city's everyday life more poignantly and introspectively by interviewing fans of the band at the grand homecoming gig. Similar to *Sound It Out* and *NG83*, it investigates the impact of music on fans. One fan interviewed had travelled from the US to the UK to see the band having been too young to see them when they last played near them. This fan, along with the other 'diehards' who arrive at the venue very early, received a reward in the shape of a credit in the film.

'The People of Sheffield' are also credited at the start of the film, ensuring that the role of fans in the legacy and life of the band is given due prominence

---

[10] A word Jarvis Cocker can't even bring himself to say, as he divulged on *The Adam Buxton Podcast* in 2022.

in the audience's expectations. It is not tokenistic. The film frequently returns to stories of the importance of the band to those from Sheffield, with meaningful stories of how they helped a fan reacclimatize to the city following a period where they 'accidentally moved to London for six months once' or the woman who made special Pulp underwear because as she says, 'I quite like Jarvis on me bum'. What stops the film being a simple love letter to the band, and makes it a more complicated work, is how the film includes testimony from people who clearly know who Pulp are, but who only associate them with Sheffield, or whose love for the band is more ephemeral. This, in classic Jarvis Cocker style, pricks the potential pomposity of the film, making it more bittersweet and tinged with melancholy. There's a wonderful sequence where a group of older people in a market café sing along to the Pulp song 'Help the Aged'. Here, as in the other films about the North of England, and Wales, images and sequences associated with the working class are prominent. The sequence would not seem out of place in a Pulp jukebox musical were it not for the fact that it is obvious they are singing from lyric sheets and have clearly just finished a quick rehearsal. This does not diminish the sweetness of the moment. Despite Jarvis saying 'surroundings don't make much difference' at some level he disagrees and has made a film in collaboration with his band and the filmmaker and the fans that seeks to ask what difference the people around you make on the music, and what flows back the other way.

'We are the walls of this house'[11] – Further Afield

If the role played by place in the film about Pulp is playfully unstable, it is even more so in a personal film about a filmmaker using the documentary form to investigate family history. Claire Belhassine's *The Man Behind the Microphone* has many resonances with *Separado!* in that it follows a person on a journey to different countries to uncover and deepen and clarify a family history that revolves around music. In this case it tells the amazing story of how the director

---

[11] *They Will Have to Kill Us First* (2015).

heard a Tunisian song in a taxi and when they asked the taxi driver who sang it, they replied with the name of her grandfather, Hédi Jouini. The film that follows is Belhassine's attempt to learn about and ultimately heal the rift in the family that concealed this information from her. She remembers her grandfather from summer visits to Tunisia when she was a child but, following a series of disagreements, the visits stopped and, as her grandfather kept the musical side of his life out of the family environment, the knowledge lay dormant. The film's investigation delves into the relationship between Jouini and Tunisia and Belhassine's own relationship to the Tunisian side of her family, as she has an English mother and a Tunisian father – Hédi's eldest son.

Vox pops on the street in Tunis, and singalongs in bars, reveal that Jouini was not just a Tunisian musician but a national icon. It feels as though he is known and beloved by all Tunisians. This naturally causes problems in the family, in terms of their relationship with him. At one point, one of his daughters admits that he belonged to Tunisia as much as he belonged to them. However, Hédi comes across as a family person for a considerable portion of his life. Indeed, that is only how the filmmaker remembers him. The film's family focus means there is frustration at what cannot be gleaned more broadly about Tunisia and Jouini's place in its history and culture, although the film does an excellent job of introducing a complex figure to wider prominence. His political beliefs were often at odds with the government but were matched by an unabated patriotism. His womanizing proves him capable of the same clichéd traps of other musicians of his stature globally. Then there's the sadly age-old and gendered fact that the filmmaker's grandmother forsook her own musical career to raise the family. Despite all this, the pull of the story remains the family and its dramatic rupture. This makes it hard to really know the Tunisia of which Jouini was such an integral artistic part, but this feels like the point. When family is concerned, nothing else really matters.

If there are thematic resonances between *The Man Behind the Microphone* and *Separado!* there are formal ones between *Crossing the Bridge: The Sound of Istanbul* and *Anorac*. In an interview for this book, *Anorac* director Gruffydd Davies cited Fatih Akin's portrait of the Istanbul music scene as an influence on his desire to do the same for Wales. Indeed, much like Davies' film, *Crossing the Bridge* feels like a collaboration between filmmaker and narrator. Here, the narrator – Berlin-born Alexander Hacke of the band Einstürzende Neubauten – traverses the Turkish capital, excitedly and curiously, in search of music, much like Huw Stephens does in *Anorac*. However, unlike Stephens, Hacke is an outsider. Having become interested in contemporary Turkish music following a collaboration with the director Akin when he scored the Turkish-German filmmaker's 2004 film *Gegen die Wand* (*Head On*), this documentary follows Hacke as he explores Istanbul, learning about its history and the connection of music to that history, as well as recording the artists as he goes. What separates this film from those where figures external to the country seek to learn about and capture indigenous music is how Hacke sublimates himself to the local music scene, acting neither as saviour nor champion.

Hacke is seen dancing extravagantly as he records one band, sometimes sitting in with others to record, often just watching. The focus is always on the local musicians, never Hacke, except at the film's finale where he admits that he never could have expected to really 'know' the city or its music from such a fleeting time within it. What emerges from the interaction of this German musician with his Turkish counterparts is a passion and restless desire to hear all kinds of sounds that can also be found in Hacke's work with his own band. There is also a sense of how meaningful, respectful conversations, where there is a genuine desire to listen to speech and musical sound, can result in a vibrant portrait of a time and place. Whether it is the father of rapper Ceza saying 'Hip Hop is the music Turkey needs right now' or a performance by icon Orhan Gencebay who, despite thousands of records and movie appearances – a similar discography and filmography to Hédi Jouini – rarely plays live, the film manages, through a majority of hand-held camerawork and fast cutting, to capture a fleeting moment that suggests an ocean of music beneath its surface. What is known of the Istanbul scene by the end of the film doesn't feel total. Instead, it feels like an introduction.

Another film from the 2000s that has shone a light on a music scene in a place where politics increasingly plays a part in what music is permitted – a theme that will recur when discussing Mali later in this chapter – is the Iranian film *No One Knows About Persian Cats*. The film, directed by Bahman Ghobadi, is not strictly a documentary. However, most people in the film, including protagonists Negar and Ashkan, play versions of themselves. The film centres on the Tehran indie music scene, of which Negar and Ash were prominent members at the time the film was made. For aesthetic (documentary feel) and practical (permits and cultural permissions in Tehran) reasons the film is shot on the move, using hand-held digital video. In interviews for the film the actors say they 'lived what you see' and the director claims it is a 'documentary fiction about underground music'. In this documentary fiction, Ash and Negar enlist the help of local fixer Nader to secure visas and passports to leave Iran so their band, Take It Easy Hospital, can play a gig in London.

On their travels around Tehran to put a band together the audience sees other, real, bands perform songs by way of audition that also create a portrait of the indie, metal, Hip Hop and traditional pop landscape of the city. At one point an 'audition' of a heavy metal musician at a remote farm outside the city is preceded by the sound of angsty cows and Ash and Negar are informed that the music upsets the animals. Most of these performances feature montages of Tehran life as cutaways and, during the film, a portrait emerges through sound and image, as well as the struggle of the two young musicians at the centre of the film to play the music they want freely. The dramatization of real life in the way the film approaches it works, for the most part, creating a sense of authenticity and drama that heightens the real-life situation but never detracts from or dilutes it. One of the negative aspects is that the characterisation of Negar, the only female musician in the film, reduces her role to that of the Western trope of the suspicious, cynical woman constantly nagging and preaching caution while her male counterpart is allowed to dream free and face the consequences like a tragic hero.

Another film with a tension between the real and the narrative is the most famous film discussed in this chapter, *Buena Vista Social Club*. The film, directed by Wim Wenders, tells the story of how musician Ry Cooder 'found' several 'forgotten' Cuban musicians and brought them to world prominence through the recording of an eponymous album and international tour. As Bill Callahan wryly notes in his song 'Ry Cooder' from 2020's *Gold Record*:

'He freed Cuba,
with a Buena Vista,
him and Wim'

Callahan acutely exposes the narrow line between documenting from a position of sublimation to the subject, or entering the narrative and coming across, intentionally or not, as a saviour. Buena Vista Social Club is an apt film with which to discuss this tension, due to its prominence and cinematic reputation. There is no denying, on one level, that the prominence is deserved because the film features incredible musicians and captures them working on stage and in the studio at significant power. The scenes of the musicians all gathered onstage in Amsterdam, the show which forms the bulk of the live footage, or in the celebrated Egrem Studios in Havana, are captivating. So too is the footage of the concert at the legendary Carnegie Hall in New York with Ibrahim Ferrer – the most prominently featured musician in the film – moved and overwhelmed by the ecstatic audience reaction.

What makes the film problematic, admittedly potentially from the retrospect of 2024, is the insertion of Cooder into the film's narrative. Similarly problematic insertions and narrative constructions that divert attention from the subject to the filmmakers in ways that unsettle can be found in works from the little known *Ethiopiques: Revolt of the Soul* (2017) to the Oscar-winning *Searching for Sugar Man* (2012). There is little contention that Cooder, in recording and celebrating the work of musicians such as Ferrer, Compay Segundo and others, was vital in making those musicians better known, but his narration, plus the way Wenders shoots and cuts in his contributions in the studio and the concerts, makes it appear that it is only because of Cooder that these musicians are known. Audience gratitude is sought most blatantly in the final shot of the film, not the musicians themselves, but Cooder taking a slow-motion bow and exiting the Carnegie Hall stage alone. Some of the filmmaking choices, including the stock footage-esque imagery of Havana life – where some participants are visibly uncomfortable with the camera's gaze – show little engagement with a Cuban history and politics that might counter the saviour narrative. Tanya Katerí Hernández writes that 'what is missing from this finely spun tale is any demonstration of agency on the part of the Afro-Cuban musicians themselves and the respect they garnered within Cuban society of their own accord' (2002: 62). Even so, it is difficult to judge too harshly the intent of the filmmakers because some of the choices – most notably the Havana locations where the musicians are filmed delivering solo performances throughout the film – do hint at an appreciation of the underlying social factors that have subdued these incredible talents in their homeland for so long.

Johanna Schwartz's *They Will Have to Kill Us First: Malian Music in Exile* is a film that similarly documents musicians whose careers are crushingly curtailed by a lack of freedom to write and perform. The film explores the impact of local Jihadist rule in Northern Mali, particularly Timbuktu, where music is banned and how this impacts a variety of musicians who are forced either to flee south to parts of the country where fighting for local control is less severe or cross the border to Burkina Faso. The film remains focused on the lives of the people it is about, including singer Khaira and the group Songhoy Blues. One of the interesting facets of the film is how it downplays successes that emerge from a Western engagement with the music, or at least keeps them in perspective in terms of the story it is telling of a people displaced.

In the film, the rise of Songhoy Blues is captured as they sign to UK label Transgressive Records and tour Britain, as well as collaborating with Damon Albarn's Africa Express project where they meet Nick Zinner of the band Yeah Yeah Yeahs, who produces their acclaimed debut album. This coverage is always tempered by the band's constant reflection on the political situation in their homeland and their desire to return home as free musicians. The footage of them riding the London Underground clutching their instruments, tired, tells so much of homesickness and the bittersweet irony of finding success outside a home context. This story is only part of the film's structure, however. As much if not more focus is given over to female musicians struggling to maintain lives and careers without Western acknowledgement. For the legendary Khaira, who holds a similar place in the hearts of Malian audiences as Jouini in Tunisia and Gencebay in Istanbul, it is vital that she holds a concert for peace in Timbuktu despite life-threatening danger. It is also vital that she performs with her friend and peer Disco who is seen throughout the film working in a refugee centre for displaced Malian women.

The concert forms the last act of the film,[12] placing the role of women and the importance of music in everyday life front and centre to the film's narrative and theme. In it, the two women perform on a Timbuktu Street, surrounded by their musicians and fans, seated, listening, singing, cheering. Schwartz's film is one that lets the musicians speak even more than the music. Very little, if any,

---

[12] This device, of building narrative towards a single event, is something the film shares with many other music films including *Buena Vista Social Club* and *Inna De Yard* (2019), a reggae film mentioned in the chapter on Black Music.

music is played by those featured in the film – troubadour Moussa Sidi is the other musician focused on – until around 35 minutes into the film. Up to that point, the audience is invited to spend time getting to know the musicians as people first, trusting that empathy will build and increase when they start playing. It makes the human politics of the film overt because ultimately, as Khaira says, capturing what her battle means in a personal–political context, 'if we can't have music, it's the end of us'.

The final film under discussion in this chapter is a masterpiece that contains within its form all the components featured thus far. Ahmed El Maanouni's *Trances* is a poetic documentary about place – Morocco – making music in your own language and with your own culture as the base, national politics, the politics of place, who speaks for whom, fandom and transcending national borders. That it manages to incorporate all these elements in a seamless whole that captures the transcendent music of the group Nass El Ghiwane in a cinematic experience is testament to the approach of the filmmaker. El Maanouni spends time observing the band in a variety of environments with no agenda and uses the music film as a direct means of capturing the resonances between people and place. The film follows the band as they move around Morocco and other North African countries on tour, as they exist and live – as teachers and struggling musicians between gigs – and as they come together to make the music that so overwhelms audiences, who continually rush the stage at the band's hypnotic, rhythmic concerts. The people in the different places the band visit, and in their homeland, feel the music intimately. As Sally Shafto (2013) writes 'what's clear from watching Nass El Ghiwane in public is the highly participatory nature of their concerts. People perform a trancelike dance onstage and often embrace the four musicians. The spectator is an essential part of the equation'. This is most thrillingly captured in the opening sequence where the audience, unable to contain themselves, storm the stage throwing the whole performance and film into disarray. The cutting captures the intensity of the moment, revealing something like the feeling of being present.

The film returns to the theme of place through montages over the music. The sound design artfully mixes ambient place sounds with live and recorded music to beautiful effect, conjuring a sense of place that feels connected to how the band talk about the music they make, rooted directly in ideas around Moroccan and African history, culture and politics. The approach to footage and editing is impressionistic. Some of it feels like a traditional observational street documentary, while, at other times, it is much more expressionistic with images transplanted over musical sequences that seem like the director is finding connections between visual and aural stimulus, sharing interpretive moments with the audience. Making place the central theme, intentionally or not, ensures that the film has an axis around which the musical compositions and performances, as well as the band's collective and individual philosophies, can be engaged. Striking scenes include one in which two members of the band take a break from making furniture to work on new rhythms with a passing street musician, and another where a local man dances in red as a sheep is sacrificed, while Nass El Ghiwane's music plays. It all affirms the statement by a theatre director in the film that 'Moroccans recognise themselves in the group' and, conversely, that the opposite is true, that the band recognize Morocco in themselves and their music. Bilge Ebiri writes that the film 'starts off like a regular concert documentary and transforms over the course of its 90 minutes into a kind of conjuring, bringing forth the spirits of a nation' (2013: 29–32). It is not a biographical document but a portrait that seeks to evoke in the audience a feeling of why this music matters, rather than telling them why it does.

As Hacke asserts at the finale of *Crossing the Bridge,* it is impossible to know everything of a place and its music in a short time. Indeed, it is always impossible and certainly beyond the capabilities of a film. However, the films engaged with here acknowledge the limitations of the form in capturing the entirety of a subject. Instead of seeking to do so, they use a variety of approaches – personal, poetic, political etc. – to tell part of a story. By focusing on place, these films give audiences a way into the story.[13] As musician Kode9 (Steve Goodman) says in the film about experimental music *The Sound Is Innocent* (2019): 'Music being just about listening is all wrong [...] music is architectural, more than something you listen to, it's something you inhabit.' By focusing on place, these films, despite their geographical differences, emphasize the interconnectedness of music and environment, of sound and place.

---

[13] Though it could be argued that one of the problematic aspects of *Buena Vista Social Club* is how it purports to be about place but ultimately is not.

5

'I just have to deal with it'[1] – Women

In writing about the Kevin Macdonald directed Whitney Houston documentary *Whitney*, from 2018, Simran Hans (2018) claims that whilst Houston's voice was 'one of a kind' the film has 'an assembly-line narrative'. This accusation is one that can be levelled at any number of music documentaries to varying degrees. However, it feels sadly more pertinent to really assess this trend in this chapter, because it remains the case that women in music films bear the brunt of a lack of creative and aesthetic care and nuance. Hans talks about how Macdonald's film ignores elements of Houston's artistic trajectory that don't 'fit the film's classical narrative and so [are] omitted'. Such omission is one example of how women are often underserved in music films and such omissions often cascade into more serious aesthetic and ideological concerns.

Films about women that centre their subjects as artists first and foremost appear throughout this book. However, this chapter attempts to grapple with how the music film has underserved women as subjects through a too regular adherence to the most basic codes and conventions of music film narratology, structure and perspective and as a result has left less room for innovation and difference than in films about some of these artists' male contemporaries. Much of this is down to control of the narrative. When women artists have managed to control the narrative, particularly as will be explored when looking at films about contemporary female pop stars, they have ensured they are represented closer to how they want. This control, in the case of, for example, Taylor Swift, is a riposte to a media that has exploited, hounded, misrepresented and shamed them. There is a tension between the misrepresentation and willful ignorance of some of the films and the need in others to reclaim a

---

[1] *Miss Sharon Jones!* (2015).

crushingly close control in response to such problematic and harmful systemic representations. Some films need accurate contextualizing, others need holding to account.

Whilst considering arguably toxic representations of women in music, including the critically acclaimed and Academy Award-winning *Amy* (2015), this chapter also considers a variety of attempts by artists to control their own narrative in the face of misogyny both internal and external to the music industry,[2] films that seek to assert women into narratives from which they have been largely excluded, as well as films that celebrate the unique contributions of women in complex and rewarding ways. In the latter cases it's noticeable that so many films that are more complex and ultimately celebratory of that complexity are directed by women. Hans writes of the two Whitney Houston films that emerged in quick succession in 2017 (directed by Nick Broomfield) and 2018 (directed by Kevin Macdonald) that it's 'curious that two middle-aged White men from the UK – Macdonald is Scottish, Broomfield English – are the designated authors of a story about a black American woman'. As with so much in cinema, representation and point of view, matters. Hans writes that 'the best and most interesting music documentaries avoid hagiography while still looking at their subjects and their craft through the lens of love'. While it would be overly presumptuous to suggest that the films made by Macdonald, Broomfield and Kapadia lack love for their subjects what is clear is that many music films made about women by men veer the narrative into ones where the role of men and trauma play central roles, and women's artistry and humanity is secondary. This is something female filmmakers, overall, don't. Some of the works resist those narratives almost entirely and those that incorporate them do so with palpable difference, as will be discussed.

'All of a sudden I wasn't there'[3] – Dead Pop Stars

Whitney: Can I Be Me (2017) opens on a ghoulish note, with the recording of the phone call from the hotel to the police when Houston died in February

---

[2] It starts by looking at films where the subjects have zero control over their narrative as they are deceased.
[3] *Amy* (2015).

2012. This not only sets the tone of the film, one that pores over the circumstances that led to her death, but also frames the context of Houston's story as primarily that of an addict, who died of an overdose, as opposed to one of the most preternaturally talented singers in the history of pop music. The film never manages to convey the complexities of biography and fame that lead to such an end, instead remaining ghoulish throughout. In contrast, *Whitney* (2018) at least starts with images of Houston the musical performer, talking about her career over slow-motion footage of a music video shoot. Throughout Kevin Macdonald's film there is some discussion of Houston's sexuality and a slightly deeper section on the sexual abuse she suffered as a child and this biographical contextualization is helped by the film having the participation of close members of Houston's family including her mother, Cissy, as well as former husband Bobby Brown. Broomfield's film, like his films on Kurt Cobain and Courtney Love (*Kurt & Courtney,* 1998), and the Notorious B.I.G. and Tupac (*Biggie and Tupac,* 2002), has very little access to inner circles, which only adds to a sense of exploitation, score settling and the tabloid-esque gaze of the work.

Both films lack the same central, contextualizing participant, Robyn Crawford – Houston's best friend, confidant and possibly lover. Crawford's absence as an active participant in the films makes both feel essentially pointless. Her presence is unavoidable through copious archive behind-the-scenes and home movie footage and she is discussed in positive and negative terms by Houston's family and collaborators and professional team in both films. Crawford's decision to remain silent across the two films, despite emerging as the person who could give the closest account of Houston's life, work and personal struggles, condemns the films to a space where they remain obviously incomplete and speculative to a degree that can't be accounted for. As mentioned, the access of the Macdonald film makes it feel more authoritative. There's much in the film that isn't in the Broomfield documentary but much of this is garnered towards making more of Houston's perceived flaws and problems than in the Broomfield film. *Whitney* includes more of a focus on the bad shows that Houston performed as she became engulfed by her addiction, there's more on her performance as a mother to Krissy, more on how her success with the film *The Bodyguard* (1992) affected her marriage to Bobby Brown than the achievement itself and there's even a short, pejorative clip where Houston criticizes Paula Abdul. On its own the criticism can be seen as more of the music industry system itself than Abdul but, in the context of the film, it tips the balance of focus further towards the negative.

More is made of the significance of *The Bodyguard* in Houston's career and life in Broomfield's film, which also takes time to highlight the unique power of her voice as heard on the film's unforgettable song 'I Will Always Love You', the Dolly Parton cover that became one of the biggest selling singles of all time and dominated the year's pop charts all over the world. However, it does give space to Kevin Costner to take credit for the dramatic acapella opening that starts the song, again undermining her talent and process as an artist. Macdonald's film spends some time on her talent and process and what made her special; this is most rewarding in the sequence that focuses on her performance of the National Anthem at the Super Bowl in 1991. Her musical director Ricky Minor talks of how, having discussed the approach with Houston, who was inspired by Marvin Gaye's take on the same song at an NBA All-Star game, he came up with a dissonant arrangement. The orchestra were not happy, and tension grew waiting for Houston's response in the build-up to the show. The Super Bowl is the most watched annual television event in the world and Houston didn't respond to Minor's arrangement until, on the eve of the show, she listens to the orchestration, once. She says 'I got it'. Minor: 'You got it?' The natural reply. And she did get it. The first take she ever sang was live, in the stadium. The result was and remains 'magical'.[4]

What is troubling about the films discussed above, and what is so troubling about the Oscar-winning *Amy*, is that the focus is overwhelmingly on biographical tragedy, to the point that talent, ability and musical and cultural impact is sidelined. Music films about male artists with similarly tragic biographies are more inclined to romanticize that tragedy, or simply to skirt around it. Often, this focus on tragedy is an issue exacerbated by films that structure their narrative chronologically. The lives of Whitney Houston and Amy Winehouse (the subject of *Amy*) ended without a redemptive final act of

---

[4] In the film, this sequence is contextualized by the writer Cinque Henderson who wrote a beautiful piece about this historic moment for the New Yorker in 2016. Available at: www.newyorker.com/culture/cultural-comment/anthem-of-freedom-how-whitney-houston-remade-the-star-spangled-banner.

rehabilitation and triumphant comeback. Therefore, any film that takes the approach of telling their story in the order events transpired will always end up being tragic, because that's how their stories ended. A similar effect will be seen later in this chapter when discussing *Billie* (2019), a film of Billie Holiday's life. The formal approach in *Amy* also leads to the film's doom-laden, exploitative and murky experience. Director Asif Kapadia employed the same approach in *Senna* (2010) about the Formula One driver Ayrton Senna. This approach is one that utilizes only footage that already exists of the subject, meaning that *Amy* is made up of home-movie footage of Winehouse at home growing up and later in the recording studio, televised and recorded performances across her life and career and, most notoriously and copiously, the sheer mountainous deluge of material collected by tabloids and paparazzi photographers and videographers. In her book, *Fangirls* (2019), Hannah Ewens writes:

> Writer and thinker Susan Sontag said that a single photo acknowledges suffering, while an endless parade of them deadens response to it. With every update, we continued to gawp and lose the bleak reality of Amy Winehouse's situation
>
> 2019: 200

Amy once more puts Winehouse through an ordeal she didn't survive. After becoming 'infamous' Winehouse was mercilessly hounded by tabloid outlets all over the world, to the point – as the film shows by sheer volume if nothing else – that her life as an artist and a person needing space to deal with traumatic experiences, became untenable. The amount of tabloid material in the film manages to convey a queasy verisimilitude of what it must have been like for Winehouse daily. The manic, stroboscopic impact of hundreds of camera bulbs popping at once leaves the viewer disorientated and nauseous.[5] However this, and the lack of any context of Winehouse as a performer and artist in new interviews – the film's interview participants are all friends and family who were part of Winehouse's inner circle who are allowed, unchallenged by the film, to justify their role in what happened to her – means the film only perpetuates the tragedy of her life and recreates the conditions under which

---

[5] Hannah Ewens' *Fangirls* astutely lambasts the hypocrisies of the press for their treatment of Winehouse before she died and after and how this hypocrisy was 'furiously rejected' (2019: 203) by her fans.

she suffered, without critique, without a counter-argument or emphasizing her talent. The result is a film that feels cruel. Amy has no contextualizing voice because she is dead. Her life and contribution have been reduced to ghostly artefacts that represent the past, where those that contain traces of a musical gift and legacy are slowly replaced by demonizing, excoriating extractions of their personhood by exploitative forces, from amongst whom it is hard to separate the makers of this film.

'Fuck that, I don't care'[6] – Pop Stars

When Taylor Swift says in the opening stages of Lana Wilson's *Miss Americana* (2020) that she has 'a need to be thought of as good' it feels like insight into her personality directly from the source. It feels revealing, and it is, but it is also, as the unfolding film reaffirms, revealing of what Swift wants revealed. The narrative feels very much controlled by the star as she uses it to, for example, address the impact of being interrupted by Kanye West at the 2009 MTV VMA awards. By giving the moment due attention, away from it being an infamous soundbite or meme, she reminds the (her) audience of what damage it did to Swift who was 19 years old at the time and thought, in the confusion, that the audience booing West, was booing her. It's presented here as a formative moment, an obstacle the artist strove to overcome, pushing as it did against her innate insecurity about being liked and popular, something that recurs throughout the film. Alongside carefully presented footage of Taylor being awkward and geeky, discussing the realities of being stalked, the paparazzi and social media, there are some genuinely insightful and revealing moments focusing on her process as a musician.[7] The film spends time with the artist as she writes songs, creates music videos and performs huge sellout shows. What comes across is her vision for her career. This is clear in meetings with her team and, in one superb moment, in the intercutting between her vision for a

---

[6] *Miss Americana* (2020).
[7] Damon Albarn (Blur/Gorillaz) should probably have watched the film before making ill-informed comments about Swift as a musician in 2021. See www.rollingstone.com/music/music-news/its-f-cked-up-to-try-and-discredit-my-writing-taylor-swift-fires-back-at-blurs-damon-albarn-1289961/

music video starring Panic! At The Disco's Brendon Urie, which she relays in a conversation with him, and the finished product.

The sense of narrative control in so much of the film is made apparent by the relative lack of control in one of the key thematic sequences. The film documents Taylor Swift's move from being an artist who presented an apolitical persona into one with a political voice, centred around the 2018 mid-term elections when Marsha Blackburn was running for senate in Swift's home state of Tennessee. The audience sees Swift fight her family (her dad, mainly) and her team for the right to make a stand and speak out against Blackburn's misogynistic, homophobic views and plans, knowing the risk it is to come out in terms seen as feminist, liberal etc., which might potentially alienate her fanbase. In one scene Swift defends her decision, in tears, trying to explain to her dad why she needs to do it and it becomes genuinely tense when she decides to make an Instagram post on the matter. What makes it tense is the understanding that the result, of the post and the election, is out of the artist's hands. And so it turns out, when Blackburn wins despite a late surge of voter registration following Swift's intervention. And while Taylor's career doesn't suffer, her engagement in the political arena marks a shift in her confidence as an artist and the film captures that precise moment of change. As the film ends, Taylor is presented as an LGBTQAI+ ally and when she talks about her experience she conveys a deeper understanding, such as when she eloquently expresses why there is such a need for female musicians to constantly reinvent themselves in a way that is not expected of male peers.

The sense that the audience is seeing what the artist and their record label and management team want them to see is present again in *Gaga: Five Foot Two* (2017), though with quite different results. There is much less of a sense here that Lady Gaga, the film's subject, is in control to the same degree as Taylor Swift. The film takes a lot of cues from *Madonna: Truth or Dare* (1991) – a film discussed in a later chapter on myth and performativity – in how it tries to present Gaga in a variety of ways; from passionate artist having 'little baby meltdowns' to confessional ambitions such as 'I want to become a woman in this business, and grow up'. Despite this formal closeness, the film ends up distancing Gaga from Madonna in a variety of ways, including how to control what audiences learn via films about you. It's clear from one key scene where a slightly drunk Gaga talks negatively about Madonna, the woman she is so often associated with creatively, that the association is an issue for her. However, the filmmakers think it will help sell the documentary because they ignore her on-screen demand that 'you can use none of this footage'.

The decision to make explicit and implicit references to Madonna in the film backfires, as do several other moments that strike a sour tone. The most striking is one sequence where Gaga writes the song 'Joanne', the centrepiece of the album, who's recording the film orbits around. She takes the song, about her aunt who died before Gaga was born, plays it for her grandmother – Joanne's mother – and films the response. The audience watches Gaga watch her grandmother for the duration the song plays via Gaga's phone. It becomes painfully clear that the moment is about Gaga, not her grandmother, not Joanne, and when she asks at the song's finish 'Did I get it right?', the awkwardness on the part of her grandmother as to what to say is palpable. The film is full of moments like these, where participants are forced to respond in front of the camera. Another involves the *New York Times* journalist Darryl Pinckney, whose interview with the artist is recorded. The sense of trying to control the narrative is pushed to the foreground but the results don't feel like they were what Gaga intended them to be when she embarked on the making of the film. Speaking of Gaga's control over her public and performance persona Hannah Ewens writes that 'there's nothing to be gleaned that isn't already known' (2019: 73). Films about female popstars are often exercises in control, in taking back or retaining it. What's interesting about the Gaga film is that what she chooses to show and what she thinks will create empathy or understanding actually ends up creating distance for audiences.

Two things that emerge prominently from viewing *Billie Eilish: The World's a Little Blurry* (2021) are the conviction and the expense of the cinematic undertaking. The conviction is on the part of Eilish's record label and the film's production company, Interscope, to essentially embed a filmmaker in the Eilish home so early in her development as an artist and follow it through to the [inevitable] triumph of a Coachella appearance and multiple wins at the Grammy awards. The film follows Eilish as she and songwriting partner, her brother Finneas, write and record songs for her debut album in his bedroom, go on tour and get ready to release the record. The expense can be felt in the amount of footage there is from throughout this period of creative development and on her first national and international tours. There is so much footage of this period and it is both intimate and expansive, with a lot of tour shows filmed with multiple cameras, making the financial and creative investment that has been made plainly felt. Intriguingly, the filmmaking team understand Eilish's age and are happy to include moments where she comes across as naïve, precocious, petulant, almost as a reminder of how young she was at the time of filming, as a way of underscoring the almost oceanic distance between this persona and the one that comes across when she sings. Despite the control exerted over the narrative that the subject is a unique talent, the film is still littered with aspects that either pull or threaten to pull it into derivative territory that doesn't necessarily present the subject in the best light.

The film, very much like *Gaga: Five Foot Two,* spends a lot of time on what Mary Wild and Sarah Cleaver (2021) describe as the 'performance of pain'. It presents Eilish as an heroic figure, battling the limitations of her body, to present a thrilling performance for her fans, night after night. This aspect is almost entirely unique to films about female musicians. Even Taylor Swift, with the high level of control over the filmic representation she exhibits, doesn't escape when she is squeezed into a disco ball dress and says 'Can I breathe? Yes. Is it easy? No' in *Miss Americana*. There's no doubt that Eilish's injuries and physical issues are serious but dwelling on it, as in the Gaga film, ends up doing her a disservice, as does the inclusion of the drawn-out saga of her teen relationship with an ending that all but Eilish can see coming in a moment where the film misjudges representing her age and lack of life experience warts and all. The results, as in so many films about female musicians, tie the subject's life experiences and routines to that of a man or a boy, and their bodies to that of commodities to be consumed until they break. However, Savina Petkova argues that this presentation of pain is a positive aspect of the Eilish film. She wrote for the Quietus in 2021 that:

> By paying attention to Eilish's body, specifically its pains, instead of a stagnated paradigm of femininity, the documentary surpasses its like unobtrusively, by opening up physical space for pain.

An artist as self-articulated as Billie Eilish can teach us a thing or two about agony. I can absolutely see that reading of the film and it may apply to others in this section, but something doesn't feel right as a male viewer extending positive attribution to some of the images and moments portrayed. Other moments, for me, are more straightforward in calling out as problematic. Possibly the most inexplicable inclusion in *The World's a Little Blurry*, given that his manager was one of the film's executive producers, is footage of 40+ year-old Orlando Bloom telling Eilish he loves her and repeatedly kissing her 18-year-old head backstage at Coachella. For a film that is so determined to present its subject within such strict parameters as an artist, the lack of criticality in terms of how some of the material can be viewed is quite staggering.

'That fucking panther is coming out of me now'[8] – Black Women

Another addition to the roster of films made by men about women that make misjudgments that impact the complex retelling of the subject's story can be found in *Billie* (2019) about the life of jazz legend Billie Holiday, although, to be fair, the result here is less egregious than in the films about Whitney Houston and Amy Winehouse. The film structures much of its narrative around the men in Holiday's life. The result is that the film only ever sees her in this context, never letting her escape her associations with men, while also remaining conservative about her famous sexual appetite. Holiday's story is undoubtedly fascinating and the film tries to get into all of it: her race, her fraught harassment by the FBI[9] and her struggles with drug addiction. Unfortunately, because of such a packed and striking biography, her music takes a back seat, despite featuring a raft of interviews with musicians who worked with her. It does, however, in one key sequence, do justice to her most famous song, the Black protest anthem 'Strange Fruit', detailing how her performance of it 'changed the course of American music' and how its introduction into her performances led to White people leaving her shows because they wanted to be 'entertained'. The way the film elevates itself above other films mentioned above, and other pedestrian jazz films discussed elsewhere, such as films on John Coltrane and

---

[8] *Grace Jones: Bloodlight and Bami* (2017).
[9] The focus of contemporaneous narrative feature film *The United States vs Billie Holiday* (2021).

Miles Davis, is in how it incorporates the inspiration and impetus for how the film came to be in the first place.

Similar to Kasper Collin's *I Called Him Morgan* (2016) – discussed in the jazz section in the chapter on Black music – the film is anchored by a series of taped conversations with Billie Holiday about her life and career. These conversations were recorded by writer Linda Kuehl for a planned biography of Holiday that she never completed because she couldn't get the 'right voice' on the page. James Erskine's film is the first time they've ever been heard, which adds a wonderful energy to the viewing of the film, through the undeniable excitement of that fresh proximity to the source. Intriguingly, *Billie* incorporates the story of Kuehl's life into its narrative, giving insight into her life through archive and interviews involving her family, ultimately celebrating her for her dedication to capturing Holiday's life at a time when she was a forgotten artist. As a result, through this device, *Billie* manages to reveal something about how women are forgotten and ignored and, in telling Kuehl's story alongside Holiday's, captures something beautiful about both women, helped by access to their private, intimate conversations, that for a variety of reasons, including Kuehl's early, tragic, and unsatisfactorily investigated death, could have remained private forever.

There's an intimacy in Sophie Fiennes' portrait of Grace Jones, *Grace Jones: Bloodlight and Bami* (2017) that is borne from Jones' trust of the filmmaker and her invitation to Fiennes to join her in private spaces. The film is a combination of live performances – some filmed exclusively for the documentary – and tour footage, alongside time spent with Jones at home in Jamaica with her family and recording an album with legendary producers Sly & Robbie (when they turn up). Fiennes hangs back, observing, never visibly interjecting, allowing the shape of the film to become centred around live performance, family and making an album. The struggles for an artist of Jones' calibre and reputation to do the latter – no support from a label, funding the record herself – are left to sit with the audience and, when juxtaposed with the incredible footage of Jones performing live, show both the absurdity that such an icon should have to struggle so much to make new music and how, for so many artists, male and female, they exist in the public imagination as vehicles for performing the hits of their so-called prime. Jones in full-flow, solo on stage, her band obscured from view, makes a mockery of the idea of a person's being confined to something youthful, something past. This film is about a dynamic present. The closest it gets to an archive is an old picture of her with Andy Warhol which Jones carries.

Instead, the film is dedicated to capturing this artist in the now of the film, even if some of that 'now' is spent reflecting on growing up and growing older and still fighting the same battles. There's a sequence where Jones defends her image, and that of the dancers that she's being asked to perform with on French television, where she is made out to be a 'madam in a brothel', which manages to convey her anger at being both artistically misunderstood and visually exploited. The film captures her sympathy at the female dancers needing the gig and how getting rid of them will look on her, and her tiredness at having, yet again, to have this battle, over an exploitative sexual reading of her persona. Jonathan Romney (2021) writes that 'Jones is a visual artist who knows what things look like, and above all, knows what *she* looks like'. In focusing on the moment of its making,[10] and through the empathy and curiosity of Fiennes as a director, *Bloodlight and Bami* manages to present a portrait of Jones that speaks louder than the sum of its parts. By finding a structure of different, connected and substantial areas to focus on and not trying to tell the whole story, the complexity of Jones' life and art is conveyed with respect and depth. So much so that even though the end of the film risks triteness by following the story of the loss of Jones' grandparents' home to a hurricane, told during a visit by Jones to the location, now reclaimed by nature, with a performance of her song 'Hurricane' over the closing credits, it doesn't feel this way. This is because Fiennes' film manages to convey story and subtext so well, and because the sight of Jones performing is frankly sensational. Romney's review of the film for *Film Comment* laments, as so many reviews of music films do, about the lack of knowledge audiences glean directly from watching – what audiences do not learn. However, this negates what is felt by the observation, what audiences can take away from the experience that is felt. Music films are often spaces where musicians perform a version of themselves, revealing little or sometimes nothing. And yet, the struggle of Jones to remain active and relevant, and a melancholic reflection on family and ageing is felt in this film, which is remarkable given that, as Mark Fisher has written, 'there is no Grace Jones the

---

[10] Or moments more accurately, as the film was shot over a five-year period.

subject who expresses her subjectivity in sound and image' but 'only one Jones the abstract hyperbody' (2018: 281).

Miss Sharon Jones! (2015), directed by Barbara Kopple, could easily slide into over-sentimentality as it tells the story of a Black women finding success and career stability later in life only to be diagnosed and treated for pancreatic cancer. The brilliance of Barbara Kopple and her focus on so many aspects of Jones's life, with music as the beating heart, plus Jones herself, ensures the film is moving but never mawkish. Jones, the person, is relentlessly pragmatic declaring throughout the film as she is undergoing treatment 'I'm responsible for everybody's payroll', 'I gotta get out there', 'I just have to deal with it'. Kopple lets this material sit for audiences, never hammering home the tragedy of Jones's situation. We see this older Black woman battling for her life and we hear her on record and see her well, earlier, self on stage and the contrast is devastating. Moments where her loyal team of bandmates and small staff break down at the terrifying enormity of the situation are captured but never exploited. The film never succumbs to the temptation to be an elegy, despite the accumulation of evidence, and as a result stands as a fitting tribute to Jones's complex Black womanhood.[11]

Jones is naturally reflective in the film but, despite some moments where her resolve breaks, she displays strength and joy and faith in her life and her path. Her commitment to sing and record again, despite the difficult physical legacies of chemotherapy on her voice, results in some of the most striking moments in the film where we see her doing what she loves and is extraordinary at – performing. Two moments are different in scale but equally powerful. In the first, Jones goes to church and tries to sing for the first time in a while. Drawing on her faith and her belief that she is in a space that will nourish her and help her through, the camera gets close to her as she tries to reach the power and technical range that used to come so naturally. The camera captures the trepidation, the tentative steps towards, and then finally the unbridled attack on the song, before swinging back and away to watch her command the space and bring into view the congregation who are ecstatic at the performance. The other one is in a secular space, New York's Beacon Theatre. A hometown show, following her return to recording and performing in earnest. This

---

[11] Jones died aged 60 in 2016, not long after the film was finished.

audience also welcomes her rapturously and the extended performance footage revels in Jones's joy at her being back where she felt she belonged. On stage. Singing. It is a moment of triumph that ends the film on a well-earned high note and acts as a fitting tribute to Jones. She loved music. Kopple, her band, her team, well they all loved her too.

'Sometimes when you're ahead of your time, you're behind on your rent'[12] – Punk Women

One way to avoid misrepresentation in music film is to have the privilege of controlling the narrative. This is something that comes across more strongly in the 'pop music' films discussed earlier but the film *Poly Styrene: I Am A Cliché* (2021) is fascinating for the different ways it seeks to control narratives around the central subject.[13] The film is co-written and co-directed by Celeste Bell, the daughter of the film's subject. Her deep involvement results in a film that seeks to reclaim several narratives surrounding her mother. Using the lens of a

Figure 5.1 Poly Styrene: I Am A Cliché (dir. Sng and Bell, 2021) © Polydoc Films.

---

[12] *L7: Pretend We're Dead* (2017).
[13] Maybe in the context of these indie films about punk women, the word 'control' should more accurately be replaced by the word 'collaboration'.

daughter seeking to learn more about, remember and re-contextualize her own family history, it [re]assesses the role of women in punk – doing in the process a better, more imaginative job than the rote *Here to be Heard: The Story of the Slits* (2017) about Poly Styrene and X-Ray Spex's peers. The film also addresses race in a way that, as evidenced in the chapter on punk, is often limited to the influence of reggae at the apex of the movement in the late 1970s. The reason for its inclusion in this chapter and not that one is the way the film is also about women searching for truths. Poly was a truth seeker and Bell, the co-director, is seeking truths about her mother, seeking to change the narrative around Poly regarding mental health and the impact of the adversity she experienced on her life and career and, ultimately, her daughter.

The focus of the narrative structure, with Bell on an often psycho-geographical investigative journey that she co-narrates,[14] ensures that the mother/daughter relationship remains at the core of the story. Poly Styrene's art and musicianship, her incredible lyrical insight and flair, is one of the avenues Bell ventures down. Vivien Goldman describes Styrene as being 'an unprecedented apparition of liberation' (2019: 04) when she appeared on the scene and the filmmaking here ensures that her uniqueness as a performer and artist is communicated. As found elsewhere, for example Kasper Collin's *I Called Him Morgan* (2016) discussed in the chapter on Black music, the investigative approach allows it to feel as though the protagonist is learning about the subject at the same time as the audience. When the protagonist is the subject's daughter there is naturally an added weight to the experience. The pace of the film, in individual moments and in its entirety, is contemplative and at times verges on the earnest, feeling very much at odds with the energy that exudes from the archive material, reinforcing the fact that this is Bell's narrative and she's in control of what gets told and how.[15] As the reality of the hardships that Poly faced throughout her career and life emerge, it is hard to begrudge her this cinematic reclamation of her mother, especially as the film also ensures an artistic legacy is reclaimed. The use of Ruth Negga as Poly (heard in voiceover) in particular, reveals the scope of Poly Styrene's gifts as a

---

[14] Actress Ruth Negga 'plays' her mother, reading from her diaries as part of the film's voiceover.
[15] I'm aware this reading of the film negates somewhat the filmmaking brought to the film by co-director and experienced filmmaker Paul Sng, which should not be underestimated. His handling of the structure and photography and cinematic tone is exemplary.

writer beyond her iconic lyrics, ensuring the journey Bell undertakes always has a powerful and poetic aural accompaniment even when the music isn't front and centre.

Akin to *Poly Styrene: I Am A Cliché*, *L7: Pretend We're Dead* (2017) is an example of how films directed by and about women also call on women to discuss the music, impact and context of women artists. There may be no scientific formula backing that up, but the inclusion of interviews with female peers and fans of 1990s punk rock band L7 – such as Brody Dalle and Allison Wolfe (in glistening HD that juxtaposes the dull TV and jittery mini DV coverage of the band in their pomp) – certainly draws out the positive gender focus of the filmmaking by Sarah Price. Men are interviewed, but they feel selected for direct relevance, and this makes the film feel similarly focused to *The Punk Singer* (2013),[16] albeit rawer, and grungier. The film feels connected to Anderson's film about Kathleen Hanna and not just because of the overlaps of Bikini Kill and L7's contemporary relevance. *The Punk Singer* was a film that, like the genre it part documented, broke through and set a template, giving permission. *L7: Pretend We're Dead* feels like it has responded to the clarion call and works hard to assert the importance of this all-female punk inflected rock band alongside their better-known male peers. It even does similar with female and male progressive punk peers. For example, In *Fugazi: Instrument*, discussed earlier in the book, there is mention of the significance of the 1991 Washington pro-choice march and rally. Fugazi's (*Fugazi: Instrument*) narratives. Price's film, however, traces the origins of that moment back to its root, to the 'Rock for Choice' concerts set up originally by L7.

Another way the film seeks to reclaim the narrative around the band is by reframing the most notorious moments from the group's career. Frustrated at their treatment by an antagonistic crowd at Reading Festival in 1992, with the band on a creative ascendancy, singer Donita removed her tampon on stage and threw it in the crowd yelling 'eat my used tampon fuckers'. The result is that the band's notoriety exploded and things got weird including another infamous incident when Donita pulled her trousers and underwear down live on British TV show, *The Word*, a show where it was hard to do something truly shocking. Rather than simply relishing in the infamy and notoriety, placing the incident

---

[16] Discussed shortly.

in the middle of the film allows a greater depth of context to emerge.¹⁷ The film doesn't shy away from the flaws of the band members in terms of the problems that led to their eventual split, but it equally ensures that the treatment they received from the industry and press – 'we wished the gender would go away' – and incidents such as the deaths of close friend Kurt Cobain and their long-time roadie Umbar are given full scrutiny. The film tells the band's story chronologically, keeping images of them to the relevant contemporary moment in the story through its copious, band-generated archive material, though we hear them in interviews recorded for the documentary as voiceover. When we finally see them as they are 'now', it's having reformed to sold-out shows and with a growing reappraisal of their musical contribution and impact.¹⁸ *L7: Pretend We're Dead* is an example of a film that envelopes considerable and fascinating archive by providing context that elevates that material beyond simple curiosity or nostalgia for those archival fragments. Using this wraparound approach, the film's structure rewards the foresight of the band in recording everything as it happened in case it mattered by asserting that, yes, what they were and continue to do, does matter.

In Don Letts' *Punk: Attitude* (2005) Sonic Youth's Thurston Moore and fellow No Wave pioneer Glenn Branca situate Patti Smith firmly in the lineage of punk rock. Moore claims her work, particularly her live performances at CBGB's alongside fellow luminaries such as Television and Talking Heads and her debut album *Horses,* 'informed punk'. Meanwhile, Branca puts it more emphatically when he calls Smith 'the queen of the universe'. Of all the artists contained in this chapter, the inclusion of a film about Smith is potentially the most debatable. However, Steven Sebring's 2008 film *Patti Smith: Dream of Life* is one that seeks to provide a cinematic portrait of an artist whose influence on the music that surrounded and followed her emergence at the height of what might be termed 'proto-punk' is undeniable. Smith's music and life contains directness, rawness, simplicity and poetry. She believes in the power of rock 'n' roll and is reflective on life, death and art to a degree that is rarely seen. Sebring, a friend and collaborator of Smith's, strives to capture the simplicity and poetry

---

[17] Although at the time of writing, as at the time it happened, it's hard to envision a more truly punk rock action in musical history than what Donita did at the Reading festival.

[18] It takes the technique Julien Temple used in *The Filth and the Fury* of obscuring the Sex Pistols' faces in interviews for the film and shifts it. It ensures the audience only see the women as they are at the time events occur, reducing reductive comparative temptation by shallow audiences and critics.

of her existence and work. John Scanlan describes the film as a 'portrait not only of one of those artists whose work spanned both the old and the new eras, but of how time and age had become a primary subject of their work' (2022: 249). The film observes Smith telling stories, singing songs, thinking. The audience watches her create worlds from the things around her. Her relationship to proximity and tactility, objects and places, discussed so beautifully in her book *M Train* (2015), is rendered visually in the film in a way that feels very punk, recalling through lingering observation the importance of the physical – clothes, records, fanzines – to the music.

In the film Smith says 'life is not vertical or horizontal'; neither is the film. It moves around time and space fluidly, evoking the dream space that cinema is so apt at conveying, tying Smith's philosophies of life and existence to the formal approach of the film. The film doesn't seek to tell audiences what is in her mind, but more what it might be like to be in her mind. It strives to see the world through her eyes. Connected, restless, curious. It's not entirely successful – how could it ever be? – but this is largely on account of Smith as a person who deflects attention, glory and importance to others, constantly. Be it her family, Sam Shepard, Robert Mapplethorpe, Lenny Kaye, her beloved Fred 'Sonic' Smith or revered poets, she is always quick to insist on the importance of others in her story, something that again feels very punk. However, the quietness of the film as it watches her on stage, in archive or on a beach with Flea (from the Red Hot Chilli Peppers) ensures that her importance is central and shines through. Anyone still in doubt that Patti Smith is punk would surely be swayed towards the end of the film when she clambers up and over railings to sit on Rimbaud's grave to try and get a bit of the feeling of proximity she relentlessly craves and feeds on. Perimeters be damned.

Like the Riot Grrrl movement that it, in part, documents, Sini Anderson's *The Punk Singer* (2013) pushes against previously established perimeters regarding the participation and representation of women in punk music. The film is a primer on feminism and activism. It feels collective, as in when it credits archive footage from other Riot Grrrl films within the frame, rather than simply in the credits. A small yet radical move in keeping with the rest of the film. That collectiveness feel extends to the testimonies within the film, shot mostly in a fairy lit grotto inside a camper van as well as the live performance that ends the film, the first on stage performance by Hanna for several years following serious illness. Structured a bit like a mystery, with the year 2005 foreshadowed throughout as a year of significance, the story takes the traditional building blocks of backstory while slowly building to a moment where the story will come to a head, Hanna's illness. One of the most beautiful aspects of the film is how it combines the familiar stories of Punk bands – mostly having no money and the tensions that arise within a band from that, especially when young – with the unique; Hanna's formation as an artist in response to childhood abuse, her politicization and ferocious feminism, most famously captured in how she wanted female audience members treated at shows, which the film documents powerfully. So Mayer (2014) writes how the film 'is edited like a zine, collaging together the wealth of textual, photographic and video documentation produced by the small DIY feminist zine scene for which self-documentation was a survival strategy'.

The inclusion in the film of so much discussion of the relationship between Hanna and the music of Bikini Kill and third-wave feminism and the framing of Hanna's battle with late-stage Lyme disease as a way of discussing both expectations on women and preconceptions of their health and bodies, resulting in a film dense with politics and ideas.[19] However, it never feels heavy or portentous. Several factors ensure this. Kathleen is captivating to watch talk, make music or perform it. Her story is incredible. Her ability to handle what life has thrown her way with such passion and articulacy comes across in the many interviews filmed to make up the central spine of the film. The music is great, which helps, and, in addition to the politics and ideology, the film contains at its heart a love story, the relationship between Kathleen and Adam Horowitz (Ad Rock of the Beastie Boys). Anderson ensures that the automatic questions around how such a staunch feminist could be in a relationship with someone who infamously objectified women repeatedly in song and video in the past are answered, but what is most telling is how the footage captured by Horowitz and Hanna during the early days of her battle with late-stage Lyme disease shows a couple deeply in love with each other. Elsewhere, Horowitz

---

[19] Fear not, adequate attention is paid to her post-Bikini Kill electronic influenced work with Le Tigre and The Julie Ruin.

champions and celebrates her with as much vigour as any of the female participants. One in a long list of ways the film subverts preconceptions, hints at the myriad complexities of life underneath short, sharp punk hits and represents punk as more than music, as a cathartic belief system that can lead to an economically difficult but morally solid way of life.

'I'd like to sing again'[20] – Conclusions

Despite reservations expressed at the outset of this chapter regarding how often women artists are represented with love and complexity, those elements are present in many films discussed here including films about Poly Styrene, L7, Grace Jones, Sharon Jones, Taylor Swift and, being discussed shortly, Shirley Collins. To varying degrees, these films try to present complex portraits of their subjects, ensuring as much as possible to present virtues, vices and vulnerabilities but always seeking to try and capture the essence of these people by placing the gender, and in some cases race, in a context where it becomes part of the story being told but is not the entire story. Arguably, Sophie Fiennes' film about Grace Jones doesn't get into race enough. However, by framing the film as she does, based on access to the experience in front of her, Fiennes responds to Jones in the moment and allows race to permeate the film implicitly as a theme via the subtext of Jones's family history and encounters. In the films about Amy Winehouse and Whitney Houston, the absence of love is palpable, felt in the often-clumsy and sometimes cruel way the storytelling is deployed. Somewhere in between are *Billie*, *Billie Eilish: The World's a Little Blurry* and *Gaga: Five Foot Two* which aren't derailed by a lack of love, but certainly aren't as complete without the level of emotional connection that in the other films allows for a deeper resonance, a deeper complexity and a deeper engagement with personhood, to emerge. It would be overly simplistic, derivative and likely false, to suggest that it is merely a lack of love that differentiates more generic works from more complex ones. An argument can, however, be made that there is a lack of a respectful and nuanced engagement by filmmakers whose gender and race differs from that of their subjects on too many occasions.

[20] *The Ballad of Shirley Collins* (2017).

Figure 5.2 The Ballad of Shirley Collins (dir. Curry and Plester, 2017) ©Curry / Plester / Shrapnel.

Virtues associated with love such as patience, respect and compassion are present in Rob Curry and Tim Plester's 2017 film about English folk legend Shirley Collins. *The Ballad of Shirley Collins* is a strong counterargument to the notion that filmmakers need to be of the same gender or race as their subject to capture their story effectively. The film starts out as a portrait of someone who was popular, influential and important, yet fell out of cultural favour. While it acknowledges the role of a man in her retreat from public view and performance – Collins lost the ability to sing after being left heartbroken when her husband had an affair with a fellow band member – it ensures this moment never defines her. Instead, the film puts her back into one of the seminal moments of twentieth-century popular music, one from which she had been largely excluded, by revisiting and reviving her trip with Alan Lomax across America in the 1950s capturing the stories and songs of folk and blues musicians. To do this, the film uses the Lomax archive, Shirley's memories, including letters home and evocative 16mm recreations of the journey. The result is part of the film's successful mission to reposition Shirley in English musical history as a living archive of song and musical tradition. The film follows Shirley around her Hastings and Sussex locale – Englishness in the film comes over as important but never insular, nationalistic, a rich cultural heritage that should be preserved, celebrated and continued peacefully – and her story blends with that of the songs she sang, creating a poignant representation of the art of the tradition of the folk song to be both specific and universal.

The making of the film, as a way of telling Shirley's story and ensuring she is regarded as a historian and archivist as well as being celebrated for her musical talent, resulted halfway through in a miraculous piece of fortuitousness as Collins, possibly through looking back on her life and achievements in a new light, feels the urge, need, desire, to sing again. The filmmakers are on hand to capture this tentative journey back to her singing self and because there was never an agenda to make the film go this way, the space is created for Shirley to discover, on her own terms and in her own way, how to do so. This luck moves the film into a new space, one where the audience, potentially unaware of Collins and only possibly familiar with her work as a young woman from decades before, can spend time watching her both overcome trauma but also work, figuring out both her 'new' voice and how to use it in service of song. The love on the part of the filmmakers is never more present than in a moment towards the end where co-director Rob presents Shirley with a recording of an interview from the early days of the film's production where she says, 'I'd like to sing again'. She can't remember saying it and it feels so genuine on everyone's part. The film captures something so important and momentous, artistically and personally, without ever intending to do so, by starting from a place of love for Collins' contribution to music and culture.

Part Three

Performativity and Performance

6

'Fuck continuity'[1] – Truth and Myth

Jonathan Romney's review for *Film Comment*, of Sophie Fiennes' *Grace Jones: Bloodlight and Bami* (2018), opens as follows:

> At least since D.A. Pennebaker's Dylan portrait *Dont Look Back*, it has been understood that the real performance moments in a music documentary don't happen on stage. They take place behind the scenes, in the dressing room, where the artist doesn't let slip the mystique slip, but instead simply mounts a different kind of show: a heightened display of the 'real' self for the camera's benefit.

This opening salvo crystallizes the exquisite tension at the heart of the music film, as discussed in this book's introduction, wherein the notional idea of a document providing truth, reality or authenticity is constantly undermined since the subjects of the films are performers. Even if they desired to show their 'real' selves, whatever that means, their instinct is to perform and a camera crew offers another route to performance, albeit one where the illusion of the 'real' can be played out. Some of the most memorable moments of music films, including *Dont Look Back* (1967), occur when an aspect of life, or the 'real', gets in the way and performance cannot be maintained.

In *Dont Look Back*, audiences see Bob Dylan working hard to create the public mystique for which he would become renowned through a relentless barrage of press questions. However, audiences also witness the impact of that barrage and the commitments of touring (with the constant entourage of people known and unknown buzzing around a star) via the image of a tired and frustrated Dylan losing his cool and taking on one of his inquisitors. In *Gimme Shelter* (1970), much of the impact stems from the juxtaposition of the

---

[1] *One More Time with Feeling* (2016).

naïve Rolling Stones press conference where they ooze an arrogance suggesting they will be the kings of the hippie movement with their benevolent free concert, and the bare, anguished moments in an edit suite where they witness the murder of festival goer Meredith Hunter. These ruptures in the film are striking because they feel like authentic glimpses of real people behind a performative facade. They remind of the known, if unacknowledged, reality that music films are different kinds of performances to the onstage shows they often document, but are performances nonetheless.

This chapter discusses films that play around with ideas of myth, reality, truth, and performance in direct ways either through their form, content, or both. In essence, this chapter is the book and indeed the music film in microcosm. The works discussed here offer a variety of examples of films where musicians purposely create or add to mythologies of their life and work, or work to undermine them through honesty, stubbornness, or humour. To open the chapter there is an extended look at two films that, taken together, offer one of the most compelling exemplars of the tension between the real and the performative that underpin the music film genre. They are two of the films that most inspired the writing of this book and they are both films about Nick Cave. The films are best discussed and understood together as a tragic life event in between the production of the two films casts such a shadow over the latterly produced film that the intentional artifice of the former becomes more readily understood and visible. To add to the rupture of authenticity they will be discussed in reverse order of their production and release.

'I don't believe in the narrative anymore'[2] – Nick Cave

One More Time with Feeling was directed by Andrew Dominik. Dominik is an Australian filmmaker and a friend and collaborator of Nick Cave's. They first worked together on Dominik's 2007 film *The Assassination of Jesse James by the Coward Robert Ford*. This is important because *One More Time with Feeling* captures Nick Cave during the recording of the 2016 Nick Cave and the Bad Seeds record *Skeleton Tree,* recorded in the wake of the death of Cave's son

---

[2] *One More Time with Feeling* (2016).

Arthur in 2015. Speaking about their collaboration on the film, and on the follow-up *This Much I Know To Be True* (2022), Dominik (2022) says he does the films because Nick asked him. He says, 'these films are not really career decisions [...] it's basically my friend's son died, and he asked me to help'. *One More Time* is structured around performances of songs from the *Skeleton Tree* record in a recording studio purposely designed to capture the performances via an elaborate 3D camera set up. Between performances, Cave, his wife Susie and his collaborator Warren Ellis talk about Arthur, their grief and the art that is being made in the wake of his death. The film almost stumbles upon the performances. It feels as though there is a purer concert film lurking inside this one, as it wends between Cave's reflections on recent events and tries to convey the weight of what he is feeling. The 3D camera is disorienting. It swoops around rooms and people, swallowing and then fleeing its subjects. The result is a woozy, unmoored feeling that perfectly captures the in-articulation of grief that Cave resolutely tries to pin down and share. It is a fearless document of loss, with tenderness and horror entwined, that echoes the songs that Cave has built during his career. In the moment of the film, and since, the distance between Cave and the tenderness and horror collapses.

The film does not explicitly state a correlation between Cave's life and the lyrics that make up *Skeleton Tree*. Cave has written directly about the flow between life and art around this time in his *Red Hand Files* series of letters to fans, and the invitation is there, due to the difficulty of reckoning with the reality of what Cave has suffered, and the desire to relieve the discomfort of that reckoning. The film does this in other ways too, often by drawing attention to the filmmaking process, as if to try and comfort the audience. It's just a film. It's not real. For example, at the outset Cave, tired and reticent, is coaxed by Dominik to redo getting dressed. It is a reminder of the inherent staging necessary in so much music filmmaking and provides a safety net as Cave exhorts 'this is really fucking difficult' and 'I don't know what the chords are' as he tries to find solace and respite in music making. Here is where stark differences between the Cave of the earlier film, discussed shortly, and this one, come into focus. The physicality and demeanour. Here, Cave's grief leaves him looking fragile and hollow, so different to the swagger and mischief of *20,000 Days on Earth* (2014). In one beautiful sequence the editing ensures that Cave is surrounded by collaborators as the song 'Jesus Alone' comes into being. Cave goes from 'I think I'm losing my voice [...] file it under lost things' to gaining command of the song. The editing conveys this by cutting to Warren Ellis, looking stoic, working with the string section, and cutting between different versions of the song being developed.

This section also highlights the importance of Ellis to Cave, as a collaborator and a friend. Here, he is almost physically willing the song into being so that his friend can work. As Cave says of Ellis in voiceover 'look at him holding everything together [...] what would I do without Warren?' It's a moment that is both tender and moving, but also distancing, reminding the audience of the film's construction, placing Cave as observer of the film alongside the audience. There's a freedom and looseness to the form of the film, likely due to how 'incredibly liberating' it was to make, something Dominik (2022) says is possible when 'the movie's not that important'. At one point, just prior to addressing the day and events of Arthur's death, Cave exclaims 'What am I doing this for? I never would have done this', acknowledging the impact of Arthur's death on his creative approach in a way that may have felt trite had it been directly related to the music making. For such a long time, the film captures and discusses creativity and art in the aftermath of tragedy without ever suggesting that the tragedy itself will be discussed directly. It doesn't feel inevitable because the construction of the film feels so responsive to the raw moments of grief and art making that it encounters. When Cave says, profoundly, 'it happened to us, but it happened to him' it feels like there is no distance at all between audience and a moment of pure truth by an artist. It doesn't feel performed, because at this point, by the film's end, we know how little energy Cave has left to perform a version of himself other than the one that tries to get up each day and make music and deal with the fact that his son is dead.

This Nick Cave is very different from the one that ends Iain Forsyth and Jane Pollard's *20,000 Days on Earth* just two years previously, in 2014. The Nick Cave viewed across that film's duration is playful, open and confident. As he says at the start of the film: 'I wake, I write, I eat, I watch TV' and that's what we watch him do, amongst other things which intentionally undermine the confidence and literalism of that utterance, until he flops onto a sofa and 'watches' *Scarface* (1983) while sharing a pizza with his two teenage twin sons, Arthur and Earl. Whilst this scene upon revisiting the film is naturally difficult to watch given what tragically happened to Arthur, the whole film feels different, almost alien when viewed in the light of *One More Time with Feeling*. Cave's struggle to escape his brutal daily reality there is matched here by a refusal to deliver anything that could easily be parsed as true or authentic. There are glimpses of the real here, such as the physical changes that can be detected in Cave when his faux psychiatrist Alain De Botton asks him about his father. In a flash the easy, cavalier facade dissolves into something more considered and thoughtful, more serious. It's a moment where the changes in tone indicate something raw and impactful. What he says following the question doesn't really matter. We already know that it is a question with deep meaning for him.

Elsewhere, where *20,000 Days on Earth* really seems to contain authenticity is in Cave's discussion of art and craft and its role in his life. There is a confidence in how he talks about songwriting and his own career – 'songwriting is about counterpoint', 'it's just shit isn't it, but important shit, for me, at the time', 'the song is heroic because the song confronts death', 'to act on a bad idea is better than not to act at all' – that the thesis of the film emerges as a place for Cave to reflect on and investigate music and creativity. John Scanlan writes how 'Cave represents how age and the repetition of doing it again and again – going to his office and sitting in front of a typewriter – become the core of a disciplined identity' (2022: 253). Biography is touched on – family, growing up, Susie his wife – when there's a direct correlation to what Cave is exploring elsewhere in the film. Shot over the course of writing and recording the album *Push the Sky Away* (2013), the film finds several devices and areas of exploration to provide dynamic visual and structural underpinning to Cave's cheeky and profound philosophical musings. Cave is presented as a character here, driving around his hometown of Brighton, a mercurial taxi driver chatting to collaborators including Ray Winstone and Kylie Minogue, who appear in his 'cab' as if conjured from his mind and are gone just as quickly. Cave visits his own archive, and this excursion into traditional music film territory is where he is most visibly awkward and reticent. And there's the aforementioned sessions with 'therapist' Alain de Botton.

The device of having de Botton talk to Cave is a way of getting traditional music film conventions into the film without it feeling trad or stale. This slight remove, and others including when Cave heads to Warren Ellis's for lunch, a natter, and to drop off taxidermy parakeets, ensure the film can both feel original while also satisfying some audience expectations of a music film. It's a critique and a complicit example simultaneously. The lunch with Warren still manages to feel special, intimate, and revealing, largely because the weirdness of the set-up makes everyone aware of the staging of the film and because they talk about music. They discuss two performances by musical heroes, one witnessed and one retold: Nina Simone[3] and Jerry Lee Lewis. It is a sequence that allows Ellis to showcase his storytelling prowess, to align Cave with the kinds of performers discussed in the anecdotes and to allow him to bear witness to art and music in a context wider than himself, placing himself in that lineage and opening out this film to be more widely about art and creativity and less specifically about Cave. It's a masterful segment and the stories are great. From there, the film moves back to Cave's day, presented as a normal, 'run of the mill' one, but obviously uniquely configured for the film. Audiences are taken back to the studio, dipping in and out of the making of the record, witnessing Cave in the studio, as he is shown later in *One More Time with Feeling* but here more carefree, more able to be playful and profound and pretentious in the same breath.

'Death was there'[4] – Inescapable Truth

If the privilege to be performative and mischievous is evoked in *20,000 Days on Earth* and subsequently unable to be deployed in *One More Time with Feeling*, sometimes that privilege cannot be evoked or deployed for different reasons, or in some cases, at all. If *One More Time with Feeling* tells the story of someone facing the trauma of grief, some music films confront the inescapable truth of a life altered by illness and ill-health and its impact on the physical ability to make music. Sometimes, the truth is that bodily survival is the only concern. Any other type of performance or performativity is rendered obsolete.

In *The Possibilities Are Endless* (2014), the audience follows singer/songwriter Edwyn Collins as he recovers from a debilitating stroke, resulting in both

---

[3] Warren Ellis has since released a book (*Nina Simone's Gum*, Faber 2021) inspired by the chewing gum he took from Nina Simone's piano after the performance discussed here in the film.
[4] *The Possibilities Are Endless* (2014).

significantly reduced motor function and a total loss of memory. The film is slow, delicate, respectful, and beautifully structured. It's a love story and a tale of a place, as well as an observational account of a human recovering from a stroke. The use of archive material in the film does several things. One is to provide a counterpoint to the Edwyn Collins that emerges in the immediate aftermath of the stroke. Collins, the songwriting genius, razor wit and intellectual force becomes a Collins that remembers none of that. Another thing is to provide space for the film to not intrude on Collins' physicality. It takes over twenty minutes to see Collins on screen in the moment of the film's making. Prior to that it is a combination of archive material and a rooting of the film in the landscape of Helmsdale, where Collins and his partner Grace Maxwell live.

The slowness of the film is imperative in feeling respectful but also honouring the uncertainty of the journey. In the film, Collins, as he recovers, writes the lyrics (to an unreleased track) 'looking back is not for me' and so the film does it for him, placing his achievements in the band Orange Juice, or his mega-hit 'A Girl Like You', in context, to ensure they are marked and also to mark time while he tries to recover movement and memory. The filmmakers are genuinely interested in the care story as much as the music story and as much time is given to Grace and her commitment, and their love, as to the music. Their story, and that of Collins' young days as an aspiring musician, is evoked by a poetic short story threaded throughout, in which a young musician writes songs on a bus and falls for a local girl. The young musician is played by Grace and Edwyn's son William. The reality of their story is rendered as quasi-fiction in the film in ways that evoke *20,000 Days on Earth* from the same year, and again extend the story of the film beyond that simply of a musician and his individual journey. As Collins relearns how to read, play guitar, write songs, and sing once again, the film doesn't become excited and frenzied. Instead, it sticks to its course of being about the care, discipline, time, patience, and the hope needed for a human being to reclaim the functions many take for granted. As a result, new music by Collins feels like a blessing, not a relief.

In *The Possibilities Are Endless*, filmmakers follow the recovery of a musician who had already achieved success, recognition and status. Jesse Vile's *Jason Becker: Not Dead Yet* (2012) tells the remarkable story of a musician who faced a life-changing medical event at the very beginning of their career. Unlike Edwyn Collins, the chances of Jason Becker ever being able to recover to a point where a career that remotely resembled the previous, or a dreamed one, were slim to none. And yet. At 19, having just been invited to play guitar for David Lee Roth and following a tour with Marty Friedman from Megadeth, Becker, a prodigious guitar talent who was regarded as generational, was diagnosed with amyotrophic lateral sclerosis (ALS), known in the US as 'Lou Gehrig's disease' after the legendary baseball player. Not only would Becker never play guitar again, but his prognosis was that he would die within two to five years. And yet. The film starts in earnest twenty-two years after that diagnosis, with Becker not just still alive but making music using his eyes, pretty much the only part of his body he can move, using a computer system developed with his father, which the film discusses. *Jason Becker: Not Dead Yet* is a film where the incredible story overwhelms the filmmaking, or indeed any need for the filmmaking to do anything but record and acknowledge.

Formally, the filmmaking is very straightforward, using many techniques from other music films. Interviews, observation, footage of recording and archive material are all present, but the story they tell is what is always front and centre in the minds of the audience. However, in some cases, the deployment of archive material has a specific impact, particularly upon rewatching. The film opens, as many music films do, with home video footage of the artist subject, capturing them in a raw state suggestive of the glory of their later career. Often this kind of early footage can capture a talent that is later rendered bittersweet by a thwarted or misunderstood career. Here, though, it's not society or the times that thwart Becker capitalizing on the unique abilities captured in that early, grainy footage, but his own body. The scale of Becker's story imbues the conventions of music film with a weight that other films deploying them can't access, elevating the filmmaking through emotion that doesn't feel manipulative. Much like *The Possibilities Are Endless*, this is a story of care. The filmmakers present the reality of what is needed to keep Becker alive in terms of medication, sustenance, and labour alongside the community of people, family, and others, who dedicate their life to doing that, with Jason. The hope of the past not resulting in success that felt preordained hangs heavy, and not just in old footage. There's a devastating moment where Jason's mum recalls responding to her son's claim that the success he was starting to have had come too easy – that he had not built any 'character' yet – by telling him: 'you'll get character, bad things will happen to you'. They really did. And yet. As the film ends, he's still alive and still composing.[5]

'He had to be known'[6] – The struggle to be true

In Jeanie Finlay's *The Great Hip Hop Hoax* (2013) and *Orion: The Man Who Would Be King* (2015) the protagonists at the heart of the films face a struggle to achieve their own authentic idea of themselves, instead finding momentary success, recognition, and infamy by taking on personas that are avowedly not how they see themselves or want to achieve success. Finlay's work here, as in *Sound It Out* (2011) – discussed in the chapter on place – is deeply empathetic to the lives of those she encounters, alive or dead, in the case of Orion. She is not interested in judging her characters for the choices they make that take them away from their families, friends, or themselves. If anything, she is interested in judging the structures around these artists that force them to make such life-changing and psychologically damaging choices. *The Great Hip Hoax* tells the story of a Scottish Hip Hop duo, Silibil (Billy Boyd) N' Brains (Gavin Bain) who, following a period of getting no career traction, decide to pretend to be from California only to find all the previously closed industry

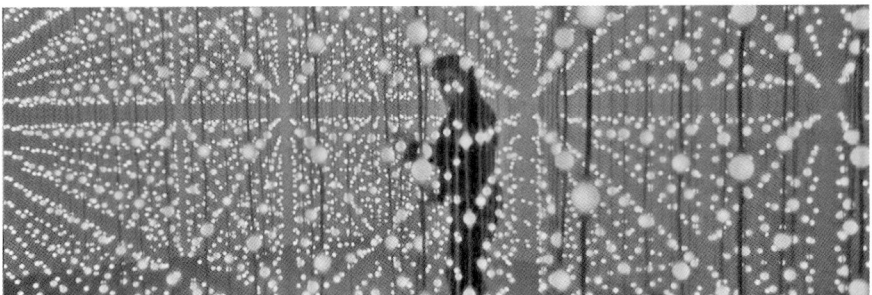

Figure 6.1 Orion: The Man Who Would Be King (dir. Finlay, 2015) © Jeanie Finlay.

---

[5] At the time of writing this book, Jason Becker is still alive and his most recent record, *Triumphant Hearts*, came out in 2018.
[6] *Orion: The Man Who Would Be King* (2015).

doors suddenly open to them. The film sees Bain and Boyd reflecting on their incredible journey but also documents the psychological toll on them and their friendship, caused not only by having to pretend to be someone else twenty-four hours a day, but by having to live in that body and behave in ways that felt antithetical to their personal and musical ethos. As Hermione Hoby (2010) wrote, when discussing the Silibil N' Bains saga, 'nothing is as chimeric as authenticity'.

By treating Silibil N' Brains as people rather than a gimmick, Finlay can unlock aspects of the music industry and the relationship between show business and certain types of personalities in ways that never seem glib. The film discusses mental health, class and regionality, music industry politics, personal compulsions and addiction while never losing sight of the fact that Boyd and Bain's story is also one that is hard to believe and full of vivid and memorable moments. The film includes one of the best uses of animated sequences, a device that's often used but rarely effective, to tell some of the most outlandish stories and as a result they have the effect of both distancing Boyd and Bain from their past while also adding a layer of persona to the material that feels appropriate given the nexus of the story. The fact that so much of the story is fun, in the moment that it happened, means that the sadness in the film – and it is a sad film – never feels maudlin or makes the protagonists pitiful. They are very aware of and own their choices, while remaining critical, as Finlay seems to be in her filmmaking, of a system that is most often arbitrary, whim-based and not rooted in talent but on gimmick, easy marketability and exploitation. When Brains says 'this has got nothing to do with talent' it doesn't feel like bitterness, but a statement of fact about how the industry works and suggests that, deep down, maybe Silibil N' Brains knew this and chose to play along anyway.

The Great Hip Hop Hoax is a vibrant, rollercoaster ride told by people who came out the other side but its central idea – that success in music, even for White male musicians, is often not about talent but performing an uncomfortable role for a baying crowd – a different kind of deal with the devil to Robert Johnson – is shared with Finlay's follow-up film *Orion: The Man Who Would Be King*. *Orion*, however, is more complex, and much sadder. The sadness comes from the fact that Jimmy Ellis never escaped the prison of the persona he took on and died tragically, shot in the chest during a robbery. Complexity comes from that fact that, unlike Silibil N' Brains, the Orion persona was one foisted on Ellis to a significant degree. His deal was one he had much less artistic say in developing. Finlay's skill as a filmmaker is in taking a simple idea – 'let's pretend to be rappers from California' or 'put on a mask and pretend to be Elvis Presley because you sound identical to him' – and spinning out from the instinctively fun premise to darker traumas and conflicts. As with *Hoax,* Finlay doesn't let Ellis the person off the hook. At one point he is described as a 'chauvinist pig' and the revelation of his collected photographic gallery of women's vulvas is disquieting to say the least. However, again, this adds layers of complexity and nuance to the story of a man who just wanted to sing and who eventually got the chance, in the form of a 'despicable gimmick' as one participant describes it.

The gimmick, for the Elvis-soundalike Ellis to wear a mask and costume and be called Orion following Elvis's death, was to suggest to audiences that 'The King' hadn't died but was alive and well in this strange new form. As with Sibilil N' Brains the film allows those still alive to create the portrait of Ellis as someone smart and driven, so surely aware of the ludicrous nature of the proposal, but also as someone seduced by the promises of fame, to do whatever it takes to get a foot in the door. Whereas *Hoax* is exuberant and knowing, *Orion* is more melancholy, and another example, like *Sound It Out,* of Finlay's talent for rooting her films in a specific place where the contours of the geography feel inextricable from the intricacies of the characters' lives. In this case, the American South. As the film moves on and the crowds seeing Eliis perform dwindle as quickly as his record sales, the toll of wearing the mask, something he had to always do contractually in public, becomes oppressive. As one participant notes 'reality doesn't mean anything in showbiz'. There is a richness to Finlay's filmmaking. Despite working in a form, the music film, where the real and authentic is exalted – if as this book attests, rarely evident – she has crafted a body of work that exemplifies how the music industry is built on performance and persona that extracts extreme cost, while showing in *Sound It Out* the real lives of the people who buy the records, go to shows and really are just all about the music.

'I'm gonna fucking put you in hospital'[7] – Unlikeable Subjects

If the artists at the heart of *The Great Hip Hop Hoax* and *Orion: The Man Who Would Be King* are presented as narcissistic, misogynistic or manipulative, they are always presented as complex human beings. Sometimes, however, filmmakers are presented with the difficult task of telling a story of complex personalities with obstruction from the persons in question. The difficult reality that sometimes, talented people are not always nice people is inescapable, often because they spend the duration of the film telling audiences just that. There are two high-profile, differing examples, featuring 'legendary' musicians showing that offstage and off-record they could be incredibly difficult people to live with and be around. The first example here is a very slippery object, *Let's Get Lost* (1988), directed by Bruce Weber, is shot on beautiful black-and-white 16mm film and is a dreamy, poetic evocation of the life of jazz trumpeter, and underrated singer, Chet Baker. Terrence Rafferty (2007) writes that 'it's nominally a documentary [...] but it documents something that only faintly resembles waking reality'. The dreamy mood evokes both the jazz played by Baker but also the heroin addiction that plagued so much of his life and career. It's an example of a celebratory form at odds with critical content and makes the audience question whether talent outweighs behaviour, making it, in many ways, a crucial film for analysis in 2022, the moment of writing this book, where this question is regularly posed in a variety of critical spaces.

One thing that is undeniable in the film is Baker's talent, presented in stunning archive and observational footage. What's also undeniable is his beauty, even as addiction ravaged his face. As he says in the film 'I played for 25 years with just 1 front tooth' and, despite that, he is still visually captivating and magnetic. He looked like a star, and he played like a genius. This may be the reason he had so many wives and children. What's fascinating about *Let's Get Lost* is that the analysis of Baker's life away from music is brutal in its presentation of him as a lousy husband and father and, due to his addiction, a frankly horrible person

---

[7] *Beware of Mr Baker* (2012).

to be around most of the time. He was a man who not only didn't support his family financially he consistently exploited them. This is a film that asks the question about the art versus the artist and presents no equivocal answer. As a result, it is a conflicting and difficult film to watch, but one which is essential and where the answer likely changes as cultures and opinions about that question change also. Weber is clearly fascinated by Baker. His cinematography and pacing aligns the trumpeter with classic jazz iconography; he clearly thinks Baker is 'cool'. He isn't, however, slavish to mythology and is happy for those around Baker, and Baker himself, to undercut that myth and iconography with brutal home truths.

What is it about musicians named Baker? In Jay Bulger's *Beware of Mr Baker* (2012), drummer Ginger Baker, most famously the drummer in rock band Cream, tears into everyone around him, everyone from his past and the filmmaker. He is seemingly determined to wreck any chance the film has of burnishing his legacy. The film opens with Baker attacking the filmmaker in his car when he is informed that Bulger wants to talk to people with whom Baker used to work. The film shows that Ginger and Chet have striking similarities. They are terrible fathers, they are self-destructive and they are regarded as artistic leaders in their field. Whereas Weber is happy for audiences to make their own mind up about Chet, Bulger introduces a meta element to soften the process and try to humanize Ginger through a commentary on the making of the film. Maybe this is an evolution of the music documentary form as much as Bulger's personal approach but, even so, it's one that Ginger treats as a challenge. It is a filmmaking gambit that mostly pays off, leading as it does to a strange relationship between filmmaker and subject that plays like a buddy comedy with Baker cast in the role of the cantankerous elder. This allows an element of sadness to enter the story in a way it never does in *Let's Get Lost,* as Ginger reveals himself to be lonelier and more scared than Chet ever did.

Similar to Weber, Bulger clearly likes Ginger Baker and wants to get to know him. Partly out of respect and partly out of curiosity as to whether the legends of his anger are true or myth. He also wants to try and be the person to track that anger back to its source. Around the interviews Bulger conducts with Baker at his compound in South Africa, Bulger creates a portrait of the drummer from archive footage that leans heavily on Tony Palmer's film, *Ginger in Africa,* screened on the BBC in the early 1970s, following Ginger as he attempts to set up a studio in Nigeria. This incredible footage helps mark Baker out as a maverick and a singular figure. His status as maybe the greatest rock drummer of all time is further bolstered by an array of testimonies to that fact by some of the most illustrious names in rock music, past and present, including his former Cream bandmates. While, thankfully, never proposing a singular cause for Baker's rage, the film does include biographical information that complicates his personality, from the death of his father and the impact of the Blitz to the fact that he always saw himself as a jazz musician, so the adulation in rock music rankled, in a similar vein to Nina Simone's desire to be seen as a classical pianist. As the film moves on, Baker becomes ill, to the point where he can't play the drums and as he says 'I like playing the drums'. It's a simple but powerful truth and in the sequence where Baker is shown playing alongside his jazz heroes including Max Roach, the bitterness of having to play rock music and having to do anything but drum, gives way to glee and a sense of belonging.

A final film worth mentioning in this vein is *David Crosby: Remember My Name* (2019). While not as caustic or confrontational as either of the Baker movies it does, however, see an artist with a reputation for being difficult wrestling with his past. Crosby's honesty regarding the fact that he wasn't a very nice person and alienated pretty much everyone around him, again linked to addiction and problems with managing success, feels powerful because it is presented in such a direct manner in a film that elsewhere charts his career in familiar, mythologizing ways. It's hard to pinpoint what makes the declaration so moving but it most likely comes down to a weariness in Crosby, the culmination of a long, superficially successful but ultimately personally unsatisfying, career, making the film's subtitle feel more like a plea than a demand. Alternatively, it could be due to a sequence in the film that feels unusual and frankly remarkable. The sequence in question is one dedicated to the music of Joni Mitchell. This generosity from Crosby, to give over so much of his own film to celebrating the work of a peer, one without a music film of their own, unsettles both the expectations of a music film and sets his later reckoning quietly in motion. These touches make this film stand out as more than mere self-pitying hagiography. There is a willingness to not wholly follow the template set down, rather to use the opportunity to ensure that Joni Mitchell, an artist who has not received comparable coverage to her male peers, is given much-needed screen time, and to use the platform to apologize and admit something many people probably wished had come in private, years ago.

'Did it get too earnest?'[8] – Humour

There's an overdue reckoning that must occur in *Anvil: The Story of Anvil* (2008) even if it's just admitting that longed-for fame and glory is never going to happen. The film follows the two founding members of the heavy metal band Anvil, still rocking and still trying to reach the level of success achieved by some of the peers with whom they shared the bill in the archive footage that opens the film – such as The Scorpions, Whitesnake and Bon Jovi – from the 1984 Supersonic Festival in Japan. It never happened for Anvil. As Lemmy says early on in the film, success in music is often down to being in the 'right place right time' and Anvil never have been. Yet still they keep touring to ever-dwindling crowds and borrowing money to make a record with legendary producer Chris Tsangarides as they did earlier in their career, in the hope that 'this is the one'. It isn't, though the band do get to have a late hurrah at the film's climax with a big(ish) Japan show that recalls the finale of Rob Reiner's *This Is Spinal Tap* (1984). This isn't the only way the film recalls that mockumentary classic[9] (even ignoring the fact that one of the leads of the film, the drummer, is called Robb Reiner). It is constantly recalling *Tap*, and almost always to the detriment of the story at the film's heart. There are genuinely comic moments due to the likeable and lovingly curmudgeonly relationship between Robb and the band's lead guitarist, and de facto leader, Steve 'Lips' Kudlow, but too often the viewer is left laughing at, rather than with, them.

Beyond the band's music and aesthetic being so closely hewn to Christopher Guest, Michael McKean, and Harry Shearer's (semi)fictional creations the story both follows a very similar arc to much of *Tap* and renders some of the same moments, such as the band recalling writing their first song 'Thumb Hang' together, in such a similar tone that it starts to feel like a pastiche. The central thrust of the film is a disastrous tour – Anvil's taking place in Europe – that is

---

[8] *King Rocker* (2020).
[9] Discussed in the chapter on milestones and innovations.

sad because, unlike Spinal Tap, this is a real band and this quest is real. It's also a funny film, again because of how it presents moments that feel like they could have sprung straight from a spoof of the band. At one point guitarist and singer Steve 'Lips' Kudlow argues with a European venue owner about payment screaming at him 'this place is jam fucking packed'. It isn't. Elsewhere there are some attempts to capture Lips' and Robb's philosophies with nonsensical aphorisms such as 'it could never be worse than it is' left hanging in the air à la Nigel Tufnel. As discussed in the milestones and innovations chapter *This Is Spinal Tap* casts a long shadow over music films that have come in its wake but the decision to adhere so closely to its tone, events and comedy here feels odd, especially as the timing of Anvil's emergence in the early 1980s makes them a prime candidate for the band that Guest et al based their characters on. There's no denying that Lips and Robb's decision to keep going, making music and believing in themselves is heart-warming but the realities of that decision, particularly economically, can only ever be alluded to or glimpsed as their story struggles against a visit to Stonehenge and amps that literally go up to eleven.

Whereas much of the humour in *Anvil* comes from the way the career and inter-personal relationship of Lips and Robb are framed, the humour in *Bros: After the Screaming Stops* (2018) comes from the two Goss brothers at the centre of the film in a different, but related, way. If there are occasional faux-philosophical soundbites from the Anvil members, in this film Matt and Luke Goss are constantly espousing their philosophies on music and life. As in *Anvil*, the statements are nonsensical but the difference here is that the brothers seem to be in on the joke, amplifying the tensions at the heart of their collaboration for comic effect, or at least leading the viewer to the question, 'they must be aware of what they sound like, surely?'. The film buys into the mythical idea of the precocious pop star in such an overt way that it feels almost entirely staged for effect. The clichés are endless and the tension that builds as the brothers reunite after decades apart for a huge show at London's O2 feels stage managed because how could film of a show that is a disaster of the scale alluded to in the build-up ever be sanctioned for release by those involved? The feeling that this is all a performance and that the two lead performers are happy to come across as facile, naive, pretentious, and prone to tantrums takes the anxiety of out watching the film and allows the viewer to revel in the performativity.

Figure 6.2 King Rocker (dir. Cumming, 2020) © Michael Cumming.

Whenever the narrator and guide of *King Rocker* (2020), comedian Stewart Lee, is in danger of bringing cliché or a familiar music film convention into the conversation the film's subject, Robert Lloyd of the Prefects and the Nightingales, points it out brusquely and the film stops to acknowledge what it is doing. Lee has discussed how his initial idea for a film about Lloyd was to do something like *Anvil,* an idea that Lloyd dismissed as he didn't want to people to think of his band and music as a joke. Instead, the film is constantly questioning what it is and what it is doing in ways that are hilarious and formally invigorating. Lee and the director Cumming knew they didn't want the film to contain the 'usual talking heads' and, as there is very little archive of Lloyd's musical incarnations earliest days, the film resorts to a variety of techniques to tell its story. The story is one very close to Anvil's; Lloyd has been consistently making music, with little fanfare, since forming the Prefects after seeing the Ramones in London in the mid-1970s. The Ramones manager, Danny Fields, is in the film and in photos he shares of the Ramones' famous London gigs, a young Lloyd can be seen loitering with intent in the background. It's a reliable piece of historical information in a film that is surprisingly lacking in them and all the better for it. Lloyd is an unreliable narrator, misremembering (wilfully or otherwise) the events of his life and he is challenged on his memory throughout, by Lee but also by the people he references who turn up to give their version of events.

Figures such as comedian Frank Skinner, musician Roger Taylor of Duran Duran and actor Robin Askwith turn up throughout to contradict events. Lloyd and Cumming are less interested in the facts than they are in crafting a portrait of Lloyd, celebrating his craft and resilience and ensuring that the film is as interesting formally as its subject's personality. The film makes up for its lack of archive with some of the best use of animation in music films and the film traces Lloyd's history, alongside that of a rare urban sculpture of King Kong, by traversing place and space and basing the storytelling around the rapport and mutual respect between Lloyd and fan and peer Lee. The constant referencing of the form as the film progresses is recognizable from Lee's work as a stand-up comedian interested in the mechanics of his form as part of his routines, but what stops the film veering into outright pretension is its blend of humour and the fact that its dialogue with music films that have preceded it is one of love and respect, but also healthy suspicion. The film at times follows Lloyd's latest, and most stable, Nightingales line-up. It's not tied to a specific tour or recording of a specific album because this band is always working. They are pragmatic, DIY, working artists. 'Did it get too earnest?' Lloyd ponders of something he says at one point. He needn't worry, he seems as incapable of earnestness as the film does. The film is more human and touching because of that, as well as one of the best commentaries on music films ever made.[10]

'Aren't we lucky?'[11] – 'Legends'

Earnestness is a word that is often associated with the band U2. *U2: Rattle and Hum* (1988), a film following the band on their American tour following the

---

[10] I interviewed Lee and Cumming for the Quietus during the making of the film. See https://thequietus.com/articles/26686-king-rocker-the-nightingales-film-michael-cumming-stewart-lee-interview and then again (with Lloyd in attendance this time) when the film was released. Available at: https://thequietus.com/articles/29527-film-king-rocker-stewart-lee-michael-cumming-robert-lloyd.

[11] *Cobain: Montage of Heck* (2015).

release of the hugely successful album *The Joshua Tree* makes no effort to rebuke that accusation or association. If anything, the film feels like a manifesto of earnestness, such are the interviews the band give in their Dublin rehearsal space that frame the road footage and frontman Bono's regular on-stage proselytization. Adrian Wootton describes the film as 'a conscious (and mythical attempt to capture the group's on-stage dynamic, while also suggesting the vital, musically self-exploratory role [U2] have set for themselves' (1988: 354). The film feels like a cinematic equivalent of *The Joshua Tree*, a bold statement that presents the U2 brand and its epic scope to the world. The film is a blend of black-and-white and colour footage. The colour footage captures the band as they move to outdoor stadium venues, while the black-and-white captures them indoors as well as backstage and on the road. Both forms are shot by leading cinematographers Robert Brinkman (black and white) and Jordan Cronenworth (colour) and the effect of the band's progression from indoor arena band and decent success to global stardom and stadium-band status feels undeniable in that simple formal shift between shooting formats. Elsewhere the message is, mostly, similarly controlled and measured as the film uses black-and-white to ensure the film hits the music film notes familiar from *Dont Look Back* onwards. There are press junkets and famous guests hanging around. There is a visit to Graceland that recalls *Spinal Tap*, obviously, though there is more hubris here as Bono persuades the steward to let drummer Larry Mullen Jr touch the Harley Davidson that is normally off limits.

The concert footage largely follows the *Stop Making Sense* template of eschewing shots of fans, and it feels like a compilation of moments from iconic music films alongside moments that attempt to assert the uniqueness of the band. However, as with many music films, the moments that stand out are those that capture something unique that is at odds with the film's overall agenda. For example, one of the most spellbinding musical moments doesn't really feature the band but instead captures the Harlem gospel choir they work with to record a new version of their hit single 'I Still Haven't Found What I Am Looking For', taking the song to beautiful new sonic places. All while drummer Larry Mullen Jr sits stoic, nonplussed in a shot that feels weirdly incongruous to the moment at hand. Later in the film there is footage of a free outdoor show in San Francisco where Bono asserts his rebellious rock star credentials by spraying graffiti under a bridge adjacent to the impromptu stage.

His powerful, philosophical, world-changing slogan? 'Rock N Roll stops the traffic'. Wootton writes how 'the material seems deliberately chosen to reinforce U2's political attitudes' (1988: 354). It feels, yes, too earnest, and takes a supposedly impromptu moment and reveals the strategy and control at the heart of the band's performance and public presence. However, there is a moment of genuine emotion and heart when the band take the stage following news of an IRA attack in Enniskillen. Bono's subsequent monologue is raw, unrehearsed, and personal. As with Bob Dylan's tiredness, discussed earlier this chapter, this feels like the real Bono and it's exhilarating in its fleeting authenticity and the performance of the song 'Sunday Bloody Sunday' that follows is elevated as a result.

There are, perhaps unsurprisingly, no such slippages into the real in *Madonna: Truth or Dare* (1991), released in the UK as *In Bed with Madonna*. There is never a moment, on stage or off, where Madonna doesn't seem completely aware of or in control of what she is doing for the cameras. What is fascinating about this film, and potentially one of the reasons that it is one of the most well-documented music films, is what Madonna wants to and is happy revealing about herself and her work as she tours the world. The film is full of the banality of touring, risqué moments presented as naughty and shocking, obsessive creative and organizational control, defiance in the face of outrage and a contradictory personality that is one minute demure and in thrall to the men in her life and in the next, defiantly individual and distanced from everyone. Jonathan Romney writes that 'once again, backstage *is* a stage. Instead of the star admitting us into her privacy, elements of the private life are exposed and brought under her rigorous control, as performance' (1995: 90). Romney has written of the backstage area as a performance space and this is felt across the majority of music films, as the introduction to this book discusses. However, it's maybe never more prominent than here. The film is a complicated representation, capturing a global star at the apex of their global fame. As time has moved on since the film's release the sequence revolving around Madonna's onstage performance of 'Like a Virgin', which gets her into trouble with the Vatican and the Canadian police, stands out for its singular, bravura provocation. Her refusal to change her act and the clearly provocative masturbatory performance raise the question of who is doing this kind of work in a pop space now and, realistically, who else has ever done it to this degree with this balance of cheek and craft?

There is a danger and an energy to the stage performance of this, and of 'Oh Father', which sees Madonna performing intimacy with a Black priest on an altar, that is missing from the supposedly outrageous backstage antics of Madonna flashing her breasts at the camera or performing fellatio on a bottle. The sense throughout though, as Madonna talks in voiceover about her feelings regarding family, crew, performing and her dead Mother – the latter accompanied by a music video-esque sequence where she visits her mother's grave to the sounds of her song 'Promise to Try' – is that Madonna knows this and is presenting exactly what she wants to present. There are so many formal elements to the film, but they feel less like paying homage to music films of the past and more like a female artist trying to find the form that is appropriate to a female global star. Writing about Madonna, Stuart Jeffries says 'the star is always a sacrificial victim, exchanging privacy for fame, and allowing the public and the media to confuse her personae with her real identity' (2021: 175). Watching Madonna in *Truth or Dare* gives a slightly distinct feeling, that she is acutely aware of what is at stake and so ruthlessly controls the narrative to protect herself from feeling vulnerable; 'let the fans and media be confused, this is who I chose to be'. If *Madonna: Truth or Dare* feels like the first significant film about a female pop star driven by that star, it is. The controlled candidness, the performance of pain, the quiet reflections on love and family, the assertion of creative dominance are all present here as they are in the films about women pop stars discussed in the chapter on films about women in this book. Madonna pioneered so much in pop music, not just for women, but she also pioneered cinematic representations about women in pop in ways still being felt 30 years on.

Madonna has always been supremely in control of how her legacy is perceived, sometimes in ways that confound critics and fans, of which *Truth or Dare* is cinematic proof. Another legacy that has been supremely controlled is that of Kurt Cobain whose band Nirvana released their most famous record *Nevermind* the same year as *Truth or Dare*, 1991.[12] Cobain died in 1994 and since then that legacy has been controlled by his wife Courtney Love and, to a

---

[12] It is kinda mad to think, looking back, that *Nevermind* and Madonna's *Blond Ambition* tour existed in the world concurrently, they feel tied to such separate, distinct eras.

lesser extent, his former band mate Krist Novoselic. Part of the ongoing legacy project is the film *Cobain: Montage of Heck* (2015) – the title taken from an early experimental mix tape Cobain made – which takes the writer and musician's audio, writing and drawing archives and animates them, seeking to reveal a hitherto unseen aspect of the legend's life. The film is lovingly controlled, seeking to reveal Cobain's complexity and uniqueness, but it always feels controlled. Participants come into the story when they came into Kurt's story. So, family, then Krist, then Courtney. The control is evident in the limited number of participants interviewed and thus entrusted to Kurt's legacy. The most notable absentee is Cobain's other Nirvana band mate Dave Grohl.[13] His absence extends theories of his conflict with Love over the handling of Cobain's legacy and confirms her role in the control of the material shared and the structure of this music film. If Love's control of the overall project is unsurprising, some of the material she chooses to share is surprising. The sharing of Kurt's creativity in the years that led to Nirvana being formed and breaking through is unsurprising as his creativity is evident in the music that followed him through his life.

It's engaging and rewarding to bear witness to but doesn't feel revelatory. What feels revelatory is the access to home video footage of Kurt and Courtney's life together as addicts and young parents to their daughter Frances – interestingly also one of the film's producers – for how it portrays them both. The footage is accompanied by Love's honest reflection on that time and their – but mostly her – behaviour. It feels like Love is taking the opportunity to address her own image and perceptions of herself within a story about Cobain but not in an opportunistic way. This is down to how unflattering and sometimes downright negligent the footage portrays them to be as parents to a baby. It takes an area of Cobain's life that was assumed and pontificated on by critics and outsiders and opens it up, revealing some ugly truths but also moments of fragility and beauty and reinforcing a narrative about his life as a troubled person, an addict, that ran throughout his life. It creates a continuity that feels resonant, coherent, and recognizable, even if the film never feels any less than ironclad in the narrative it presents. However, while the film strives to

---

[13] There are conflicting narratives that Grohl was unavailable to be interviewed for the film and that Morgen shot interviews and decided not to include them.

be definitive and sealed off, one absence that is felt due to the length of time devoted to sharing incredibly intimate home movie footage of Kurt, Courtney, and Frances[14] is that of the person who shot that footage. So much of it is clearly shot by a third party who feels like a ghostly presence in a film where those present on screen are so clearly defined.[15] Another reminder that you can never retain complete control of what is felt when watching a film, even one where you are the direct arbiter of a legacy and legend.

'Us who are just nobodies'[16] – Concluding thoughts and *Leaving Neverland*

In the years following the suppression of films about the Rolling Stones (*Cocksucker Blues*) and Bob Dylan (*Eat the Document*) by the artists because they felt they didn't portray them how they wanted – following on from films that showed them in a variety of lights respectively – artists have gained more and more control over cinematic output. To the point that it would be fair to label these films as only ever performances of persona or brand with 'real' or 'authentic' moments at a minimum. This is largely why these films have been branded for 'fans only' for decades, as if they have nothing to offer a wider audience who isn't buying (into) the music. A different way to consider these films, and that is the emphasis of this chapter, is to look at what they choose to show and why and how these choices, which often don't do the work the artists intended, impact viewer understandings of the artistic process and popular music as a form. This chapter has discussed a range of examples along this spectrum from films where the real is inescapable, where it comes clashing against the artificial as in the films about Nick Cave – and where formal and content choices are interesting in how they chose to tell the story of their subjects. The three films discussed at the end of the chapter, focusing on pop music 'legends' are exemplars of how artists control image and legacy, serving

---

[14] At one point, Love flashes the camera à la Madonna in *Truth or Dare*.
[15] This footage was shot by Hole guitarist and friend of Kurt and Courtney Eric Erlandson. Available at: https://eu.usatoday.com/story/life/music/2015/04/23/brett-morgen-kurt-cobain-montage-of-heck/26152349/
[16] *Leaving Neverland* (2019).

up cinematic output that they hope will become part of the definitive narrative or at least provide a subjective statement of artistic, creative, or political intent. if nothing else, they have all become renowned and infamous.

To close this chapter, there will be discussion of a film that slowly and methodically dismantles the legacy of an artist, one holding the most legendary status of all the artists discussed so far, Michael Jackson. Towards the end of *Leaving Neverland* (2019), a two-part television documentary that feels like a singular object with an emotionally necessary interval, Stephanie Safechuck, the mother of James 'Jimmy' Safechuck, one of two young men recounting their experience of abuse at the hands of Michael Jackson, says 'I was so happy he'd died'. The relief is palpable but is inseparable from the guilt of what happened to her son and her role in it. It's a complicated statement at the end of a film that devastatingly captures the complexity of child abuse, a complexity made more extraordinary because the abuser was the most famous musician on the planet. One of the most famous people, period. *Leaving Neverland* is an austere work that focuses on in-depth on camera testimony from Jimmy Safechuck and fellow abuse victim Wade Roberts, as well as family members, as they tell the story of not just what happened and how, but its crushing legacies. Formally, the film uses archive footage for context, usually as events are reported in the interviews. The film follows a chronological timeline and the most stylistic intervention, the only one really, is the use of drone footage over the Neverland ranch that creates a feeling that is sombre, macabre and voyeuristic, adding discomfort to an already uncomfortable story. That discomfort is a key part of what the film is aiming to achieve. While there is no doubt that the blame lay with Jackson, the families must reckon with their own culpability as the events are laid out in a row that stretches across a vast amount of time and they reflect on opportunities for intervention.

Culpability is also expected from the viewer in terms of excusing or ignoring claims against Jackson through a process of mythologizing that is still going on in certain quarters of his fan base. Even then it's not a simple accusation towards passive fans and consumers but part of a tapestry of complexities in the cases of the two men who came forward and shared their story and the others suggested as victims who have yet to find the courage to do the same.[17]

---

[17] The film also makes clear why that may never happen via the cataloguing of Jackson's deep and systematic manipulations.

What the film gives to Jackson's victims most clearly is time. The accusation that such a long running time – the film is around four hours long over its two parts – is an excuse to gratuitously labour on the intricacies of the abuse is offset by the respect afforded the victims via time and minimal interference in their recounting of the horrific events of their childhood. Jackson's death clearly made it possible for them to see some escape from their trauma and the film allows them to state their experiences without a phone call from Jackson or his people, something the film details as happening a lot as court cases against him grew. The depth of their trauma and the horror of their experiences ensure that any viewer who endures the discomfort of the film – a minimal discomfort compared to the victims' lives – will likely be unable to regard Jackson in the same light, ever again. This is a dismantling of a legend that forever changes how other cinematic and audio/visual representations of their work will be encountered.[18] Here the real is inescapable but, unlike the hope of films such as *Jason Becker: Not Dead Yet* or *The Possibilities Are Endless,* any hope here is smaller and rooted far, far away from music or musicians.

---

[18] I hope that a film is made one day of Jackson's complicated relationship to Blackness and the Black community, a complexity beautifully wrestled with by Greg Tate when Jackson died. Available at: www.villagevoice.com/2009/07/01/michael-jackson-the-man-in-our-mirror/

7

'Walk on stage and fucking 'ave it'[1] – Concert and Tour Films

Leaving the chapter on concert and tour films to the end of the book serves a dual function. It ends the book with a series of films that are, in the main, celebratory, capturing in a variety of ways why audiences are often drawn to music films: namely, to see musicians perform. The other function is to suggest another, different, next book. There could and should be a book on concert and tour films that defines and discusses them as their own definite object. They are connected to music documentaries and, of course, are documents of music, but they also have their own set of conventions, aesthetics, formal structures and sets of meanings and contexts. They are, in the words of Wim Wenders, films that deal with 'a certain period of time and, to a greater or lesser degree, with the history and experiences of the viewer' (1991: 64). Tour films, as will be discussed later in the chapter, have their own conventions and rhythms, taking audiences backstage and on the road between venues, including much of what is common in music documentary such as rehearsal and press work but always and only as part of an event, the tour. Wider context is hinted at through archive or interview but this almost always ruptures the hermeticism of the event at hand. Additionally, concert films, even more so than documentaries, are regarded as fan documents, for those who were there or wish they were. This does the best and most interesting of them a disservice and Thomas F Cohen does brilliant work in extrapolating what is of wider, deeper interest in films documenting performance in his book *Playing to the Camera* (2012).

---

[1] *Lord Don't Slow Me Down* (2007).

Figure 7.1 Be Pure. Be Vigilant. Behave (dir. Evans, 2019) © Manic Street Preachers/ Kieran Evans.

To discuss some of the things that concert films do, and how different ambitions can collide in fascinating ways, this chapter starts with an analysis of Kieran Evans' 2019 capturing of the Manic Street Preachers' anniversary tour, in 2014, where they played their famous 1994 album *The Holy Bible* in full. *Be Pure. Be Vigilant. Behave* is a visceral document. Filmed entirely by Evans, who recorded each night on the tour from a different vantage point, the film achieves the oft-desired, but rarely achieved, result of putting the cinema audience 'there' with the band and the fans.[2] Shot by one person, mostly close to the action, be it on stage or in the crowd, there is a resultant intimacy that is deeply felt. There are messy zooms, pans and whips and the action is cut frenetically. At just over an hour the intensity doesn't let up. The harsh, relentless visual style reflects the harsh, relentless collection of music and lyrics that is *The Holy Bible*. There are very few on-stage pleasantries from the band. This is a serious record, taken seriously, and the intensity is maintained by Evans' choice to intercut each song with stroboscopic inter-titles that announce the next song via a snippet of a lyric repeated in huge font at great speed.

---

[2] I'm aware that audiences can't actually 'be there' but this film gets closer than nearly any other at conveying a sense of what it was like to be there in a way that goes beyond normal representations in concert films.

What the above formal approach to the film does is capture the record that is being played, that at the time of the performances was twenty years old, as well as the event of that playing. What is also present in the film is the time that has passed between the recording and the (re)playing. Knowledge of the difficult context within which the album was recorded and the subsequent disappearance of band member Richey Edwards – towards the end of the film there are lovely tributes to him from both band and fans – helps explain why this concert film is so meaningful to fans. However, without that context, there are still moments of strange, real joy and meaning that can be gleaned. While trying to capture something of the brutality and anger in the record, the film also never tries to pretend it is not twenty years on from its recording. The band are older, the difference between singer James Dean Bradfield's ability to capture the ferocious speed and high notes of the album's songs, particularly 'Faster', is palpable.[3] He can't keep up and can't hit the same practical highs. The distance travelled is undeniable. The same is true for the audience. The film gives the fans time and space, capturing the rapture but also the catharsis of celebrating this record, Richey's life, and their own lives as soundtracked by this music. The thrill of hearing fans singing lines such as 'we all are of walking abortion' and 'I wanna die in the summertime' with such joy and exhilarating catharsis are moments of delightful incongruity that are central to the magic of a rewarding concert film.

'I need another pair of pants'[4] – Some Classics

Fans play a complicated role in concert films. As discussed earlier, Jonathan Demme's self-proclaimed 'performance film', one of the most famous examples of the genre, *Stop Making Sense* (1984), excludes the concert audience for nearly the whole film. DA Pennebaker and Chris Hegedus's *Depeche Mode: 101* (1989) marks a turning point in fan representation where they move from being conceived of en-masse with intermittent talking heads to agents of the narrative with suggested complex inner lives and back stories. In early examples of the

---

[3] Cohen (2012) argues that on stage is where an artist is their most authentic self and this film has moments where that feels resonant, notably in James Dean Bradfield's battles with his younger singing self.
[4] *Elvis: That's the Way It Is* (1970).

concert film the fan is firmly in the former camp and in maybe the most famous concert film of all time, or certainly right at the top of the list, *Woodstock* (1970), they are represented as a unified organism, a potent collective symbol of the utopian potentialities of 1960s America. There's little to write on *Woodstock* that hasn't been covered in excellent depth and prose elsewhere. It was a box office smash. It was very influential, owing to its innovative (for the time) use of split screen. It was edited by Martin Scorsese who approached the edit by treating each performance individually, crafting a rhythm and editing style unique to each performer, with the contextual narrative of the staging and the local impact also having its own arc and flow. It is interesting to think of *Woodstock* while writing about it from the vantage point of 2022, a time when content is king and media forms are more slippery than ever. The introduction to this book talks about music films as messy objects. *Woodstock* is an excellent example of this in a literal sense, as the film has been recut and reissued several times since its initial theatrical release. Just as everyone who went experienced their own unique festival experience, so audiences now have their own unique cinematic *Woodstock*. One of the legacies of *Woodstock* is that it is seen by many as the first concert film, which it is not. That honour goes to the film *Concert Magic* from 1948, featuring a performance by Yehudi Menuhin. *Woodstock* isn't even the first pop concert film. Several preceded it, including *The T.A.M.I Show* (1964) featuring performers including the Beach Boys, Marvin Gaye and the Supremes, which has seen its critical standing rise since being made available widely thanks to a home release in 2010 via the boutique label The Shout Factory.

With that in mind, a note here on Murray Lerner's *Festival* (1967), which collects footage shot at the Newport Folk Festival between 1963 and 1966. The film is a beautifully shot collection of performances of emerging and established stars. Most famously it captures Bob Dylan in transition from 'folk' to 'rock' and such is the power of the footage that Martin Scorsese draws on it heavily in his account of Dylan's early life and ascent to cultural zenith in *No Direction Home* (2005). The footage of artists including Dylan, Joan Baez, Odetta and Howlin' Wolf is exceptional. The sound and image quality is some of the best in the concert film oeuvre. What marks *Festival* out though, in a way that is different to Lerner's other work such as *Listening to You: The Who at the Isle of Wight 1970* (1998), conceived for television, is how it reaches out beyond documentation to commentary in small ways. One older attendee's pronouncement of 'everyone gathering together to be a non-conformist' stands as a defining critical statement of the 1960s youth generation and its failed ideals. Elsewhere, the film grapples with the complexity of race, seeking to honour the role of 'negro' performers at a festival that was accused of presenting the notion that old, American music was a purely White phenomenon. Beyond the excellent performances, including the Staple Singers in a wonderful gospel segment, the film doesn't really know how to do this without coming across as awkward, but it's still commendable that it tries.

DA Pennebaker's *Monterey Pop* (1968) also precedes *Woodstock* and is a key document of the late 1960s American period known as the hippie or flower power era and, while it doesn't have *Woodstock*'s (or indeed 'Woodstock's) epic zeitgeist-capturing singularity, it remains a fascinating document of the period and one that contains positive and negative elements in terms of representation and focus as well as some of the most famous and iconic performance sequences captured on film. The film is similar in tone and feel to Les Blank's short documentary of the first Los Angeles love-in *God Respects Us When We Work, But Loves Us When We Dance*, also from 1968, in that it follows the crowd as they spend time at the event and moves from artist to artist and surrounding moment to moment without haste, conveying a sense of the 'being in the moment' that is crucial to perceptions of the hippie culture. As Dave Saunders notes, Pennebaker likes to linger on shots of female concert goers, providing images of young women with flowers in their hair that would become synonymous with the era and its 'free love' evocations, resulting in a 'slightly insalubrious, voyeuristic and highly masculine' (2007: 87) experience. There's a similarly dated but more overtly poor taste moment when a shot of Mama Cass of the band the Mamas and Papas is seen enjoying a performance while the soundtrack resounds with the line 'No-one's getting fat'. It feels like a misjudgement, given Cass's noted battles with her weight and self-image.

The above elements are part of the time capsule qualities of the concert film and evidence of how rooted in a specific moment they can feel decades after the fact. Equally though, along with moments that do not age well, the film has sequences that capture performances and performers that feel as exciting, daring, fresh and unique as ever, despite time barrelling away from the moments the film captures. When thinking of Jimi Hendrix one of the first images that comes to mind is him on his knees as his guitar flames away in front of him and this film is the moment where that legendary immolation entered the public consciousness, moving it from myth to event. Similarly, rumours of The Who's destructive tendencies were legendary; one of the most thrilling sequences in *Monterey Pop* is the sight of guitarist Pete Townsend in a frenzy, on a warpath of destruction on the festival's tiny stage, and a flurry of stagehands scrambling around trying to protect the equipment of other bands from his ire. Rewatching *Monterey Pop* is a chance to put these images, so often considered in abstract or witnessed fragmentarily on YouTube, in their original context, as part of a freewheeling document of a moment in time that brought together a disparate array of artists of different races and nationalities in a utopian experiment. The bitterness that the experiment was a failure is offset slightly by the innocence captured, most potently in the sight of young musicians such as Cass and Janis Joplin enjoying the music of their peers from the crowd. Both would die not long after, both aged only 27.[5]

One of the thrilling elements of *Monterey Pop* is how open it is to potential futures of inclusion and equality. Performances of Black music by White performers is offset by Otis Redding's electric set delivered to the largely White audience. There's also a joy in images of the same audience rapt as Indian musician Ravi Shankar dives into an extended raga, as well as a moment of good-natured communal embarrassment as the crowd responds with deep love and applause only to be told that what Shankar and his peers had been doing was merely tuning up. These potentialities are not present in a film that exists at the opposite end of the spectrum from not only *Monterey Pop* but pretty much any concert film: *Pink Floyd: Live at Pompeii* (1972). Like other films mentioned in this section, *Woodstock* and later *Bird on a Wire* (2010), this film exists in a variety of forms and versions. It also suffered production constraints including footage that didn't come out. Ultimately, as a concert film, it always has and likely always will stand out as one recorded without an audience present. Or at least a traditional audience, as the sound team and roadies are present, watching on as the band perform in an empty amphitheatre in the deserted Roman city of Pompeii. The director, Adrian Maben, has always described the film as a conceptual piece as opposed to 'just' a concert film.

---

[5] Joplin and Cass both died within six years of the film's release, in 1970 and 1974 respectively, and the footage here of Joplin is the best captured of her performing.

There's that justifier again, as discussed in the introduction. The editing of the band performing in conjunction with busts and statues of Roman Gods, surviving or preserved following the eruption of Mount Vesuvius in 79CE as well as slow motion inserts of the band strolling across the Volcanic wasteland is direct in its intention to create and preserve a Godlike status for these musicians in the minds of audiences. Kevin Holm-Hudson writes how the film 'can be regarded as an attempt to make a concert movie with 'art film' sensibilities' (2015: 50). The grandiosity and (self)reverence is in keeping with Pink Floyd around the time of recording and releasing their most successful record, *Dark Side of the Moon* (1973).[6] This weirdness is heightened by the live performance of the song 'Mademoiselle Nobbs' featuring Rick Wakeman's dog on vocals. For a short moment the grandeur and epic scope of the setting and the music is brought in close, as the camera and the band gather round the performing canine as he howls along in tune to the song's harmonica melody.

DA Pennebaker pops up yet again with his 1979 film of David Bowie's final show as Ziggy Stardust, *Ziggy Stardust and the Spiders from Mars*, capturing a star performer at a peak of their powers, a performer for whom the epithets strange, hypnotic and unique ring particularly true. Pennebaker's film is a consummate concert film. It doesn't necessarily move the genre forward, but it doesn't put a foot wrong in terms of capturing the moment.[7] The positions of the camera team, the footage they capture individually and collectively and the way the material is edited is masterful. There are, of course, elements that make it stand out, not least because it captures the moment when Bowie, as Ziggy, informs the crowd that they've just witnessed the final show by the Spiders of Mars. The moment comes at the end of the performance with one song left for the audience to process the information. The song is, aptly, 'Rock 'n' Roll Suicide'. The sense the film conveys is that the audience present didn't hear, or register, the news that famously spread following the show and sent shockwaves through the British music scene. By the time the film was released, six years after the show, Bowie had transformed into various something elses and the

---

[6] In one version of the film, the live performance of earlier songs is juxtaposed with footage of the band in the studio recording this album.
[7] Even if some people have criticized the film for being underlit and murky, but again if the approach is taken to feel rather than learn, as discussed in the chapter on truth and myth, the experience works beautifully.

initial shock of the 1973 Hammersmith Odeon show had subsided. As an artefact containing a memorable declaration, the film is often viewed for clues as to the reasons the announcement was made but, at least in the film Pennebaker cut together, clues are hard to discern.

The band are musically tight and physically loose. They are friendly and at ease with each other on stage, the relationship between Bowie and his lead guitarist Mick Ronson captured in intimate detail through close ups, at a time when the pair were courting controversy in similar ways on national television via their very close performance of 'Starman' on BBC's Top of the Pops in 1972. There's a relaxed atmosphere on stage, with Bowie in total control of the performance. The film also includes numerous backstage interludes capturing Bowie before the show putting his make up on and darting off for outfit changes (and what outfits they are). During these moments Bowie appears relaxed and focused but also in charge, joking (maybe) with the make-up artist that she can't know anything about make up because she's a woman. It's a remarkable document of an artist at their peak. Because the conventions of the concert film and indeed the music film were still being established in the early 1970s, Bowie appears happy to be seen at ease and in control, as if it's effortless and natural to do what he does, in a way that has come to be seen as crude. Performing for large adoring crowds must be seen as labour and physically intensive, gruelling and draining, with the artist expending every ounce of themselves on the stage. Not here. Not Bowie. Indeed, here it's the crowd showing the effects of exertion. As John Scanlan notes 'the audience is glimpsed in various stages of ecstasy – heaving and writing and sobbing, with hands thrusting out to try to touch the object of their devotion' (2022: 162). Part of the magic of the film is the blend of footage that is measured, up close, controlled with footage shot from the throng of the crowd giving it a bootleg, cameras-smuggled-in feel, capturing an artist from what feels like two different perspectives, symbiotic in their reverence.

It is widely regarded that the television special *Elvis: '68 Comeback Special* (1968) captures Elvis Presley at the height of his performing powers, his live peak, but 1970s *Elvis: That's the Way It Is,* sits closely behind it.[8] Similar to

---

[8] If not alongside it in the restored form the film took when re-released in 2001 with more rehearsal and on-stage performance included. Another concert film that can't sit still and just be.

Pennebaker's *Ziggy Stardust*, as the decades progress, the sense of uniqueness of certain performers captured on celluloid grows and it feels more and more incredible to travel back in time and see them performing for adoring audiences with a blend of natural talent and laser focus and discipline. Shot over several performances in the summer of 1970 during Presley's return to regular live performance following years of starring in movies, the film follows the star, his band and singers as they prepare for the shows at MGM studios in Culver City and Las Vegas. After this, the film settles into a compendium of performances from different shows at the International Hotel in Las Vegas. There's also intimate footage of Presley in his hotel room with his entourage and guests including Cary Grant and Sammy Davis Jr mingling backstage. These elements are interesting as curios but where the film really excels is in how it captures Presley as both a performer and a band leader. The restored version of the film works hard to establish Presley as the latter, knowing that he is commonly only ever considered as the former.

In rehearsal footage prior to the shows, Presley is shown working closely with his band, listening to records of songs to cover and working out arrangements with them. At times, the editing here uses crossfades, usually reserved for traversing a passage of time but here used to move the viewer close, softly and quietly, to Presley as he works out the vocal arrangements and dramatic renderings of songs. The film focuses on the development of Presley's version of the Bee Gees' 'Words'; how he plans to sing it and how he wants it performed. The first stage is shown in rehearsal at MGM, before returning, evolved, more fully realized in a rehearsal at the International Hotel. As the film nears the moment of performance, as the live audience files into the ballroom, Elvis admits 'it starts to get tense around this time' and admits to worrying about forgetting the words. This glimpse of the icon as human feels exhilarating, especially as all that nervousness is obliterated within the opening bars of 'That's All Right Mama' as he strides on to the stage in a trademark white suit. If the sight of him leaving the stage to kiss multiple women in the crowd during 'Love Me Tender' feels unlikely to be deemed acceptable by performers now, the extended, emotional and scintillating performance of 'Suspicious Minds' remains a glimpse of a pop star in full flow, capturing what makes them so special and why there have been so few truly unique, globally adored pop stars.

The preceding two films capture artists so singular they have exalted status in popular music history and the cinematic documents of them at their performing peak are special because they capture that peak in all its glory. A film that does the same and, in some way, completes a trilogy of concert films capturing male icons at their peak is *Sign 'O' The Times* (1987). If anything, this film surpasses those earlier works regarding representing the focus and control of star performers in that this concert film was directed by the performer themselves. Between 1986 and 1990, Prince directed three feature films,[9] of which this, the only documentary (he also directed the narrative-led *Under The Cherry Moon* (1986) and *Graffiti Bridge* (1990), is the most highly regarded.[10] The reason is likely down to the combination of the tour promoting the record that shares its name with the film and how, akin to Pennebaker's *Ziggy Stardust,* the filmmaking is intuitive to the performance but doesn't try to overpower what's happening on stage. Despite being largely reshot and re-recorded at Prince's Paisley Park studios after Prince was unhappy with what was recorded during the European tour from which the audience material is taken, the result is a seamless document of a star at the height of their performing and conceptual powers.[11]

Here, the performance – featuring material mostly taken from the record being promoted – is weaved around a mini-narrative that takes the live and cinema audience on a journey, as the band members become characters in a tale of love and betrayal that unfolds around the songs. The scene is set for cinema audiences by a short prologue, also shot at Paisley Park, that sets the tone of the show as one connected to the aesthetics of film noir and Blaxploitation as Prince's 'character' lurks on a street set with lighting that prefigures both Tim Burton's *Batman* (1989) and Warren Beatty's *Dick Tracy* (1990). Prince's character moves to the live stage area for the performance, but the stage set follows a similar aesthetic and resembles a street scene replete with a sleazy bar and low-rent apartments. In similar fashion to *Elvis: That's The Way It Is,* the dominant mode of composition are mid and wide shots to

---

[9] He also directed a number of his own music videos in the 1980s and 1990s.
[10] The most highly regarded Prince film is still probably *Purple Rain* (1984) but, despite containing footage of Prince performing 'live', it's a musical, with Prince acting the part of a performer.
[11] Despite the Ziggy Stardust persona, the Hammersmith show is a largely straight-forward rock show and Elvis was never really one for concepts.

capture the star's physicality, though *Sign* does include wonderful close-up cutaways of Prince's shuffling, boogieing feet. The standard approach to shooting the performance captures the greatness of what Prince did in consummate fashion, though a standout moment in terms of filmmaking also captures an idiosyncratic element of the live show. A short musical interlude takes place in an apartment that makes up part of the stage set; however, the action is obscured from the live audience's view, meaning the film audience is granted special permission to gaze on an intimate moment between lovers. It's a wonderful privileging of the gaze for those watching in cinemas or at home at the expense of those privileged to attend in person.

'Neo Super Blackness'[12] – Black Performance

Some of the commentary around the 2021 release of Questlove's *Summer of Soul,* documenting the 1969 Harlem Cultural festival, suggested that on screen cinematic performance by Black artists was an ultra-rare occurrence. The clickbait nature of that opinion aside, there is admittedly a dearth of material that captures Black icons at the same level as White icons but, as *Sign 'O' The Times* shows, there are high-quality examples from cinema history. Ignoring the lineage that *Summer of Soul* is part of does a disservice to the work that has come before and regarding it in isolation as opposed to part of a body of work also does a disservice to Questlove's remarkable document. Mel Stuart's *Wattstax* (1973) captures the 1972 Watts Summer Festival, featuring artists on the Stax record label roster, and so is from the same era as the Harlem Cultural Festival (re)covered in *Summer of Soul*. *Wattstax* features icons such as Isaac Hayes and The Staple Singers, the latter group part of the *Summer of Soul* line-up also. The performances throughout *Wattstax* are exceptional but the film is special because of how it is structured as a portrait of a community, a celebration of Blackness and a critique on contemporary America and the conditions that led to ghettoization and resultant uprisings in places like Watts. From the opening salvo, with Richard Pryor discussing police violence alongside

---

[12] *Summer of Soul* (2021).

introducing the 'film of the experience', *Wattstax* sets itself up as a document of Black experience as well as a musical one.

Mel Stuart, a White director, collects images associated with Black urban life as the film gets underway, including the barbershop, the church and the police pulling over Black men. He avoids exploitation by giving Black men the time and space to discuss their experiences openly and without judgement. By spending so much time with members of the Watts community, both via interview and through watching them arrive ready to enjoy the festival, the film creates an indelible link between the Blackness of the residents and that of those performing. Jesse Jackson is present, delivering a speech about Black unity and pride that echoes, if not repeats in chunks, that which emerges in *Summer of Soul*. The theme of the speech, the 'I Am Somebody' he wants the Black audience to feel and yell back, runs through images of Black audience, Black performer and Black labourer – the crew staging the organization, logistics and mechanics of the event – that recur throughout the film, mingling to create a complex picture of Blackness that defies easy categorization. The performances mean so much to the audience with one festival goer exclaiming at one point 'It's a hell of a feeling' witnessing it unfold, but also to the artists, with the Staple Singers proudly declaring 'we're doing our thing the Black way' in voiceover before the film showcases their spellbinding performance.

While some of the coverage of the release of *Summer of Soul* drew out its parallels with *Wattstax* in doing so it leap-frogged (or ignored) a film that it is much closer to in terms of the uncovering and subsequent release and re-contextualization of long-hidden footage. That film is 2008's *Soul Power*, directed by Jeffrey Kusama-Hinte. Kusama-Hinte (known as Levy-Hinte at the time of production) is, like Mel Stuart, a White filmmaker, who has made a film that is unapologetic in its celebration and presentation of Blackness. The film follows the production of the musical and cultural festival that accompanied the Muhammed Ali and George Foreman boxing match known as the 'Rumble in the Jungle', that took place in Zaire in 1974. The 'Zaire 74' festival featured leading American and African musical artists including James Brown, Bill Withers and Miriam Makeba. The film, wisely in many ways, is constructed entirely from footage shot at the time, rather than introducing contemporary context or reflection in the form of new interviews. The result is a film that feels like a peer to *Wattstax*. There is the now-familiar footage from concert films of the event being constructed. Here, however, there is the added tension of the disconnect of staging an event in Zaire in an American style, as musical performance on the African continent is often delivered in a very different context. There is also behind-the-scenes footage from the wider cultural aspects of the festival, with Black American performers spending time in the milieu of their African counterparts and experiencing Black African life.

Part of the attraction for performers, as the film shows, is the desire to connect with Africa as an ancestral space and presence. It is made explicit in the many proclamations by Muhammed Ali throughout the film ahead of his fight. Ali is shown in press conferences, the festival, training in Zaire and hanging out with artists. Ali is a star of the film, his fame and charisma imposing itself in much the same way that Richard Pryor's presence in *Wattstax* performs a similar function. Ali and Pryor's presences politicize the films and expand the thematic canvas beyond music. The sense of connecting with an ancestral homeland in *Soul Power* is felt elsewhere too, however, in the declaration from the stage made during the Spinners' performance that 'we are Black people ... come back home' and Bill Withers' admission to the camera that 'What I wanna bring back is the feeling'. The choice to not add contextual voice to these moments, from a belated present looking back, retains much of the power of the impact of the trip and the festival on the participants while leaving the legacy hanging in the air. The final act of the film is given over to headliner James Brown, who is shown throughout to be thoroughly business-like, as is the case with a film discussed later this chapter. It is clear from his lack of engagement with the everyday aspects of the festival, and the truth of his performance, that he is a star on a different plain to his fellow participants. From the opening bars of his song 'The Payback' he is on fire, in control. The camera enraptured by every movement and utterance. Like Ali, he is shown as a unique Black figure, in control of his domain like few others before or since. The film lets his performance play out, so it can be appreciated for the event it is, *the* event of the Zaire 74 festival.[13]

---

[13] In a post-credits moment Brown is seen spent, solo backstage, reduced to stillness and sweat following his epic performance. There's a wonderful echo of this moment in Christine Franz's Sleaford Mods film *Bunch of Kunst* (2017) where she captures frontman Jason Williamson in a backstage portacabin following the group's breakthrough Glastonbury performance.

Amongst almost universal praise, some voices, including that of Melissa Anderson, critiqued Questlove's *Summer of Soul* (2021) for interrupting the footage from the Harlem Cultural Festival with unnecessary or distracting contextual voiceover or cutaways. The film displays a few traits of the first-time filmmaker including this risk-averse approach to the material with Questlove drawing heavily on the structure and filmmaking of *The Black Power Mixtape 1967–1975* (2011), which he was a contributor to, in having archive footage contextualized by voices from the production's present. This approach works well in *Black Power Mixtape,* as discussed earlier in the book in the milestones and innovations chapter, but here can sometimes detract from the raw power of the footage that has been unearthed.[14] The film takes footage recorded at the time of the festival in 1969 but largely never released and crafts an incredible document of an event that featured some of the most iconic and innovative musicians of the twentieth century, at an event that happened around the same time as Woodstock, but which has been largely forgotten. Despite frustrations that might emerge from the filmmaking in terms of wanting this material, unseen for so long, to be presented with minimal interruption,[15] the film renders critique somewhat moot or somewhat bad faith through the undeniable power of the performance footage.

One of the most thrilling aspects of the construction of this recovered material for the scholarship and appreciation of music films is how it connects to, creates dialogue with and expands existing cinematic material of the artists performing and either returns to or places these artists in a Black performance context. One of the key sequences of the film is a duet between Mahalia Jackson and Mavis Staples of the Staple Singers, the latter supporting a fragile Jackson towards the end of her performing life. Jackson can be seen performing in earlier films such as *Jazz on a Summer's Day* (1959) – discussed in the introduction – and the Staple Singers are a highlight of both *Festival* and *Monterey Pop,* discussed earlier in this chapter. Those latter films are documents of events that featured or focused predominantly on White artists but here

---

[14] Melissa Anderson's balanced review for 4Columns discusses the flaws and problems with the film most succinctly and eloquently: See https://4columns.org/anderson-melissa/summer-of-soul.
[15] I acknowledge here the irony of this criticism given how I argue that concert films should be regarded as documentaries in the introduction, elevated by context, and here I am saying this film should just let the performances play out.

they are seen performing for a predominantly Black audience in a Black cultural and geographical location giving their performances different weight and significance. Similarly, the electric performance here of Sly & The Family Stone becomes a fantastic companion piece to their performance in *Woodstock* where they were one of only a handful of Black artists[16] on a mammoth bill. The dialogues that emerge between these films due to the existence of this work, and the ability to critique differences between the performances across time and audience demographic is one of the great gifts of *Summer of Soul*. Another gift is the presence in the film of Greg Tate who, in Anderson's (2021) words, is 'always a welcome interlocuter' and here, as in many music documentaries focusing on Black music, provides deep contextual insight and elucidates in words the joy captured on the Black faces in the Harlem crowd. As he says so beautifully 'this is an eruption of spirit'.

A different kind of eruption is feared in *The Night James Brown Saved Boston* (2008), a film that captures the relationship between Black music and American politics in the 1960s. While technically a TV movie – it was financed in part by music channel VH1 – it is a vital film in the context of Black performance on screen due to how it sets up the central figure of James Brown as, if not a saviour, then, a necessary salve and intervention during a hostile and intensely emotional time for Black America, before letting performance footage back up the strength of that thought. The first half of the film's running time of just over an hour is dedicated to historical context. The film tells the story of how uprisings erupted in cities across America following the assassination of Martin Luther King. Jr in April 1968 and how the mayor and city of Boston tried to avoid becoming one of a growing number of places facing confrontations in the streets between law enforcement and grieving citizens. Using archive footage and contemporary interviews the film delivers a précis of Race in America, 1960s Civil Rights Struggles, Boston's racial history, the relationship between James Brown and Martin Luther King Jr, the impact and legacy of the latter's death and the role James Brown occupied in American culture. This was one where, as Al Sharpton declares in the film, 'James Brown made the mainstream cross over to Black', in contrast to many of his predecessors and peers who had made crossover concessions to White audiences.

---

[16] I know that Sly & The Family Stone, like the Jimi Hendrix Experience, are a multi-racial group.

The central part of the film is given over to the performance, which was filmed for live broadcast and immediately re-shown due to demand. It captures both Brown's magnetism and power as a performer as well as the fear that the Black audience and White security staff would come to blows. It's so potent it translates via the black-and-white television-camera-filmed footage that exists of the performance. From here the film moves into a theorization of how this event, in the midst of national mourning, politicized Brown and led to a role as a crisis communicator in the midst of turmoil, citing Robert Kennedy's assassination and his visits to Vietnam to perform for troops as examples, crystallized in his Black pride anthem 'Say It Loud (I'm Black and I'm Proud)'. However, it never settles on an easy narrative of hero worship and includes how this politicization led to an uncomfortable alliance in later years with Richard Nixon. Earlier in the film Brown is shown taking control of financial negotiations regarding his performance, in no uncertain terms aware of his value and how important a figure he is in potentially ensuring there are no uprisings on the streets of Boston. On stage, when the crowd starts to surge and engage with the security personnel he proclaims, 'you're not being fair to me, or yourselves, or your race'. He comes across in the film's construction as unpredictable and complicated but, as the film ends, there is a return to performance footage from the show and, once again, Brown's talent, presence and importance is rendered without question.

Talent, presence and importance are ideas that are ever present in *Homecoming: a Film by Beyoncé* (2019), which captures the iconic performer's extraordinary Coachella festival performances in 2018. Other ideas that are ever present on viewing the film are vision, labour (two kinds), family and Blackness. The film is credited as co-directed by Beyoncé and Ed Burke, but audiences are left in no doubt that the experience is entirely down to Beyoncé. The film is constructed of footage of her two shows at the festival across different weekends, intercut with intense preparations for the event. Beyoncé is the creative director, on hand throughout, clutching her 'Bey-chella' folder containing her ideas and plans. She is involved in the choreography, the musical direction, the design and costuming. There is the performativity of pain discussed in the chapter about women, when she undertakes her first rehearsal following giving birth and when she experiences muscle spasms as the rehearsals take a physical toll. This is a minor aspect though, as the central theme that Beyoncé presents is Blackness and how she plans to seize the belated honour[17] of being the first female Black performer to headline the event by showcasing and celebrating Black art and culture in her vivid and slick performances, with a special focus on the Black female, represented most clearly in the film and her shows by the predominantly Black female-led band that will be responsible for the intricate musical delivery. Hanif Abdurraqib writes how 'as she's gotten older, Beyoncé has found ways to insert the political into the performance. The attempt being not only to start a conversation but to be a driving force and a guiding hand within the conversation' (2021: 205–6). *Homecoming* is a significant addition to that particular canon of work.

Like the footage of other Black performers across the films discussed here, her presence and power as a performer is undeniable. The film captures her at full pelt; her movement and management of her body, her voice and the show is exhilarating. She knows how good she is, on stage and as a filmmaker. Her willingness to devote stage time to her dancers and band – she leaves the stage first so they can bask in the audience glow and due to her many costume changes, they have plenty of show time to shine – is matched throughout the behind-the-scenes sections by footage celebrating her family and her crew. There is genuine delight on the bus to the festival arena with the dancers as they anticipate the show. On stage she extends space to her sister Solange and her husband Jay-Z for separate duets, screen space to a quote by and image of Audre Lorde and, in a moment that sees the crowd absolutely lose it, a reunion with her Destiny's Child collaborators.[18] Framed as a 'homecoming' game, a traditional annual celebration of 'school pride' in American high schools and colleges, Beyoncé imagines the performance as celebrating Black excellence and the film as a way of lifting up those same performers, predominantly Black women, and showcasing them to the world, using her power to do so. Her talk in the film of wanting to celebrate Black excellence is matched by images doing just that, and it just so happens that most often the images are of Beyoncé herself.

---

[17] Beyoncé cancelled her Coachella headline slot in 2017 when she became pregnant adding more pressure (by herself more than anyone) to her 2018 event.
[18] The successful group she was with at the start of her career before going solo.

'Tony, it's been wonderful'[19] – On Tour

Occupying an odd, liminal space between music films as discussed throughout this book and concert films as discussed so far this chapter are tour films. These are traditionally films with footage of musicians performing live, interspersed with the conventional footage of music films such as press events, rehearsals etc., but, in these instances, based around a specific sequence of events temporally bound. The tour, in other words. They seek to capture the strange truth of re-staging the same show (essentially) in a different town every night to different people with a common interest and point of reference. They also, by dint of capturing the liminal space of the tour bus and the backstage area, shine a light on the toll, the banality and the Kafka-esque absurdities of the tour, trying to balance the privilege of being a professional touring musician with its sometimes tedious and draining realities. Occupying a strange space in this strange field is Tony Palmer's document of Leonard Cohen's 1972 European tour, *Bird on a Wire* (2010).[20] It is a strange work not only because it has gone through so many versions, but also because it captures an artist at a fascinating juncture in their career. Palmer describes the film in his re-edited version via a title card as 'an impression of what happened', which it is, but more than that it is provides an 'impression' of Leonard Cohen in 1972 via a series of intriguing and revealing scenes both on and off stage. Several sequences are deeply revealing of Cohen as a performer and person. The opening sequence finds Cohen trying to perform to a crowd that is on edge, through a mixture of excitement and anticipation and a desire to get close to their idol, something Cohen encourages, and the desire of the show's security management to keep these young people, with their libidinous lack of control, at bay.

The scene recalls the horrific scenes of the Stones at Altamont from *Gimme Shelter* (1970), because pretty much any scene of crowd unrest or surge in a

---

[19] *Bird on a Wire* (2010).
[20] Like *Woodstock* and *Live at Pompeii,* this film has gone through many iterations. However, in this case, the changes were not the creative tinkering of the director Tony Palmer, who fought for years to regain control of the film and realized his preferred version in 2010, hence the year marker used here.

concert film can't help but, but also the ramshackle enthusiasm of the audiences at the start of *Trances* (1981), discussed in the chapter on place. Cohen's declaration at the trouble that 'this scene isn't working' recalls the exhortations of Mick Jagger in *Gimme Shelter* but also suggests a mode of operation that Cohen requires to perform, a theme that returns again and again in Palmer's film. Later in the film, Cohen listens to and tries to reason with a baying post-show crowd in Germany who are unhappy with the sound quality of the gig. Cohen listens and offers refunds. His patience and willingness to engage in the experience of his audience is remarkable. One key thread of the film is Cohen's desire to perform in Israel and the 'will it, won't it' subplot adds dramatic tension to proceedings. The final section of the film is given over to this special moment for Cohen and moves through several states. It's a bad show. He calls it a 'failure'. It's so rare to hear a musician so critical of themselves in public and backstage. It's startling. 'We bombed in Jerusalem' he jokes, uneasily. There's a beautiful irony as the film shares a performance of 'That's no way to say goodbye' at this very moment. This is in stark contrast to a performance just preceding this, with Cohen crying on stage, breathlessly sharing with the audience that this was the transcendental feeling he'd been searching for. Backstage he is in tears, as are his band, overwhelmed by the beauty of the show. There's a cumulative power to witnessing the events in *Bird on a Wire* and knowing they occurred in a short period of time, where cinema audiences can see the physical and emotional toll of touring on the performers from one town and/or sequence to the next, as well as the very real lift venue audiences can provide to performers with dwindling energy reserves. There's a unique power to witnessing a document of time as bound by a tour or collection of tours that can sometimes be lost when moments are extracted for a biographical music documentary re-telling.

The highest-profile film about Oasis is the documentary *Supersonic* (dir. Whitecross, 2016), which tells the story of their rise in the early 1990s to their peak, their landmark concerts at Knebworth in 1996. The latter event is collected in excellent fashion in *Oasis: Knebworth '96* (2021), released to coincide with the event's 25th anniversary. However, a more intriguing film, overlooked now and at the time of release, is Bailie Walsh's film of the band's 2005 world tour, *Lord Don't Slow Me Down* (2007). This intrigue is, in large part, because the band were well past their mid-1990s peak. Walsh's film provides a fascinating insight into how to maintain a working, successful rock band when the two central members don't get on. Some of the band's press responsibilities featured in the film include more than one band member, but it's rarely Noel and Liam Gallagher together. There are separate buses and separate cars to and from the venues. The amount of time they share together is limited to photo shoots, performing on stage and being backstage; even then, sometimes, they are very clearly staying away from each other in that space. The film doesn't lean into the easy target of the warring siblings but does capture the tensions of touring and their inherently fractious relationship, including a sequence where Noel is sound checking for a show while Liam is off enjoying oysters in the city they are playing. Elsewhere, Liam says to his brother 'you should have a bit more fucking respect for our band' but this comes towards the end of the film, which tries to hide long-standing tensions under the veil of tour toll. It's a brilliantly cut sequence, with Noel answering a Japanese journalist's question 'How is the tour?' by saying 'great until last night' and the film then cuts to the brothers arguing in a hotel bar. It's dark and feels voyeuristic and uncomfortable. However, ,due to the embedded nature of the film crew, there are moments that capture the brothers laughing and enjoying moments of shared joy amidst the machinery of the tour. This ensures the portrait of them is never easily reduced to the expected tabloid soundbites with which they are synonymous. Sections of the film are given over to extended montages of performance and travel set to Oasis songs from the era including the song that gives the film its title, and an earlier single from the album they are touring, 'Let There Be Love'. The latter's music video was the section of the film that it soundtracks. This acts, simultaneously, as a trailer for the film, which was to follow.

A common practice in the tour film is showcasing musicians as tired, bored and frustrated by the touring process. This element of the tour film has its zenith in a film that was made to foreground all the ways that touring and promoting records reduces artists to gibbering soundbite machines, Grant Gee's *Meeting People Is Easy* (1998). The film, funded by Radiohead's label at the time, Parlophone, to capture the band as they toured the world capitalizing on the global breakout success of their 1997 album *OK Computer*, should be a triumphal blend of a band seizing on becoming world famous and playing to rapturous, adoring crowds, night after night. It has that element, with the band brilliant in performance and crowds going crazy. There's a lovely moment following their performance of 'Creep' at their famous Glastonbury 1997 show, with the band clearing enjoying their work and its response. Alternately, off stage as the band engage with the press and traverse the globe as the tour and the demands for their time grow due to the record's success, the film is unflinching in its portrayal of the tensions of that aspect of touring and promoting. From close ups of stickers stating 'I'm not here' to utterances such as 'we actually don't know where we are at the moment', which can be taken literally and figuratively, the film presents a fragmented blur, with the band testy, bemused and sometimes confrontational. As Lindsey Eckenroth writes, Gee 'emphasizes the themes of alienation, fear, and disillusionment that are audible in Radiohead's music and lyrics by linking them to the band's experience on tour' (2014: 221). It is an anti-promotional film in many respects, disinterested in gaining new audiences.

As the film moves on, it becomes more fragmented, more dreamlike in how it manages chronology and space. The band and the audience struggle to keep up with where and when things are occurring. It feels like a grim piece of realism in terms of the cognitive experience of a world tour – even for privileged White musicians who are the talk of the town. The band never look relaxed, never seem to be having fun, even as the album they are touring becomes the album of the year in practically every country on practically every poll. There's a frankness and openness that has come to be synonymous with Radiohead but, at the time, they were a relatively unknown quantity in mainstream terms. They are happy for statements such as 'Jonny doesn't want to do TV interviews cos he thinks he comes across like an idiot' to be included, and for Thom to be shown arguing with a journalist that the music should speak for itself à la Dylan in *Dont Look Back*. This is how they are happy for the world to see them in a cinematic context. Gee is a sympathetic filmmaker for this task, interested in the workings of the band and the production of art at the expense of the capitalist components attached to it and a question emerges of whether the band really hated every minute of this tour or if they all just agreed to only show the miserable bits. Either way it is a striking document of a band at the precise moment they become a globally recognized musical act and one where, no matter how miserable they might seem offstage, on stage, as in the footage of them performing 'Airbag', at Brixton Academy,[21] the hype feels justified.

The title of Mike Mills' tour documentary *Air: Eating, Sleeping, Waiting and Playing* (1999), released the year after *Meeting People Is Easy,* reads like a statement of solidarity with Radiohead and the film feels very similar in tone, aesthetic and its intention to further reveal the banality of life on the road. The result is that it tips the portrayal of musicians as put-upon and compromised into the 'woe is me' zone, diluting audience sympathy towards the trade-off between being paid to make art and fulfilling capitalist or business interests that are attached to that. Mills' film, which follows the French duo Air during the tour for their breakout record *Moon Safari* (1998), does, in contrast to the Gee film, include more of the artists enjoying themselves within the machinery and engaging more with the filmmaker about their work and its motivation and context. It is a more balanced film, but the black-and-white aesthetic and endless nondescript back stages and incremental tensions of touring make it, in many ways a companion piece to *Meeting People Is Easy*. What the film highlights also, by being made and released in such proximity to and in dialogue with the Radiohead film, is the limitations of filmmaking when it comes to following musicians on tour. There are only so many things to film when every green room looks the same and every journalist asks the same question.

'It's very strange but it seems to work'[22] – Variations on a Theme

As mentioned above, the limitations and repetitions of touring often mean that the cinematic representations of concerts and tours tend to cover the same ground in terms of content and often fall back on the same visual cues; the endless road outside the bus window, unnamed stagehands loading and unloading gear, the clutter and ephemera of the pre-/post-show green room. Within this cinematic space there are films that have sought to push against the familiar and introduce narrative or aesthetic devices that make for singular,

---

[21] Show 37 of the tour. Each show segment is numbered to give a sense of the tour's duration.
[22] *All Tomorrow's Parties* (2009).

resonant works. Dick Carruthers is a filmmaker with a long history of filming live concerts, documentaries and music videos for high-profile acts. It is his document of a White Stripes concert at Blackpool's famous Empress Ballroom, *White Stripes: Under Blackpool Lights* (2004) where the relationship between the music and the image, the musical artist and the cinematic representation is aligned to the greatest effect. In Emmett Malloy's superb tour film of the White Stripes, *The White Stripes Under Great Northern Lights* (2009), band leader Jack White talks about their approach to music making and live performance as one involving risk and challenge, limitations and pressure the band puts on themselves. The decision, therefore, to film *Under Blackpool Lights* on Super8mm film makes sense for a band who liked to push against the expected conventions of live shows. The fact that the film is shot on Super8 has several effects on the feelings and ideas the film manages to capture, regarding band, and live performance as a cinematic form.

The White Stripes were a band renowned for their eschewing of the modern and the digital in their recording and performance practices, where possible, so the aesthetic choice makes sense, aligning the format so often associated with nostalgia, the home movie and the analogue past, with a band whose ethos echoes those themes. The images created by the cameras are fuzzy edged and indistinct. The movement blurs the images further, the band and audience appearing frenetic, jagged, barely contained. There is lens flare and the jerky vertigo of the hand-held whip pan as the operators try to focus on the important moment to capture with each passing beat. The band are no-frills, minimal talk. They stride on stage and get straight into it. They play fast and they play a lot of songs. All the while the cameras just capture, as best they can, the energetic display that unfolds. The format and approach feel perfectly attuned to the raw, powerful blues rock played by the duo. The images of the crowd pogoing, intercut perfectly in time to Meg White's drumming for 'The Hardest Button to Button', the blurry figures on stage, even in close-up due to the limitations of the Super8 format and the dizzying edit dance between figures on stage and figures on the dance floor capture more of the exhilarating and fragmentary experience of a live rock show than pretty much any other film has done. At gigs, the band on stage are often hard to see clearly, even in small venues, while the power coming from the stage often makes it a feat to stay focused on what is happening up there and not losing your footing in the melee. This film makes you feel that, viscerally.

Similarly, Adam Smith's film *Don't Think* (2012), his concert film capturing the Chemical Brothers live at Japan's Fuji Rock festival in 2011, seeks to capture the visceral, bodily experience of the electronic musicians and their renowned audio-visual live show. The film's title is a helpful command to the audience. Just feel.[23] The construction of the film, if the audience can give themselves over to it regardless of what they feel about the music, is such that it reduces the viewer to an instinctive, physical respondent. The bodily plays a key role in the film, most notably hands. The hands of the two musicians, dwarfed behind huge banks of equipment on stage and shrouded in the shadows and glimmers cast by their vast accompanying projections, are shown in frequent close up. Alongside this are the hands of the crowd, thrust up in unison at every beat drop, slowly clapping in unison as another song ramps up and gets underway.[24] The relationship between sound and image in the film is exquisitely rendered. Smith is a director who understands the contours of the Chemical Brothers' music, honed over almost two decades of collaboration at the time of the film's production (and of electronic music live events) innately. Built to resemble and reference a single performance, as well as a night out in a club, the film echoes the feeling evoked by Mia Hansen-Love's narrative ode to electronic club and dance culture, *Eden* (2014), a film that captures so much of the joy and comedown melancholy of the rave.

The way *Don't Think* moves between musicians, crowd, visuals, and the entirety of those components is mesmerizing, the flow of images matching the ebb and flow of the sounds, with small punctures at key moments so it never feels like a static, over-controlled experience. Smith knows that the film can suggest the immersive but that this cannot be fully realized or maintained by a 2D film, so some of those punctures and ruptures emerge midway through the film where it breaks from representing the communal experience and drifts off into the fringes of the festival grounds with a single reveller. The film follows this reveller as she dances with fellow crowd members, strolls the festival grounds, becomes overwhelmed and disorientated by the visuals and the sounds. There are giant tigers in the mud and the previously smooth and

---

[23] There's a lovely echo here with the title card from Jake Meginsky's film *Milford Graves Full Mantis* (2018), discussed in the chapter on Black music.
[24] Most memorable in this regard is the intro to the song 'Believe' where a sustained focus is kept on the hands of the crowd.

defined textures of the music and the imagery start to glitch and deform; this sends the reveller off to the food trucks at the periphery of the arena, to regain sense and composure before returning for the epic finale. This moment, where the banal necessity of the live event intrudes in the fantasy, echoes the Beastie Boys' *Awesome; I Fuckin' Shot That!* (2006) in showing fans drifting off to the concessions when things get too much (or boring) and reinforces Smith's intelligence at knowing the film can't make it feel like 'you' are there. What it does is to provide a surrogate point of view that attempts realism, cinematically speaking, that suggests an authenticity of experience and also draws attention to the ecstatic, artistic moments of musical and experiential euphoria.

Somewhere between, and beyond, these approaches to recreating atmospheres and feelings sits *All Tomorrow's Parties* (2009), another film indebted to the innovations of *Awesome; I Fuckin' Shot That!*. Jonathan Caouette's *All Tomorrow's Parties* is a document of the cult festival known as ATP, which saw famous and renowned musicians and bands such as Nick Cave, Portishead, Sonic Youth and the Yeah Yeah Yeahs curate their dream concert line ups over weekends at British holiday camps, of the Butlins variety, in Minehead, Somerset and Camber Sands, East Sussex. The film is comprised of material shot by filmmaker Vincent Moon over a series of events, complemented by footage shared by both performing artists and attending fans. The result is a frenetic and shoddy blend of images and sounds that feels direct and unfiltered. This result is apt given that one of the unique aspects of the festival was the proximity of artists to each other and the audience. The holiday camps were both venue and accommodation for the musicians and festival goers, with everyone sharing digs next to each other, and no sign of a VIP area from which to observe the performances. The cavalcade of images, of professional and amateur provenance, captures the chaos and intimacy of the festival, with bands frequently urging fans to come on stage, leaving the venue to conduct impromptu congas throughout the park or decamping to chalets to continue shows. Sam Davies (2009) describes the 'collage techniques and occasionally dreamlike drift of the edits' that make the film work, ensuring the 'finished film's rhythm roughly corresponds to the three-day arc of a typical All Tomorrow's Parties' festival. The footage of Iggy and the Stooges, shot by fans, is a good case study of the surreal nature of the event in having legends perform in dingy holiday clubs for small, devoted crowds, where the usual distances and protocols have been removed or left to gather dust. Though, true, Iggy never let anything like barriers or security guards stop him.

The film contains many complete or extended performances of songs, is very light on interviews (relying instead on soundbites collected along the way); instead it presents live performance in a variety of guises from the traditional to the non-traditional and is edited in such a fashion that it never feels conclusive or exhaustive. The diversity of bands and artists and the relentless presentation of them performing suggests the festival has a deep history of which this is a mere percentage. Most of the performances are electric, with the rapport between artist and audience palpable. The holiday camp is an enclosed world where anything goes and the film certainly includes moments of wreckage, banality and, in the case of comedian David Cross, a particularly vicious (and utterly nonsensical given that he was invited by the festival's curators) bout of heckling and abuse. For the most part, though, the film is presented as a loving portrait of music, where crowd and performer are given a more equitable billing and where performer becomes both crowd and fan. There's a delightful moment where one performer can't hide his joy at seeing Kevin Shields from My Bloody Valentine saunter past. It suggests that the event was egalitarian, and the film is built as a time capsule. It may be a nod to a future where such free integration between artists and audience members will seem a thing of the distant past, or more positively, a precursor for the norm.

'This is my last endless pause'[25] – On endings

As this book draws to close there is just time for one final goodbye, in the form of a film about goodbyes, with the (first) goodbye of LCD Soundsystem and their mammoth final show at New York's legendary Madison Square Garden venue. *Shut Up and Play the Hits* (2012) is celebratory, reflective, playful and joyous and packed with examples of a musician seeking to savour and recall moments as something is ending. Writing the ending of this chapter (and this

---

[25] *Shut Up and Play the Hits* (2012).

book) brings forward moments from the films that have been covered thus far. In the service of brevity and to bring focus, this conclusion will shine a light on moments from concert films that stick in the mind and heart. Whether it's Noel Gallagher and road crew, in *Lord Don't Slow Me Down,* failing to open a comically large bottle of backstage champagne in a prolonged struggle and anti-climax that can't help recalling *This Is Spinal Tap* (1984) and its absurd realism, or the camera floating above the crowd in *Don't Think* (2012) and making the mass of dancing bodies look like worms wriggling intimately and cosily under a sunlamp. It could be the power and glory of the Edwin Hawkins Singers singing 'Oh Happy Day' in *Summer of Soul,* Greg Tate's 'eruption of spirit' in full force, or the marching band and Black Panthers co-commanding the stage for Beyoncé's *Homecoming* (2019), or Prince smirking ironically as he purrs 'not bad for a girl' about Sheila E's drumming at the end of a scintillating performance of 'Play in the Sunshine'.

Moments like these are jewels of memory for audiences lucky enough to attend the concert but also resonate for what they reveal about performers for cinema audiences. They provide insight into moments and perspectives that audiences don't and can't see, or haven't seen previously, in the case of *Summer of Soul*. In *Shut Up and Play the Hits* there are the expected conventions of prepping for the show with band members and the stage crew setting things up. They are tinged with melancholy as the show being prepped is the last one the band will perform. Unlike when Bowie stopped being Ziggy Stardust, this time everyone was prepped and the show was intended as a celebration of what had been achieved, collectively, between band and fans. Alongside this, the footage of the show – onstage and backstage – is intercut with a rumination on the end of this era by the bandleader James Murphy as he contemplates what lies ahead and contextualizes what has happened in the past. These interludes position Murphy firmly within the hipster milieu he is often associated with as he pores over coffee making and walks his tiny dog around Brooklyn. It's a distancing technique to allow Murphy and the audience to process the finality of the undertaking without getting too emotionally connected. This juts against the emotionality of the performance, which is exuberant and communal. There is a convenient 'press interview' so that Murphy can provide exposition on why he's calling it a day and what he thinks the band's legacy is and this appears situated to put this on the record, for

Murphy as much as anyone else. In fact, this is a staged conversation between Murphy and writer Chuck Klosterman. Ian Buckwalter (2012) claims that 'Klosterman is [the film's] ace in the hole, a well-informed observer digging deeply into Murphy's complex and often conflicted relationship with stardom'.

The show is for the fans and the band. A final, exultant moment of communal joy. The shooting of the performances is solid – as expected with Reed Morano as director of photography – if unexceptional. The expected shots, angles and camera movements are all present and correct. This is not a time to innovate but to document. What resonates are the moments where attention was paid at just the right second, with just the right composition. Be that when Murphy looks up to the sky as 'New York I Love You (But You're Bringing Me Down)' reaches its false climax, awaiting the falling of an ocean of white balloons or in the final moments when a devastated fan, in tears of joy and sadness, can't bear to leave the venue floor and the camera watches him cry, thankfully from a respectful distance. Murphy spends the film's offstage moments reckoning with his artistic endeavours and persona, the melancholy air of the film aided by so much of this aspect taking place in the hungover comedown glow of the days after the show. Onstage he is having a good time with his friends – both the band and their guests, including Arcade Fire who show up on backing vocals at one point – making it a memorable show for the audience. The film captures all of that and some of it is messy and flows over the sides of the film a bit; quite self-indulgent despite the postmodern distancing techniques. Despite and maybe because of all that, it's also a thrilling account of a great band doing what they are great at. It wasn't goodbye as the band reformed in 2016. This is though.

Endnotes – Omissions, Alternative Histories and Further Watching

If you have read the book (or skimmed the index) you may have noted some films that you may have presumed would be featured more heavily that weren't. There is very little on the Oscar-winning *Searching for Sugar Man* (2012) and very little mention of the work of Nick Broomfield, whose films have focused on music and musicians several times. This book is one history of music film. There are many alternative histories that could be written about music films that focus more on those works, that engage with early works in concert film such as *The T.A.M.I. Show* (1964) or early music mockumentary films such as Peter Watkins' *Privilege* (1967), that choose to write about Lara Lee's excellent electronic music documentary *Modulations* (1998) when discussing that genre as opposed to the choices I made of Jeremy Deller's *Everybody in the Place* (2019) or John Akomfrah's *The Last Angel of History* (1996). There's a lot on the Beatles films, nothing on the many films about and featuring John Lennon after they split up. An alternative history should include, as mentioned in the introduction, a focus on films about country music. There also needs to be more on short works including the infamous *Heavy Metal Parking Lot* (1986) that I reference in a footnote, Les Blank's gorgeous portrait *The Blues According to Lightnin' Hopkins* (1970) or the brilliant films on John Cooper Clarke, *Ten Years in an Open Necked Shirt* (1982) and Lynton Kwesi Johnson, *Dread Beat and Blood* (1982), made for Channel 4 in the UK by the Arts Council about two poets skirting on the edges of popular music and sometimes diving in. I know that some people may find it unforgivable (maybe that's pushing it) that there is no mention of Paul Kelly's beautiful *Lawrence of Belgravia* (2011), which might have worked well in the careers section of the making music chapter, or more on Laurie Anderson's *Home of the Brave* (1986), a spellbinding concert film as well as a fantastic piece of performance art and, in places, stand-up comedy. I would have loved space to write about Kieran Evans' *Vashti Bunyan: From Here to Before* (2008), or more on Rob Curry and Tim Plester's *Southern Journey [Revisited]* (2020), two fabulous physical and temporal road movies. Or my friend Dan S's wonderful portrait of his record-store owning father *Old Man* (2014). If I'd included work from 2022, I would have loved to discuss Toby Amies' brilliant King Crimson film *In the Court of the Crimson King* (2022). The generous and encouraging reviews of the typescript threw up a desire for more on vocal performance and the role of the mixing desk in the making music chapter, ideas I think would have been of benefit to focus on more. Alas, I must admit that time, space and scope has beaten me. I would like to close with a few words on the film that started my journey with music films. I saw Don Letts' *The Clash: Westway to the World* (2000) when it first appeared on television and it introduced me to the Clash – a band I was loosely aware of through the 'hits' – and made me fall in love with them. It also set me on the path to, eventually, writing this book, because there was something in the way that Letts told the story that gripped me. The film is designed to be impactful in specific ways and it certainly had that effect on me. It's a thrill to finally be able to write about it, alongside the films that followed in its wake. Produced a couple of years before Joe Strummer died, the film is essentially a primer about the band. It covers their formation and their peak years, their memories, philosophies, and some amazing live footage, pretty much ignoring the huge rift and fall out after Mick Jones left in 1983 and totally ignoring the 'final' Clash album, *Cut the Crap*, released in 1985. It is fast and direct and romanticizes the band and their place in the punk pantheon and British culture more broadly. Never false, but always curated and cut with a pace that absolutely corresponds to that of the music and the restlessness of the band as individuals and collectively.

Towards the end of the film Joe remarks on how quick it all was, those years from 1976 to 1982, and the film makes the audience feel that pace and how exciting it must have been, but also how unsustainable it was. Despite the pace of information and the barrage of live footage the film also dedicates time to ensuring that some of the formative and significant elements of the band's personality and career are covered in detail. Highlights include how it links bassist Paul Simonon's background interest and abilities in art with the look of the band and their stage backdrops. Alongside Johnny Rotten, Simonon and the Clash cultivated the 'look' of British punk, that unique meld of art-school statement and working-class salvage.[1] The film gives Paul his due. A later

---

[1] In terms of the images that travelled the country in newspapers and the music press, the influence of Vivienne Westwood and Malcolm McLaren is, of course, vital in this regard.

section sees the band in New York in the early 1980s, jumping on the Hip Hop train and having a sizeable hit with their song 'The Magnificent 7,' and selling out the Bonds venue on Broadway for 17 shows in a row. The footage from the latter, directed by Letts and intended for a concert film that sadly never saw the light of day, is incendiary. It ignites this film since, unlike so much of the archive material, it was little seen, if at all, but also acts as a sad glimpse of what might have been one of the finest concert films ever made. I hope this book starts conversations, brings people to films previously unfamiliar to them, and contributes to challenging common perceptions of the music film that fail to acknowledge its complexity and cultural relevance. I hope it prompts more people to write about music films, so that I can continue to read what they have to say.

References

Abdurraqib, H. (2021), *A Little Devil in America: In Praise of Black Performance,* London: Allen Lane/Penguin.

Abdurraqib, H. (2019), *Go Ahead in the Rain: Notes to A Tribe Called Quest,* London: Melville House.

Abramovich, A. (2020), 'Even When It's a Big Fat Lie, *London Review of Books,* 8 October. Available online: www.lrb.co.uk/the-paper/v42/n19/alex-abramovich/even-when-it-s-a-big-fat-lie.

Adams, T. (2020), 'Andrew O'Hagan: If you are honest, you never stop being who you were', *The Observer,* 30 August. Available online: www.theguardian.com/books/2020/aug/30/andrew-ohagan-if-you-are-honest-you-never-stop-being-who-you-were.

Anderson, M. (2013), 'Poetic Justice: Melissa Anderson on *Right On!* At MoMA', *Artforum,* 4 March. Available online: www.artforum.com/film/melissa-anderson-on-right-on-at-moma-39666.

Anderson, M. (2021), 'Summer of Soul', *4Columns,* 25 June. Available online: https://4columns.org/anderson-melissa/summer-of-soul.

Appiah, K. A. (2020), 'The Case for Capitalizing the B in Black', *The Atlantic,* 18 June. Available online: www.theatlantic.com/ideas/archive/2020/06/time-to-capitalize-blackand-white/613159/.

Aufderheide, P. (2007), *Documentary Film: A Very Short Introduction,* Oxford: Oxford University Press.

Barthes, R. (1977), *Image Music Text,* Glasgow: Fontana.

Beattie, K. (2016), *Dont Look Back,* London: BFI/Palgrave.

Berman, M. (1999), 'Views from the burning bridge', *Dissent,* 46(3): 76–87.

Brody, R. (2016), 'A Classic Jazz Documentary that Honors and Insults the Art Form', *The New Yorker,* 25 October. Available online: www.newyorker.com/culture/richard-brody/a-classic-jazz-documentary-that-honors-and-insults-the-art-form.

Brunette, P. (ed), (1999), *Martin Scorsese Interviews,* Jackson: University of Mississippi Press.

Buckwalter, I. (2012), 'At His Zenith, And Unlikely Rock Star Bows Out, *NPR,* 17 July. Available online: www.npr.org/2012/07/17/156725951/at-his-zenith-an-unlikely-rock-star-bows-out.

Buxton, A. (2022), 'Ep.180 – Jarvis Cocker', *The Adam Buxton Podcast,* 10 June. Available online: www.adam-buxton.co.uk/podcasts/wmcgmfe7zj7chps-89fa4-2e48e-rwzy8-824b8-4mdjd-2hcs8-chrb2-7y8jj-5pcse-2wtsh-cz8zd-e3cdy-g68s7-3dezn-7k5mw-y739l-p75rr-jr8a7-7akgj-l4zms-mbmhm-486s5-jg45z-n3dba-3g2sh.

Callahan, B. (2020) 'Ry Cooder', *Gold Record*. Available at: Apple Music (Accessed 29 Nov 2023)

Caramanica, J. (2021), 'Remembering the Velvet Underground Through the Mirror of Film, *New York Times Popcast Podcast,* 16 November. Available online: www.nytimes.com/2021/11/16/arts/music/popcast-velvet-underground-documentary.html.

Caramanica, J. (2022), 'Where is Jazz Most at Home?', *New York Times Popcast Podcast,* 29 June. Available online: www.nytimes.com/2022/06/29/arts/music/popcast-jazz-venues.html.

Clark, A. (2011), 'The Story of Lovers Rock', *Permanent Plastic Helmet,* 14 April. Available online: permanentplastichelmet.com/2011/04/14/the-story-of-lovers-rock/.

Cohen, J. and Gee, G. (1999), 'Wish you were here', *Filmmaker Magazine,* April: 52–55. 92–95.

Cohen, T.F. (2012), *Playing to the Camera: Musicians and Musical Performance in Documentary Cinema,* New York: Columbia University Press.

Cowie, P. (2004), *Revolution! The Explosion of World Cinema in the 60s,* London: Faber.

Dargis, M. (2015), 'Review: What Happened, Miss Simone? Documents Nina Simone's Rise as Singer and Activist, *New York Times,* 23 June. Available online: www.nytimes.com/2015/06/24/movies/review-what-happened-miss-simone-documents-nina-simones-rise-as-singer-and-activist.html.

Davies, S. (2009), 'Sonic Youths: Jonathan Caouette's All Tomorrow's Parties', *BFI*. Available online: www2.bfi.org.uk/news-opinion/sight-sound-magazine/interviews/sonic-youths-jonathan-caouette-s-all-tomorrow-s-parties.

Davies, S. (2009), 'Am I Black Enough for You', *Sight and Sound,* July: 54.

Ebiri, B. (2013), 'On Trances', in: *Martin Scorsese Presents World Cinema Project Volume One,* 26–49, London: Masters of Cinema.

Eckenroth, L. (2014), 'Representing Joy Division: Assembling Audiovisual Argument and Psychogeography in Rockumentary', *Rock Music Studies,* 1(3): 211–30.

Eshun, K. (2007), 'Drawing the Forms of Things Unknown', in: Eshun, K and Sagar, A (eds), *The Ghosts of Songs: The Film Art of the Black Audio Film Collective 1982–1998,* 74–105, Liverpool: Liverpool University Press.

Ewens, H. (2019), *Fangirls: Scenes from Modern Music Culture,* London: Quadrille.

Ferguson, A.G. (2013), 'Every Tongue Brings in a Several Tale': *The Filth and the Fury*'s Counterhistorical Transgressions', in: Edgar, R., Fairclough-Isaacs, K. and

Halligan, B. (eds) *The Music Documentary: Acid Rock to Electropop,* 141–56, Abingdon: Routledge.

Fisher, M, (2018). *k-punk,* London: Repeater Books.

Forman, M. (2002), *The 'hood Comes First: Race, Space and Place in Rap and Hip Hop,* Middletown: Wesleyan University Press.

Fox, N. (2015), 'I'm a Proponent of Change: Penelope Spheeris and the Decline of Western Civilization', *Directors Notes,* 1 September. Available online: https://directorsnotes.com/2015/09/01/penelope-spheeris-the-decline-of-western-civilization/.

Fox, N. (2015), 'On Location: Manchester', in: Mitchell, N. (ed), *Directory of World Cinema: Britain 2,* Bristol: Intellect.

Fox, N. (2015), 'Head Music: Stop Making Sense Reassessed', *the Quietus,* 5 December. Available online: https://thequietus.com/articles/19381-stop-making-sense-article.

Fox, N. (2016), 'Would you ask the Beatles that? How Bob Dylan and the Beatles shaped perceptions of the music press, *Transformation and Tradition in Sixties British Cinema,* 4 January. Available online: https://60sbritishcinema.wordpress.com/2016/01/04/would-you-ask-the-beatles-that-how-bob-dylan-and-the-beatles-shaped-perceptions-of-the-music-press/.

Frere-Jones, S. (2021), 'Sleaford Mods', *4Columns,* 29 January. Available online: www.4columns.org/frere-jones-sasha/sleaford-mods.

'Gallagher Thought Spinal Tap Were Real Band', (2005), *contactmusic.com,* 24 June. Available online: www.contactmusic.com/liam-gallagher/news/gallagher-thought-spinal-tap-were-real-band.

Garfield, R. (2022), *Experimental Filmmaking and Punk: Feminist Audio-Visual Culture in the 1970s and 1980s,* London: Bloomsbury.

Glynn, S. (2021), *The Beatles and Film: from Youth Culture to Counterculture,* Abingdon: Routledge.

Goldman, V. (2019), *Revenge of the She-Punks: A Feminist Music History from Poly Styrene to Pussy Rio,* London: Omnibus.

Halligan, B. (2021), 'American Music Documentary: Five Case Studies of Ciné-Ethnography', in: *Popular Music,* 40(1): 174–76.

Hanley, M.T. (2022), 'Andrew Dominik', *The Deeper into Movies Podcast,* 28 March. Available online: https://open.spotify.com/episode/1iNwKmfI8c046LuxnuwI6H.

Hans, S. (2018), 'My Love Is Not Your Love: Two Documentaries Misunderstand Whitney Houston's Magic, *MUBI Notebook,* 11 July. Available online: https://mubi.com/notebook/posts/my-love-is-not-your-love-two-documentaries-misunderstand-whitney-houston-s-magic.

Harbert, B. (2018), *American Music Documentary: Five Case Studies of Ciné-ethnomusicology,* Middletown: Wesleyan University Press.

Hatherley, O. (2011), *Uncommon: An Essay on Pulp*, Alresford: Zero Books.

Hoby, H. (2010), 'Silibil N' Brains: the end of authenticity', *The Guardian,* 18 April. Available online: www.theguardian.com/music/musicblog/2010/apr/18/silibil-n-brains-california-schemin.

Holm-Hudson, K. (2015), 'Through a Lens Darkly: The Changing Performer-Audience Dynamic as Documented by Four Progressive Rock Concert Films' in: Edgar, R., Fairclough-Isaacs, K., Halligan, B. and Spelman, N (eds) *The Arena Concert: Music, Media and Mass Entertainment,* 45–56, London: Bloomsbury.

Howell, A. (2012), 'Performing Countercultural Masculinity: Mick, Music and Masquerade in Gimme Shelter', *Genders,* 55: 1–21.

Hutcheon, L. (2002), *The Politics of Postmodernism,* 3rd edn, New York: Routledge.

Kael, P. (1984), 'Stop Making Sense', *The New Yorker,* 26 November. Available online: www.thestacksreader.com/stop-making-sense/.

Kateri Hernandez, K, (2002). 'Buena Vista Social Club: The Racial Politics of Nostalgia', in: Habell-Pallán, M. and Romero, M. (eds), *Latino/a Popular Culture,* New York: NYU Press.

Kenny, G. (2018), 'Review: Milford Graves Full Mantis Delivers a Lot of Heart', *New York Times,* 12 July. Available online: www.nytimes.com/2018/07/12/movies/milford-graves-full-mantis-review.html.

Jafaar, A. (2006), 'Dave Chappelle's Block Party', *Sight and Sound,* July: 50–52.

James, D. (2016), *Rock 'N' Film: Cinema's Dance with Popular Music,* New York: Oxford University Press.

Jeffries, S. (2021), *Everything, All the Time, Everywhere: How We Became Postmodern,* London: Verso.

Lodge, G. (2020), 'Streaming: the best jazz films', *The Guardian,* 14 November. Available online: www.theguardian.com/film/2020/nov/14/streaming-the-best-jazz-films-billie-holiday-documentary-james-erskine.

Marcus, G. (2005), *Like a Rolling Stone: Bob Dylan at the Crossroads,* London: Faber.

Martell, N. (2007), 'Wilco Survives {or Enjoying the View with Jeff Tweedy}, *Filter,* Spring: 50–57.

Mayer, S. (2014), 'Film of the Week: The Punk Singer', *Sight and Sound,* June: 85.

Mulholland, G. (2011), *Popcorn: Fifty Years of Rock 'n' Roll Movies,* London: Orion.

Mundy, J. (1999), *Popular Music on Screen: From Hollywood Musical to Music Video,* Manchester: Manchester University Press.

'Music Documentaries', (2022), *The Film Comment Podcast,* 18 January. Available online: www.filmcomment.com/blog/the-film-comment-podcast-music-documentaries/.

Nichols, B. (2017), *Introduction to Documentary,* 3rd edn, Bloomington: Indiana University Press.

Penman, I. (2019), *It Gets Me Home, This Curving Track,* London: Fitzcarraldo Editions.

Petkova, S. (2021), 'Billie Eilish: The World's A Little Blurry and The Body in Pain, *The Quietus,* 11 June. Available online: https://thequietus.com/articles/30081-film-billie-eilish-documentary-review.

Pinkerton, N. (2015). 'Les bon temps rouler: rolling with Les Blank's good-time movies', *Sight and Sound,* February. Available online: www.bfi.org.uk/sight-and-sound/features/les-blank-joyful-documentaries-margins-american-life.

Rafferty, T (2007), 'A Jazzman So Cool You Want Him Frozen at His Peak', *New York Times,* 3 June. Available online: www.nytimes.com/2007/06/03/movies/03raff.html.

Reynolds, S. (2007), 'Tombstone Blues: The Music Documentary Boom', *Sight and Sound,* May: 32–36.

Reynolds, S. (2011), *Retromania: Pop Culture's Addiction to Its Own Past,* London: Faber.

Romney, J. (1995), 'Access: All Areas: The Real Space of Rock Documentary', in: Romney, J. and Wootton, A. (eds), *Celluloid Jukebox: Popular Music and the Movies Since the 50s,* 82–93, London: BFI.

Roessner, J. (2013), 'The Circus is in Town: Rock Mockumentaries and the Carnivalesque', in: Edgar, R., Fairclough-Isaacs, K. and Halligan, B. (eds), *The Music Documentary: Acid Rock to Electropop,* 159–70, Abingdon: Routledge.

Saffle, M. (2013), 'Retrospective Compilations: (Re)defining the Music Documentary', in: Edgar, R., Fairclough-Isaacs, K. and Halligan, B. (eds), *The Music Documentary: Acid Rock to Electropop,* 42–54, Abingdon: Routledge.

Saunders, D. (2007), *Direct Cinema: Observational Documentary and the Politics of the Sixties,* London: Wallflower.

Scanlan, J. (2022), *Rock 'N' Roll Plays Itself: A Screen History,* London: Reaktion Books.

Sexton, J. (2006), 'A Cult Film by Proxy: Space is the Place and the Sun Ra Mythos', in: *New Review of Film and Television Studies,* 4(3): 197–215.

Shafto, S. (2013), 'Trances: Power to the People', *Criterion: The Current,* 16 December. Available online: www.criterion.com/current/posts/2992-trances-power-to-the-people.

Schager, N. (2015), 'Film Review: Junun', *Variety,* 8 October. Available online: https://variety.com/2015/film/reviews/junun-film-review-1201613807/.

Tate, G. (2009), 'Michael Jackson: The Man in Our Mirror', *the Village Voice,* 1 July. Available online: www.villagevoice.com/2009/07/01/michael-jackson-the-man-in-our-mirror/.

Teodoro, J. (2016), 'I Called Him Morgan'. Available online: https://cinema-scope.com/cinema-scope-online/called-morgan-kasper-collin-swedenus-tiff-docs/.

Wenders, W. (1991), *Fmotion Pictures,* London: Faber.

Wigley, S. (2014), 'Saint Etienne and Paul Kelly on A London Trilogy', *BFI,* 23 April. Available online:www2.bfi.org.uk/news-opinion/news-bfi/interviews/saint-etienne-paul-kelly-london-trilogy.

Williams, R. (2003), *Who Speaks for Wales? Nation, Culture, Identity,* Cardiff: University of Wales Press.

Wootton, A. (1988), 'U2 Rattle and Hum', *Monthly Film Bulletin,* December: 354–55.

Wootton, A. (1995), 'The Do's and Don'ts of Rock Documentaries', in: Romney, J. and Wootton, A. (eds), *Celluloid Jukebox: Popular Music and the Movies Since the 50s,* 94–105, London: BFI.

Yanow, S. (2004), *Jazz on Film: The Complete Story of the Musicians & Music Onscreen,* San Francisco: Backbeat Books.

Filmography

A Band Called Death (2012), Dir. Mark Christopher Covino and Jeff Howlett, USA: Haven Entertainment.
A Dog Called Money (2019), Dir. Seamus Murphy, UK: Pulse.
A Hard Day's Night (1964), Dir. Richard Lester, UK: United Artists.
A Matter of Life and Death (1946), Dir. Michael Powell and Emeric Pressburger, UK: The Archers.
A Mighty Wind (2003), Dir. Christopher Guest, USA: Castle Rock.
A Poem Is a Naked Person (1974) Dir. Les Blank, USA: Les Blank Films.
Afro-Punk (2003), Dir. James Spooner, USA: Afro-Punk.
Air: Eating, Sleeping, Waiting and Playing (1999), Dir. Mike Mills [Video], France.
All Tomorrow's Parties (2009), Dir. Jonathan Caouette, UK: Warp.
Am I Black Enough For Ya (2009), Dir. Göran Olsson, Sweden: Story AB.
Amazing Grace (2018), Dir. Alan Elliott and Sydney Pollack, USA: Warner Brothers.
American Interior (2014), Dir. Dylan Goch and Gruff Rhys, UK: Soda Pictures.
American Utopia (2020), Dir. Spike Lee, USA: HBO.
Amy (2015), Dir. Asif Kapadia, UK: FilmFour.
Anorac (2018), Dir. Gruffydd Davies, UK: Film Cymru.
Animal Farm (1954), Dir. Joy Batchelor and John Halas, UK: Halas & Batchelor.
Anvil: The Story of Anvil (2008), Dir. Sacha Gervasi, Canada: Abramorama.
Awesome; I Fuckin' Shot That! (2006), Dir. Nathanial Hörnblowér, USA: Oscilloscope.
Basically, Johnny Moped (2013), Dir. Fred Burns, UK: Heavenly Films.
Batman (1989), Dir. Tim Burton, USA: Warner Brothers.
Bayou Maharajah (2013), Dir. Lily Keber, USA: Mairzy Doats Productions.
Be Pure. Be Vigilant. Behave (2019), Dir. Kieran Evans, UK.
Beats, Rhymes & Life: The Travels of A Tribe Called Quest (2011), Dir. Michael Rapaport, USA: Rival Pictures.
Berberian Sound Studio (2012), Dir. Peter Strickland, UK: FilmFour.
Best in Show (2000), Dir. Christopher Guest, USA: Castle Rock.
Beware of Mr. Baker (2012), Dir. Jay Bulger, USA: Insurgent Media.
Big Star: Nothing Can Hurt Me (2012), Dir. Drew DeNicola and Olivia Mori, USA: September Gurls Productions.
Big Time (1988), Dir. Chris Blum, USA: Island.
Billie (2019), Dir. James Erskine, USA: Altitude.

Billie Eilish: The World's a Little Blurry (2021), Dir. R.J. Cutler, USA: Interscope.
Bros: After the Screaming Stops (2018), Dir. Joe Pearlman and David Soutar, UK: Fulwell 73.
Buena Vista Social Club (1999), Dir. Wim Wenders, Germany: Road Movies Filmproduktion.
Bunch of Kunst (2017), Dir. Christine Franz, Germany.
Carry on at Your Convenience (1971), Dir. Gerald Thomas, UK: Rank.
CB4 (1993), Dir. Tamra Davis, USA: Universal.
Charlie Is My Darling (1966), Dir. Peter Whitehead, UK.
Chasing Trane (2016), Dir. John Scheinfeld, USA: Meteor 17.
Cobain: Montage of Heck (2015), Dir. Brett Morgen, USA: HBO.
Cocksucker Blues (1972), Dir. Robert Frank, USA.
Concert Magic (1948), Dir. Paul Gordon, USA.
Country Music (2019), Dir. Ken Burns, USA: PBS.
Crossing the Bridge: The Sound of Istanbul (2005), Dir. Fatih Akin, Germany: NDR.
D.O.A. (1980), Dir. Lech Kowalski, USA.
Dave Chappelle's Block Party (2005), Dir. Michel Gondry, USA: Partizan.
David Crosby: Remember My Name (2019), Dir. A.J. Eaton, USA: Vinyl Films.
Delia Derbyshire: The Myths and Legendary Tapes (2020), Dir. Caroline Catz, UK: Anti-Worlds.
Depeche Mode: 101 (1989), Dir. D.A. Pennebaker, Chris Hegedus and David Dawkins, USA/UK: Pennebaker Associates/Mute.
Dexys: Nowhere Is Home (2014), Dir. Kieran Evans and Paul Kelly, UK: Heavenly Films.
Devil's Pie (2019), Dir. Carine Bijlsma, USA: Significant Productions.
Dick Tracy (1990), Dir. Warren Beatty, USA: Touchstone.
Dig! (2004), Dir. Ondi Timoner, USA: Interloper Films.
Documentary Now! (2015), [TV Series], USA: IFC, 20 August.
Don't Break Down: A Film About Jawbreaker (2017), Dir. Tim Irwin and Keith Schieron, USA: Rocket Fuel.
Dont Look Back (1967), Dir. D.A. Pennebaker, USA: Leacock-Pennebaker.
Dread Beat an' Blood (1979), Dir. Franco Rosso, UK: Arts Council.
Eat the Document (1972), Dir. Bob Dylan, USA.
Eden (2014), Dir. Mia Hansen-Løve, France: CG Cinéma.
Elvis: That's the Way It Is (1970), Dir. Denis Sanders, USA: MGM.
Elvis '68 Comeback Special (1968), Dir. Steve Binder, USA: Binder/Howe Productions.
Elephant Days (2015), Dir. James Caddick and James Cronin, UK: 2am TV.
Ethiopiques: Revolt of the Soul (2017), Dir. Maciej Bochniak, Germany: HBO Europe.

Everybody in the Place: An Incomplete History of Britain 1984–1992 (2019), Dir. Jeremy Deller, UK: Frieze.
Fear of a Black Hat (1993), Dir. Rusty Cundieff, USA: Oakwood Productions.
Festival (1967), Dir. Murray Lerner, USA: Patchke Productions.
Finding Fela! (2014), Dir. Alex Gibney, USA: Jigsaw.
Finisterre (2003), Dir. Kieran Evans and Paul Kelly, UK: Heavenly Films.
Fiorucci Made Me Hardcore (1999), [Video], Dir. Mark Leckey, UK.
Gaga: Five Foot Two (2017), Dir. Chris Moukarbel, USA: Live Nation.
George Harrison: Living in the Material World (2011), Dir. Martin Scorsese, USA: Sikelia Productions.
Gimme Shelter (1970), Dir. Albert and David Maysles, Charlotte Zwerin, USA: Maysles Films.
Ginger Baker in Africa (1973), Dir. Tony Palmer, [TV Series], UK: BBC, 15 July.
Good Ol' Freda (2013), Dir. Ryan White, UK: Tripod Media.
Goodfellas (1990), Dir. Martin Scorsese, USA: Warner Brothers.
Grace Jones: Bloodlight and Bami (2017), Dir. Sophie Fiennes, UK: Blinder Films.
Graffiti Bridge (1990), Dir. Prince, USA: Warner Brothers.
Heavy Metal Parking Lot (1986), Dir. John Heyn and Jeff Krulik, USA.
Help! (1965), Dir. Richard Lester, UK: United Artists.
Here to be Heard: The Story of the Slits (2017), Dir. William E. Badgley, UK: Head Gear Films.
Home of the Brave: A Film by Laurie Anderson (1986), Dir. Laurie Anderson, USA: Talk Normal.
Homecoming: A Film by Beyoncé (2019), Dir. Beyoncé and Ed Burke, USA: PRG.
I Am Trying to Break Your Heart (2002), Dir. Sam Jones, USA: Plexifilm.
I Called Him Morgan (2016), Dir. Kasper Collin, Sweden: SVT.
I'm Not There (2007), Dir. Todd Haynes, USA: Killer Films.
I've Been Trying to Tell You (2021), Dir. Alasdair McLellan, UK: BFI.
In the Court of the Crimson King: King Crimson at 50 (2022), Dir. Toby Amies, UK: Succulent Pictures.
Inna De Yard (2019), Dir. Peter Webber, France: Borsalino Productions.
Instrument (1999), Dir. Jem Cohen, USA: Dischord.
Jammin' The Blues (1944), Dir. Gjon Mili, USA: Warner Brothers.
Jason Becker: Not Dead Yet (2012), Dir. Jesse Vile, USA: Kino Lorber.
Jazz Dance (1954), Dir. Roger Tilton, USA.
Jazz on a Summer's Day (1959) Dir. Bert Stern and Aram Avakian, USA: Galaxy.
Joe Strummer: The Future Is Unwritten (2007), Dir. Julien Temple, UK: FilmFour.
Junun (2015), Dir. Paul Thomas Anderson, USA: Ghoulardi.
Jubilee (1978), Dir. Derek Jarman, UK: Megalovision.

Justin Timberlake + The Tennessee Kids (2016), Dir. Jonathan Demme, USA: Playtone.
Kate Nash: Underestimate the Girl (2018), Dir. Amy Goldstein, UK: Span Productions.
Keyboard Fantasies: The Beverly Glenn-Copeland Story (2019), Dir. Posy Dixon, UK: LUCA.
King of Jazz (1930), Dir. John Murray Anderson, USA: Universal.
King Rocker (2020), Dir. Michael Cumming, UK: Fire Films.
Late Blossom Blues (2017), Dir. Wolfgang Pfoser-Almer and Stefan Wolner, Austria: Let's Make This Happen.
Lawrence of Belgravia (2011), Dir. Paul Kelly, UK: Heavenly Films.
Le Donk & Scor-zay-zee (2009), Dir. Shane Meadows, UK: Warp.
Leaving Neverland (2019), Dir. Dan Reed, USA/UK: HBO/Channel 4.
Leonard Cohen: Bird on a Wire (2010), Dir. Tony Palmer, UK: The Machat Company.
Let It Be (1970), Dir. Michael Lindsay-Hogg, UK: Apple Corps.
Let's Get Lost (1988), Dir. Bruce Weber, USA: Little Bear Productions.
Listening to You: The Who at the Isle of Wight 1970 (1998), Dir. Murray Lerner, UK: Pulsar.
London (1994), Dir. Patrick Keiller, UK: BFI.
London Symphony (2017), Dir. Alex Barrett, UK: Disobedient Films.
Lord Don't Slow Me Down (2007), Dir. Bailie Walsh, UK: Cheese Film & Video.
Lost in France (2016), Dir. Niall McCann, Ireland/UK: Still Films/Edge City.
L7: Pretend We're Dead (2016), Dir. Sarah Price, USA: Blue Hats Creative.
Madonna: Truth or Dare (1991), Dir. Alek Keshishian, USA: Miramax.
Magical Mystery Tour (1967), Dir. George Harrison, John Lennon and Paul McCartney, UK: Apple Corps.
Makina! (2020), Dir. Hector Aponysus, UK: British Council/Boiler Room.
Marley (2012), Dir. Kevin Macdonald, UK: Tuff Gong.
Mean Streets (1973), Dir. Martin Scorsese, USA: Warner Brothers.
Meeting People is Easy (1998), Dir. Grant Gee, UK: Parlophone.
Metallica: Some Kind of Monster (2004), Dir. Joe Berlinger and Bruce Sinofsky, USA: RadicalMedia.
Miles Davis: Birth of the Cool (2019), Dir. Stanley Nelson, USA: Davis Raynes Productions.
Milford Graves Full Mantis (2018), Dir. Jake Meginsky and Neil Young, USA: Mantis Film.
Miss Americana (2020), Dir. Lana Wilson, USA: Tremolo Productions.
Miss Sharon Jones! (2015), Dir. Barbara Kopple, USA: Cabin Creek Films.
Momma Don't Allow (1956), Dir. Karel Reisz and Tony Richardson, UK: BFI.
Monterey Pop (1968), Dir. D.A. Pennebaker, USA: Leacock-Pennebaker.

Monty Python and the Holy Grail (1975), Dir. Terry Jones and Terry Gilliam, UK: Python Pictures.
Muscle Shoals (2013), Dir. Greg 'Freddy' Camalier, USA: Ear Goggles.
My Name Is Albert Ayler (2005), Dir. Kasper Collin, Sweden: Filmpool Nord.
Nashville (1975), Dir. Robert Altman, USA: Paramount.
Neil Young: Heart of Gold (2006), Dir. Jonathan Demme, USA: Playtone.
Neil Young Journeys (2011), Dir. Jonathan Demme, USA: Shakey Pictures.
New York, New York (1977), Dir. Martin Scorsese, USA: Chartoff-Winkler Productions.
NG83 When We Were B Boys (2016), Dir. Sam Derby-Cooper, Claude Knight and Luke Scott, UK: NG83 Productions.
No Direction Home: Bob Dylan (2005), Dir. Martin Scorsese, USA: PBS.
No One Knows About Persian Cats (2009), Dir. Bahman Ghobadi, Iran: Mitosfilm.
Oasis Knebworth 1996 (2021), Dir. Jake Scott, UK: Black Dog Films.
Oil City Confidential (2009), Dir. Julien Temple, UK: Cadiz.
Old Man (2014), Dir. Dan S., USA.
On the Road (2016), Dir. Michael Winterbottom, UK: Lorton Entertainment.
One + One (1968), Dir. Jean-Luc Godard, UK: Cupid Productions.
One More Time with Feeling (2016), Dir. Andrew Dominik, UK: Iconoclast.
Orion: The Man Who Would Be King (2015), Dir. Jeanie Finlay, UK: Glimmer Films.
Ornette: Made in America (1985), Dir. Shirley Clarke, USA: Caravan of Dreams.
Other Music (2019), Dir. Puloma Basu and Rob Hatch-Miller, USA: Cartoon Network.
Patti Smith: Dream of Life (2008), Dir. Steven Sebring, USA: Clean Socks.
Pink Floyd: Live at Pompeii (1972), Dir. Adrian Maben, West Germany: Bayerischer Rundfunk.
Points on a Space Age (2009), Dir. Ephram Asili, USA: ConFluence Films.
Popstar: Never Stop Never Stopping (2016), Dir. Akiva Schaffer and Jorma Taccone, USA: Universal.
Poly Styrene: I Am a Cliché (2021), Dir. Paul Sng and Celeste Bell, UK: Tyke Films.
Privilege (1967), Dir. Peter Watkins, UK: World Film Services.
Pulp: A Film About Life, Death and Supermarkets (2014), Dir. Florian Habicht, UK: Pistachio Pictures.
Punk: Attitude (2005), Dir. Don Letts, UK: 3DD.
Punk Can Take It (1979), Dir. Julien Temple, UK: Boyd's Company.
Ray (2004), Dir. Taylor Hackford, USA: Universal.
Renaldo and Clara (1978), Dir. Bob Dylan, USA: Lombard Street Films.
Requiem for Detroit? (2010), Dir. Julien Temple, UK: BBC.
Richard III (1955), Dir. Laurence Olivier, UK: London Film Productions.
Right On! (1970), Dir. Herbert Danska, USA: Leacock-Pennebaker.

Rolling Thunder Revue: A Bob Dylan Story by Martin Scorsese (2019), Dir. Martin Scorsese, USA: Sikelia Productions.
Rudeboy: The Story of Trojan Records (2018), Dir. Nicholas Jack Davies, UK: Pulse Films.
Science of Ghosts (2018), Dir. Niall McCann, Ireland: Still Films.
Scott Walker: 30 Century Man (2006), Dir. Stephen Kijak, UK: BBC.
Scratch (2001), Dir. Doug Pray, USA: Palm Pictures.
Searching for Sugar Man (2012), Dir. Malik Bendjelloul, UK: Red Box Films.
Senna (2010), Dir. Asif Kapadia, UK: Universal.
Separado! (2010), Dir. Dylan Goch and Gruff Rhys, UK: Soda Pictures.
Sex Pistols Number 1 (1977), Dir. Derek Jarman, Julien Temple and John Tiberi, UK.
Shine a Light (2008), Dir. Martin Scorsese, USA: Paramount.
Shut Up And Play The Hits (2012), Dir. Will Lovelace and Dylan Southern, USA: Pulse Films.
Sign 'o' The Times (1987), Dir. Prince and Albert Magnoli, USA: Paisley Park.
Sisters with Transistors (2020), Dir. Lisa Rovner, UK/France/USA: Willow Glen Films.
Small Axe: Lovers Rock (2020), Dir. Steve McQueen, UK: BBC.
Sound It Out (2011), Dir. Jeanie Finlay, UK: Glimmer Films.
Soul Power (2008), Dir. Jeffrey Kusama-Hinte, USA: Antidote Films.
Southern Journey (Revisited) (2020), Dir. Rob Curry and Tim Plester, UK: Fifth Column Films.
Space is the Place (1974), Dir. John Coney, USA: North American Star System.
Standing in the Shadows of Motown (2002), Dir. Paul Justman, USA: Artisan.
Stepping Razor: Red X (1992), Dir. Nicholas Campbell, Canada: Bush Doctor.
Stop Making Sense (1984), Dir. Jonathan Demme, USA: Cinecom.
Style Wars (1983), Dir. Tony Silver, USA: Public Art Films.
Summer of Soul (. . .Or, When the Revolution Could Not Be Televised) (2021), Dir. Questlove, USA: Mass Distraction Media.
Supersonic (2016), Dir. Mat Whitecross, UK: Mint Pictures.
Superstar: The Karen Carpenter Story (1987), Dir. Todd Haynes, USA: Iced Tea Productions.
Syl Johnson: Any Way the Wind Blows (2015), Dir. Rob Hatch-Miller, USA.
Syncopation (1942), Dir. William Dieterle, USA: RKO.
Synecdoche, New York (2008), Dir. Charlie Kaufman, USA: Sony.
Tanner '88 (1988), Dir. Robert Altman, USA: HBO.
Teddy Pendergrass: If You Don't Know Me (2018), Dir. Olivia Lichtenstein, UK: BBC.
Ten Years In An Open Necked Shirt (1982), Dir. Nick May, UK: Arts Council.
The Assassination of Jesse James by the Coward Robert Ford (2007), Dir. Andrew Dominik, USA: Warner Brothers.

The Ballad of Shirley Collins (2017), Dir. Rob Curry and Tim Plester, UK: Fifth Column.
The Beatles: Eight Days a Week – The Touring Years (2016), Dir. Ron Howard, USA: Apple Corps.
The Beatles: Get Back (2021), Dir. Peter Jackson, USA: Disney.
The Black Power Mixtape 1967–1975 (2011), Dir. Göran Olsson, Sweden: Story AB.
The Blank Generation (1976), Dir. Ivan Král and Amos Poe, USA.
The Blues Accordin' to Lightnin' Hopkins (1970), Dir. Les Blank, USA: Flower Films.
The Chemical Brothers: Don't Think (2012), Dir. Adam Smith, Japan.
The Clash: Westway to the World (2000), Dir. Don Letts, UK: 3DD.
The Decline of Western Civilization (1981), Dir. Penelope Spheeris, USA: Spheeris Films.
The Decline of Western Civilization Part II: The Metal Years (1988), Dir. Penelope Spheeris, USA: I.R.S. World Media.
The Decline of Western Civilization Part III (1998), Dir. Penelope Spheeris, USA: Spheeris Films.
The Devil and Daniel Johnston (2005), Dir. Jeff Feuerzeig, USA: Complex Corporation.
The Ecstasy of Wilko Johnson (2015), Dir. Julien Temple, UK: Nitrate.
The Filth and the Fury (2000), Dir. Julien Temple, UK: FilmFour.
The Great Hip Hop Hoax (2013), Dir. Jeanie Finlay, UK: Glimmer Films.
The Great Rock 'n' Roll Swindle (1980), Dir. Julien Temple, UK: Virgin.
The Last Angel of History (1996), Dir. John Akomfrah, UK: Channel 4.
The Last Waltz (1978), Dir. Martin Scorsese, USA: United Artists.
The Man Behind the Microphone (2017), Dir. Claire Belhassine, France.
The Man from Mo'Wax (2016), Dir. Matthew Jones, UK: Capture.
The Night James Brown Saved Boston (2008), Dir. David Leaf, USA: David Leaf Productions.
The Parkinsons: A Long Way to Nowhere (2016), Dir. Caroline Richards, UK: Demarz Productions.
The Possibilities Are Endless (2014), Dir. James Hall and Edward Lovelace, UK: Pulse Films.
The Punk Rock Movie (1978), Dir. Don Letts, UK: Punk Rock Films.
The Punk Singer (2013), Dir. Sini Anderson, USA: Long Shot Factory.
The Rolling Stones Rock and Roll Circus (1996), Dir. Michael Lindsay-Hogg, UK.
The Rutles: All You Need Is Cash (1978), Dir. Eric Idle and Gary Weis, UK/USA: Rutle.
The Seventh Seal (1957), Dir. Ingmar Bergman, Sweden: Svensk Filmindustri.
The Sound Is Innocent (2019), Dir. Johana Ozvold, Czech Republic: Cinémotif.
The Sparks Brothers (2021), Dir. Edgar Wright, USA: Focus.
The Story of Lovers Rock (2011), Dir. Menelik Shabazz, UK.
The T.A.M.I. Show (1964), Dir. Steve Binder, USA: Screen Entertainment Co.

The Velvet Underground (2021), Dir. Todd Haynes, USA: Killer Films.
The White Stripes Under Great Northern Lights (2009), Dir. Emmett Malloy, USA: Woodshed Films.
The Wrecking Crew! (2008), Dir. Denny Tedesco, USA: Lunch Box Entertainment.
They Will Have to Kill Us First: Malian Music in Exile (2015), Dir. Johanna Schwartz, UK: Together Films.
This Is Spinal Tap (1984), Dir. Rob Reiner, USA: Embassy Pictures.
This Is Tomorrow (2008), Dir. Paul Kelly, UK: Heavenly Films.
Time Is Illmatic (2014), Dir. One9, USA: Tribeca Film Institute.
Trances (1981), Dir. Ahmed El Maanouni, Morocco: Interfilms.
Truth & Memory (2019), Dir. Kieran Evans, UK.
Twenty Feet from Stardom (2013), Dir. Morgan Neville, USA: Tremelo Productions.
Under the Cherry Moon (1986), Dir. Prince, USA: Warner Brothers.
U2: Rattle and Hum (1988), Dir. Phil Joanou, USA: Paramount.
Vashti Bunyan: From Here to Before (2008), Dir. Kieran Evans, UK: CC-Films.
Velvet Goldmine (1998), Dir. Todd Haynes, UK: Killer Films.
Waiting for Guffman (1996), Dir. Christopher Guest, USA: Castle Rock.
Walk Hard: The Dewey Cox Story (2007), Dir. Jake Kasdan, USA: Columbia.
Walk the Line (2005), Dir. James Mangold, USA: Fox 2000.
Walker (1987), Dir. Alex Cox, USA: Walker Films Limited.
Wattstax (1973), Dir. Mel Stuart, USA: Stax.
We Jam Econo: The Story of the Minutemen (2005), Dir. Tim Irwin, USA: Rocket Fuel.
What Happened, Miss Simone? (2015), Dir. Liz Garbus, USA: RadicalMedia.
What Have You Done Today Mervyn Day? (2005), Dir. Paul Kelly, UK: Heavenly Films.
What's Happening! The Beatles in the U.S.A. (1964), Dir. Albert and David Maysles, USA: Maysles Films.
White Riot (2019), Dir. Rubika Shah, UK: Bridge + Tunnel.
White Stripes: Under Blackpool Lights (2004), Dir. Dick Carruthers, UK.
Whitney (2018), Dir. Kevin Macdonald, UK: Altitude.
Whitney: Can I Be Me (2017), Dir. Nick Broomfield and Rudi Dolezal, UK: Showtime.
Year of the Horse (1997), Dir. Jim Jarmusch, USA: Shakey Pictures.
Yellow Submarine (1968), Dir. George Dunning, UK: Apple Corps.
Ziggy Stardust and the Spiders from Mars (1979), Dir. D.A. Pennebaker, UK: Miramax.
2+2=22: The Alphabet (2017), Dir. Heinz Emigholz, Germany: Heinz Emigholz Filmproduktion.
9 Songs (2004), Dir. Michael Winterbottom, UK: Revolution.
24 Hour Party People (2002), Dir. Michael Winterbottom, UK: Revolution.
20,000 Days on Earth (2014), Dir. Iain Forsyth and Jane Pollard, UK: BFI.

Index

16mm xii, 15, 43, 90, 102, 183, 198
2+2=22: The Alphabet 100
20 Feet from Stardom 64, 90–2, 93
20,000 Days on Earth 189–193
24 Hour Party People 6, 63
35mm 43, 90
8mm [Super] 235
9 Songs 63

A Band Called Death 134–5
A Dog Called Money 20, 96–7
A Hard Day's Night 3, 4, 6, 11, 25, 33, 34–7, 38, 58, 62
A Mighty Wind 59, 61
A Poem is a Naked Person 26–9
Abdurraqib, Hanif 13, 45, 115, 138, 229
Afro-Punk [Film] 135–6
Air: Eating, Sleeping, Waiting and Playing 234
Akin, Fatih 155
Akomfrah, John 84, 116, 117–18, 241
Albarn, Damon 159, 168
All Tomorrow's Parties [Film] 234, 237–8
Am I Black Enough for You [Film] 126–7
Amazing Grace [Film] 24, 26–9
American Interior [Film] xi, 144–6
Amies, Toby 242
Amy 81, 164, 166–8
Anderson, Laurie 53, 241
Anderson, Melissa 116, 226, 227
Anderson, Paul Thomas 98–9
Anderson, Sini 178, 180–1,
Anka, Paul 10–11, 47
Anorac 144, 147–8, 150, 151, 155, 156
Anvil: The Story of Anvil 105, 201–3
Armstrong, Louis 16, 18
Asili, Ephram 119
Aufderheide, Patricia 6
Authenticity 8, 12, 24, 59, 61, 63, 66, 80, 84, 131, 157, 187, 188, 181, 196, 206, 237
Awesome: I Fuckin' Shot That! 3, 80–1, 237

Badu, Erykah 82, 83, 142
Baez, Joan 38, 42, 216
Basically, Johnny Moped 106
Basu, Puloma 151
Bayou Maharajah 128–9
BBC 71, 85, 149, 199, 220
Be Pure. Be Vigilant. Behave 213, 214–15
Beastie Boys 3, 80–1, 110, 181, 237
Beatles, The 4, 11, 17, 25, 33–8, 44, 45, 49, 58, 62, 241
Beats, Rhymes & Life: The Travels of a Tribe Called Quest 136, 138–9
Beattie, Keith 3, 37, 38
Becker, Jason 80, 193–5, 211
Belhassine, Claire 150, 154–5
Beware of Mr Baker 198, 199–200
Beyoncé 228–9, 239
Biggie and Tupac 165
Bijlsma, Carine 128, 129–30
Billie 167, 172–3, 183
Billie Eilish: The World's a Little Blurry 170–1, 183
Bird on a Wire 21, 218, 230–1
Blank, Les 26, 27, 217, 241
Blur 153, 168
Bowie, David 62, 63, 219–20, 239
Brilleaux, Lee 1, 71
Brody, Richard 19
Broomfield, Nick 164–6, 241
Bros: After the Screaming Stops 203
Buckwalter, Ian 240
Buena Vista Social Club 99, 133, 143, 157–8, 159, 161
Bulger, Jay 199
Bunch of Kunst 25–9, 225
Burns, Fred 106

Callahan, Bill 157
Caouette, Jonathan 237
Caramanica, Jon 21
Carruthers, Dick 235

Cassavetes, John 107, 108
Catz, Caroline 84–6
Cave, Nick 151, 188–92, 209, 237
Cave, Susie 189, 191
CB4 61
Charlie is my Darling 47
Chasing Trane 117, 123–4, 125
Clark, Ashley 132
Clarke, Shirley 119–20
Cliché 77, 123, 203
Coachella [Festival] 170, 172, 228, 229
Cobain, Kurt 79, 165, 178, 207–8
Cobain: Montage of Heck 20, 204, 207–9
Cocksucker Blues 23, 26, 28, 39, 48, 49, 209
Cohen, Jem 5, 107, 108
Cohen, Leonard 21, 230–1
Cohen, Thomas F 3, 4, 18, 214, 215
Collin, Kasper 121–3, 172, 177
Collins, Edwyn 80, 192–3
Collins, Shirley 182, 183–4
Coltrane, John 117, 123, 125, 140, 172
Cooder, Ry 100, 157–8
Country [Music] 3, 22, 61, 62, 241
Cowie, Peter 4, 34
Crock of Gold: A Few Rounds With Shane McGowan 73
Crossing the Bridge: The Sound of Istanbul 143, 155–6, 161
Cumming, Michael 203–4
Curry, Rob 183–4, 241

Danska, Herbert 116
Dave Chappelle's Block Party 22, 140–2
David Byrne's American Utopia 54
David Crosby: Remember My Name 200–1
Davies, Gruffydd 155
Davies, Sam 127, 237
Davis, Angela 82, 123
Davis, Miles 20, 140, 172
Delia Derbyshire: The Myths and Legendary Tapes 33, 84–6
Deller, Jeremy 65, 84, 241
Demme, Jonathan 14, 53–7, 64, 99, 215
Depeche Mode 101 3, 33, 64–6, 215
Detroit 21, 22, 73, 90, 117
Devil's Pie: D'Angelo 128–30
Dexys: Nowhere Is Home 67, 84
Dig! 77–8, 79

Directors Notes 52, 106, 146
Dixon, Posy 140
DOA 50
Documentary Now! 64
Dominik, Andrew 188–90
Don't Think 236–7
Dont Look Back 2, 3, 11, 37–9, 40, 41, 60, 62, 64, 187, 205, 233
Dr Feelgood 1, 70–1, 143
Dread Beat and Blood 241
DVD 6, 52, 56, 79, 118
Dyal, Geeta 16–17
Dylan, Bob 11, 23, 37–44, 50, 61, 62, 187, 206, 209, 216, 233

Eat The Document 23, 39–40, 43, 209
Ebiri, Bilge 161
Eckenwroth, Lindsey 233
Eden 236
Eight Days A Week: The Touring Years 36
El Maanouni, Ahmed 160
Elephant Days 74, 95, 97–8, 102, 103
Ellis, Warren 189–92
Elvis: That's The Way It Is 215, 220–1, 222
Emigholz, Heinz 100
Eshun, Kodwo 117–18
Ethiopiques: Revolt of the Soul 158
Evans, Kieran 74, 75, 84, 148–9, 213, 214–15, 241
Everybody in the Place: An Incomplete History of Britain 1984–1992 84
Ewens, Hannah 167, 170

Fear of a Black Hat 61
Festival [Film] 216–17
Feuerzeig, Jeff 79–80
Fiennes, Sophie 173–4, 182, 187
Finding Fela! 143
Finisterre [Film] 73–5
Finlay, Jeanie 66, 150–2, 195–7
Fiorucci Made Me Hardcore 84
Fisher, Jean 117
Fisher, Mark 1, 10, 75, 174
Folk [Music] 37, 39, 44, 59, 61, 147, 149, 183, 216
Frank, Robert 28, 39, 48,
Franklin, Aretha 19, 24, 26–8, 94
Franz, Christine 25–9, 225
Frere-Jones, Sasha 29

Fugazi 3, 107–8, 178
Fugazi: Instrument (see *Instrument*)

Gaga, Lady 169–70
Gaga: Five Foot Two 20, 169–70, 171, 183
Gahan, Dave 33, 65
Garbus, Liz 124
Garfield, Rachel 135, 136
Gaye, Marvin 91, 118, 166, 216
Gee, Grant 5, 232–3, 234
George Harrison: Living in the Material World 40, 44
Get Back [Film] 16, 17, 36
Ghobadi, Bahman 156
Gimme Shelter [Film] 10, 11, 38, 44, 45–7, 48, 49, 66, 95, 187, 230, 231
Gimme Shelter [Song] 44, 93
Ginger in Africa 199
Glastonbury [Festival] 225, 233
Glastonbury [Film] 73
Glynn, Stephen 4, 37
Goch, Dylan xi, 144, 147
God Respects Us When We Work, But Loves Us When We Dance 217
Godard, Jean-Luc 43, 45, 46, 94–6, 100
Goldman, Vivien 177
Goldstein, Amy 104
Gondry, Michel 140
Good Ol' Freda 36
Grace Jones: Bloodlight and Bami 172, 173–4, 187
Grant Ferguson, Ailsa 69
Graves, Milford 20, 120–1
Greenwood, Jonny 98–9, 233
Gwenno 147, 150

Halligan, Benjamin 78
Hanna, Kathleen 104, 180–1
Hans, Simran 21, 163–4
Hansen-Løve, Mia 236
Harbert, Benjamin J 3, 4, 46, 66, 107–8
Harlem 82, 205, 223, 226, 227
Hatch-Miller, Rob 125–6, 151
Hatherley, Owen 153
Haynes, Todd 62, 63, 86
Heart of Gold [Film] 56
Heavy Metal Parking Lot 77, 241
Hedegus, Chris 64, 65
Help! [Film] 35

Hendrix, Jimi 11, 217, 227
Here to be Heard: The Story of the Slits 176
Hip Hop 8, 29, 61, 75, 81, 116, 117, 126, 136–9, 141, 142, 147, 152, 156, 157, 195–197, 198, 243
Hoby, Hermione 196
Holiday, Billie 167, 172–3
Holm-Hudson, Kevin 219
Home of the Brave 53, 241
Homecoming: a Film by Beyoncé 228–9, 239
Hörnblowér, Nathanial (see Yauch, Adam)
Houston, Whitney 21, 163, 164–6, 172, 182
Howell, Amanda 45
Hunter, Meredith 45, 46, 188
Hutcheon, Linda 1, 2, 4, 7, 9, 10, 66

I Am Trying to Break Your Heart [Film] 101–3
I Called Him Morgan 121–3, 172, 177
I'm Not There 62
I've Been Trying To Tell You [Film] 76
Ibiza: The Silent Movie 73
In Bed With Madonna (see *Madonna: Truth or Dare*)
In The Court of the Crimson King [Film] 242
Inna De Yard 131, 133–4, 159
Instrument [Film] 3, 107–8, 178

Jackson, Mahalia 15, 226
Jackson, Michael 24, 210–11
Jagger, Mick 28, 45–9, 92, 231
James, David E 3, 4, 96
Jammin' the Blues 12–13
Jarmusch, Jim 56, 107
Jason Becker: Not Dead Yet 80, 193–5, 211
Jazz Dance 13, 14
Jazz on a Summer's Day 3, 14, 15–19, 226
Jeffries, Stuart 207
Joe Strummer: The Future is Unwritten 20, 71–2
Jones, Grace 172, 173–4, 182, 187
Jones, Sam 101
Journeys [Film] 56
Jubilee 50
Junun [Film] 98–9, 100
Justin Timberlake + The Tennessee Kids 14, 56–7

Kael, Pauline 54
Kapadia, Asif 164, 167
Kate Nash: Underestimate the Girl 103, 104–5
Keber, Lily 128
Kelly, Paul 74–5, 76, 84, 241
Keyboard Fantasies 33, 140
King Rocker 33, 201, 203–4,
Kopple, Barbara 174–5
Kurt & Courtney 165
Kusama-Hinte, Jeffrey 224

L7: Pretend We're Dead 176, 177–9, 182
Late Blossom Blues 7, 8, 130
Lawrence of Belgravia 241
Le Donk & Scor-zay-zee 29
Leaving Neverland 24, 209–11
Lee, Spike 54
Lee, Stewart 203–4
Lennon, John 36, 40, 48, 241
Lerner, Murray 22, 216
Lester, Richard 3, 11, 25, 34–6, 43, 62
Let It Be [Film] 17, 23, 36, 46, 58
Let's Get Lost 198–9
Letts, Don 50, 72–3, 133, 179, 242–3
Lindsay-Hogg, Michael 36
Listening to You: The Who at Isle of Wight Festival 1970 22, 216
Lloyd, Robert 6, 203–4
Lodge, Guy 6
London [Place] 68, 70, 72, 74–6, 84, 96, 97, 106, 151, 154, 157, 159, 203
London [Film] 75
Lonely Boy 10, 11–12, 14, 47
Lord Don't Slow Me Down 60, 213, 231–2, 239
Lost in France 108–10
Love, Courtney 165, 207–9
Lovers Rock [Film] 131

Maben, Adrian 218
Macdonald, Kevin 133, 163–6
Madonna 7, 169, 170, 206–7, 209
Madonna: Truth or Dare 7, 169, 206–7, 209,
Magical Mystery Tour [Film] 36
Malloy, Emmett 235
Manchester 63, 151
Manic Street Preachers 75, 148–50, 213–15

Marley 133
Maxwell, Grace 193
Maysles Brothers, The 11, 34, 35, 44–7
McCann, Niall 108
McLellan, Alasdair 76
McQueen, Steve 131
Meeting People Is Easy 5, 39, 232–4
Meginsky, Jake 20, 120–1, 236
Metallica 26, 76–7
Metallica: Some Kind of Monster 26, 76–7
Miles Davis: Birth of the Cool 20, 124
Milford Graves Full Mantis 20, 120–1, 236
Mili, Gjon 12
Mills, Mike 234
Miss Americana 168–9, 171
Miss Sharon Jones! 163, 174–5
Mistaken for Strangers 83
Mitchell, Joni 42, 200
Modulations 241
Momma Don't Allow 13–14
Monk, Thelonious 15–16, 18
Monterey Pop 11, 64, 217–18, 226
Morgan, Lee 121–3, 124, 132, 172, 177
MTV 61, 69, 139, 168
Mulholland, Garry 3, 48, 91
Murphy, Seamus 97
Muscle Shoals [Film] 46, 90, 93–4
Muscle Shoals [Studio] 46
My Name Is Albert Ayler 123
Myth 2, 33, 43, 63, 67, 78, 80, 84, 123, 169, 187, 188, 199, 218, 219

Nashville [Film] 42, 62
Nashville [Place] 26, 56
New York 19, 46, 49, 65, 68, 80, 86, 94, 116, 117, 119, 122, 126, 137, 138, 140, 151, 152, 243
New York, New York [Film] 43
New York Times 19, 121, 170, 243
New Yorker, The 19, 54, 166
NG83 When We Were B Boys 150, 152–3
Nichols, Bill 7, 8
No Direction Home: Bob Dylan 22, 40–1, 42, 216
No One Knows About Persian Cats 156–7
Notorious B.I.G 141, 165

Oasis 60, 153, 231–232
Oasis: Knebworth '96 [Film] 231

Oil City Confidential 1, 70, 71, 73, 105, 143
Old Man 242
Olsson, Göran 82
One + One (see *Sympathy for the Devil* [Film])
One More Time with Feeling 187, 188-2
Orion: The Man Who Would Be King 195-7, 198
Ornette: Made in America 3, 119-20, 121
Other Music 151

Paratext 9-10
Parody 7, 58, 73
Paparazzi 167, 168
Patti Smith: Dream of Life 179-80
Pendergrass, Teddy 127
Penman, Ian 25
Pennebaker, DA 2, 11, 37, 38-9, 43, 60, 62, 63, 64-6, 187, 215, 217-18, 219-20, 221, 222
Performativity 7, 8, 116, 169, 185, 192, 203, 228,
Petkova, Savina 171
Pink Floyd: Live at Pompeii 218-19, 230
Pinkerton, Nick 26
Plester, Tim 182, 183-4, 241
Points on a Space Age 119
Poly Styrene: I Am A Cliché 33, 67, 176-7,
Pop, Iggy 29, 62
Popstar: Never Stop Never Stopping 21, 61
Postmodern 54, 55, 62, 63, 240,
Postmodernism 2
Presley, Elvis 197, 215, 220-1, 222
Price, Sarah 178
Prince 222-3, 239
Privilege [Film] 57, 241
Pulp: A Film About Life, Death & Supermarkets 153-4
Punk Can Take It 69
Punk Rock Movie 50
Punk: Attitude 136, 179

Questlove 82, 129, 130, 223, 226-7, 16
Quietus, The 54, 96, 120, 127, 171, 204

Radiohead 5, 39, 232-4
Rafferty, Terrence 198
Rapaport, Michael 138-9
Ray 61

Reality 1, 4, 8, 46, 52, 57, 60, 65, 84, 87, 94, 177, 187, 188, 189, 191, 193, 194, 198
Reconstructions 85, 90, 119, 132
Redding, Otis 93, 218
Reed, Lou 62, 86
Reiner, Rob 6, 60, 202
Reisz, Karel 13-14
Renaldo and Clara 41
Requiem for Detroit? 21, 73
Reynolds, Simon 71, 149
Rhys, Gruff xi-xiii, 144-7, 148, 150
Richards, Caroline 105-6
Richardson, Tony 13-14
Right On! 116-11
Roessner, Jeffrey 58
Rolling Stones, The 28, 39, 44-9, 66, 93, 95-6, 188, 209
Rolling Thunder Revue: A Bob Dylan Story by Martin Scorsese 41-4
Romney, Jonathan 174, 187, 206
Rudeboy: The Story of Trojan Records 133-4

S, Dan 241
Saffle, Michael 54
Saunders, Dave 3, 15, 217
Scanlan, John 3, 41, 179, 191, 220
Schwartz, Johanna 158-60
Scorsese, Martin 37, 40-4, 49, 51, 60, 69, 90, 216
Scott Walker: 30 Century Man 94, 100-1
Scott, AO 19, 86
Scratch 139
Searching for Sugar Man 79, 158, 241
Sebring, Steven 179-80
Separado! Xi, 144-6, 150, 154, 155
Sex Pistols Number 1 69
Sex Pistols, The 67-70, 179
Shabazz, Menelik 131-2, 133
Shine A Light 44, 49
Shut Up and Play the Hits 238-40
Sign 'O' The Times 222-3
Simone, Nina 115, 124-5, 130, 192, 200
Sisters With Transistors 33, 85
Sleaford Mods 26, 28-9, 225
Sly & The Family Stone 227
Smith, Adam 236-7
Sonic Youth 179, 237
Soul Power 224-5

Sound It Out 150, 151–2, 153, 195, 197
Southern Journey [Revisited] 241
Space Is The Place [Film] 118–19
Spheeris, Penelope 49–53, 64, 67
Standing in the Shadows of Motown 90–1, 92
Staple Singers, The 217, 223, 224, 226
Staples, Mavis 226
Stepping Razor: Red X 131, 132–3
Stop Making Sense 205, 215, 53–6, 57,
Strummer, Joe 20, 67, 71, 72, 242
Stuart, Mel 142, 223–4
Style Wars 75, 136–7, 142
Summer of Soul 16, 27, 33, 82, 223, 224, 226–7, 239
Sun Ra 117, 118–19
Sun Ra Akestra, The 119
Super Furry Animals 144, 146, 148, 150
Supersonic [Film] 231
Superstar: The Karen Carpenter Story 62
Swift, Taylor 163, 168–9, 171, 182
Syl Johnson: Anyway the Wind Blows 125, 126–7, 151
Sympathy for the Devil [Film] 45, 89, 94–6, 100, 102
Sympathy for the Devil [Song] 46
Syncopation 12, 18

Tate, Greg 117, 124, 211, 227, 239
Teddy Pendergrass: If You Don't Know Me 127–8
Tedesco, Denny 91
Television [Medium] 22, 23, 34, 40, 58, 64, 65, 70, 148, 166, 174, 210, 216, 220, 228, 242
Temple, Julien 4, 50, 67–73, 105, 179
Ten Years in an Open Necked Shirt 241
The Ballad of Shirley Collins 182, 183–4
The Black Power Mixtape (1967–1975) 21, 82–3, 84, 226
The Blank Generation 50
The Blues Accordin' To Lightnin' Hopkins 26, 241
The Clash: Westway to the World (see *Westway to the World*)
The Decline of Western Civilization Part I 49–53, 64, 67
The Decline of Western Civilization Part II: The Metal Years 49–53, 64

The Decline of Western Civilization Part III 49–53, 64
The Devil and Daniel Johnston 77, 79–80
The Ecstasy of Wilko Johnson 70–1
The Filth and the Fury 4, 50, 67–0, 73, 179
The Great Hip Hop Hoax 195–6, 197, 198
The Great Rock 'n Roll Swindle 50, 67, 68, 69–70
The King of Jazz 12
The Last Angel of History 84, 115, 116, 117–18, 119, 241
The Last Waltz 42–3, 44, 51, 60, 90
The Man Behind the Microphone 146, 150, 154–5
The Man from Mo'Wax 110–11
The Parkinsons: A Long Way to Nowhere 105–6
The Possibilities Are Endless 80, 192–3, 194, 211
The Punk Singer 104, 178, 180–1
The Rolling Stones Rock and Roll Circus 47, 48
The Rolling Stones: Sympathy for the Devil (see *Sympathy for the Devil* [Film])
The Rutles: All You Need Is Cash 7, 12, 57, 58, 59, 60, 69,
The Science of Ghosts 108
The Sound Is Innocent 161
The Sparks Brothers 33, 67
The Story of Lovers Rock 131–2
The T.A.M.I Show 216, 241
The United Sates vs. Billie Holiday 172
The Velvet Underground [Film] 19, 20, 33, 62, 86–7
The White Stripes Under Great Northern Lights 235
The Wrecking Crew! 91–2
They Will Have to Kill Us First 154, 158–60
This Is Spinal Tap 6, 12, 52, 57–60, 61, 77, 202, 205, 239,
This Is Tomorrow 75–6
This Much I Know To Be True 189
Tilton, Roger 13
Time Is Illmatic 137–8, 150
Timoner, Ondi 77–9
Tonite Let's All Make Love in London 23
Trances 160–1, 231
Truth 8, 41, 73, 81, 132, 153, 177, 187, 188, 190, 192, 200, 219, 225, 230

Truth & Memory 148–50
TV xi, 15, 34, 36, 47, 69, 74, 178, 190, 227, 233

U2: Rattle and Hum 204–6
Utopian 66, 70, 119, 216, 218

Vashti Bunyan: From Here to Before 241
Velvet Goldmine [Film] 62–3
Vile, Jesse 80, 193–5

Walk Hard: The Dewey Cox Story 61–2
Walk The Line [Film] 61
Washington 97, 178
Watkins, Peter 57, 241
Watts, Charlie 28, 46
Wattstax [Film] 142, 223–5
We Jam Econo: The Story of the Minutemen 106–7
Webber, Peter 131, 133–4
Weber, Bruce 198–9
Welch, Leo 'Bud' 7, 8, 130
Wenders, Wim 7, 95, 157–8, 214
West, Cornel 123, 138
West, Kanye 141, 168
Westway to the World 72, 242
What Happened, Miss Simone? 124–6

What Have You Done Today Mervyn Day? 75–6
What's Happening: the Beatles in the USA 11, 34, 58
White Riot [Film] 72
White Stripes: Under Blackpool Lights 80, 235
Whitehead, Peter 23, 47
Whitney 163, 164, 165–6
Whitney: Can I Be Me 164, 165–6
Who, The 134, 216, 218
Williams, Raymond 145, 147, 148
Wilson, Lana 168
Winehouse, Amy 166–8, 172, 182
Wonder, Stevie 91, 92
Woodstock [Film] 11, 43, 216, 217, 218, 226, 227, 230
Wootton, Adrian 68, 205, 206

Yauch, Adam (also Hörnblowér, Nathanial) 80–1
Year of the Horse 56, 107
Yorke, Thom 39, 110,
Young, Neil [Musician] 43, 56–7

Ziggy Stardust and the Spiders from Mars [Film] 63, 219–20, 221, 222
Zwerin, Charlotte 11, 45–8